WORLD LITERACY

International literacy assessments have provided ample data for ranking nations, charting growth, and casting blame. Summarizing the findings of these assessments, which afford a useful vantage from which to view world literacy as it evolves, this book examines literate behavior worldwide, in terms of both the ability of populations from a wide variety of nations to read and the practice of literate behavior in those nations. Drawing on *The World's Most Literate Nations* (www.ccsu.edu/globalliteracy), author Jack Miller's internationally released study, emerging trends in world literacy and their relationships to political, economic, and social factors are explored. Literacy, and in particular the practice of literate behaviors, is used as a lens through which to view countries' economic development, gender equality, resource utilization, and ethnic discrimination. Above all, this book is about trajectories. It begins with historical contexts, described in terms of support for literate cultures. Based on a variety of data sources, these trends are traced to the present and then projected ahead. The literate futures of nations are discussed and how these relate to their economic and sociocultural development.

To be sure, a literate culture requires proficiency, but it also obliges its members to engage in literate activity. To ignore indices of such activity can lead to a distorted and reductionist notion of literacy status. This book is unique in providing a broader perspective on an intractable problem, a vantage that offers useful insights to inform policy, and in bringing together an array of relevant data sources not typically associated with literacy status.

John W. (Jack) Miller is President of Central Connecticut State University, USA. His work has been funded by state, federal, and private agencies, including the Department of Defense, the Department of Education, Bell South Foundation, and the Foundation for the Improvement of Postsecondary Education. He conducts a widely disseminated annual study of America's Most Literate Cities.

Michael C. McKenna is Thomas G. Jewell Professor of Reading at the University of Virginia, USA. His research has been sponsored by the National Reading Research Center (NRRC) and the Center for the Improvement of Early Reading Achievement (CIERA). He is the co-winner of the Edward Fry Book Award and the American Library Association's Award for Outstanding Academic Books.

WORLD LITERACY

How Countries Rank and
Why It Matters

John W. Miller and Michael C. McKenna

NEW YORK AND LONDON

First published 2016
by Routledge
711 Third Avenue, New York, NY 10017

and by Routledge
2 Park Square, Milton Park, Abingdon, Oxon, OX14 4RN

Routledge is an imprint of the Taylor & Francis Group, an informa business

© 2016 Taylor & Francis

The right of John W. Miller and Michael C. McKenna to be identified as authors of this work has been asserted by both of them in accordance with sections 77 and 78 of the Copyright, Designs and Patents Act 1988.

All rights reserved. No part of this book may be reprinted or reproduced or utilized in any form or by any electronic, mechanical, or other means, now known or hereafter invented, including photocopying and recording, or in any information storage or retrieval system, without permission in writing from the publishers.

Trademark notice: Product or corporate names may be trademarks or registered trademarks, and are used only for identification and explanation without intent to infringe.

Library of Congress Cataloging-in-Publication Data
Miller, John W. (John Winston), 1947–
  World literacy : how countries rank and why it matters / by John W. Miller and Michael C. McKenna.
     pages cm
  Includes bibliographical references and index.
  1. Literacy. 2. Reading. I. McKenna, Michael C. II. Title.
  LC149.M5 2016
  302.2'244—dc23   2015027927

ISBN: 978-1-138-90955-7 (hbk)
ISBN: 978-1-138-90956-4 (pbk)
ISBN: 978-1-315-69393-4 (ebk)

Typeset in Bembo
by Apex CoVantage, LLC

CONTENTS

Preface   *vii*

1 Keys to the Kingdom: The Long Struggle for Literacy   1

2 What Is Literacy? The Challenge of Framing the Problem   16

3 The Rise and Decline of Measured Reading Ability – National Winners and Losers   23

4 The Crisis of Elementary Schooling – Literacy's Training Ground   65

5 The Crisis of Secondary and Post-Secondary Schooling – Literacy's Practice Field and Proving Ground   86

6 Supporting Literate Cultures – The Past, Present, and Future of Libraries, Newspapers, and Bookstores   100

7 Skill versus Will: Important Lessons for Policy   142

8 Are Books Obsolete? Examining Trends in Media Use   153

9 Overcoming the SES/Literacy Relationship – Making
   Exceptions the Rule   169

10 The Future of the Knowledge-Based Economy and
   Change in the World Order   192

Index   *209*

PREFACE

A great many books underscore the current status of literacy achievement around the world. This isn't one of them. Our purpose is to view the subject through a much broader lens, one that includes practice as well as proficiency. Though we duly summarize the history of international assessments in an effort to distill their principal lessons, we view achievement as a necessary but insufficient condition for leading a literate life and contributing to a literate society.

With respect to achievement, it is important to be clear about what this book is not. Our goal is not to conduct secondary statistical analyses of international data. It is to interpret available results in a reasonable manner for a broad general readership consisting of policymakers, educators, and other concerned adults. When comparing countries on the basis of achievement and other metrics, we rely both on rankings and significant differences. We are aware that some analysts prefer only the latter, but the fact is, rankings are real. They are routinely reported, and we believe they are useful in guiding policy as long as they are used in tandem with other data, especially data related to behavior.

For this reason, the book dovetails with data newly gathered about how literacy is practiced around the world. These data were compiled by the first author from numerous international sources, including factors such as library use and availability, periodical subscriptions, and many others. The World's Most Literate Countries (WMLC) study is a freely available report that summarizes these data and ranks countries on a combined metric, similar to the one used in the annual America's Most Literate Cities (AMLC) report published in *USA Today*. Throughout this book we cite the WMLC report frequently as we examine world literacy trends. It is the first book to bring these information sources together.

Examining literacy issues through a wide-angle lens is an ambitious task, requiring a careful look at economic, social, and historical contexts. We begin by describing the nearly unthinkable sacrifices made by individuals to acquire and preserve literacy, goals that are too often taken for granted in developed nations. We then trace the results of international assessments for more than half a century and describe achievement shifts in recent years. We examine the education systems that underlie literacy growth at the elementary and secondary levels, and although we use the United States as a basis of comparison in some cases, we provide contrasting vignettes of a variety of other nations.

We then turn to the practice of literacy, as a set of behaviors, beginning with long-term trends in the use and prevalence of libraries, bookstores, and newspapers. We explore the issue of motivation as an essential component of a truly literate society, a component largely overshadowed by a preoccupation with achievement. We describe important trends concerning how motivation is reflected in literate behavior, both in the WMLC study and in recent results of international assessments. We next consider how motivation and the behaviors it engenders are evolving in the digital age.

In the last two chapters, we describe additional factors that can help provide a more nuanced picture of any nation's status. We approach the issue of literacy from both an economic and a socioeconomic standpoint. We explore the strong relationship between socioeconomic status and literacy growth but argue that it need not be an insurmountable obstacle. We examine instances of resilience at the individual, school, and national levels, and we endeavor to distill their common elements. Finally, we turn to the inescapable connection between literacy and economic viability in a dawning era of the knowledge-based economy.

Never before has so much depended on literacy. This is a statement that one might be tempted to cast aside as a bland and self-evident bromide. But it is quite literally true in that the role played by literacy has come to be marked by differences in kind as well as degree. As knowledge increasingly becomes a product as well as a tool, the economic welfare of any nation will be ultimately and inextricably tied to the literacy of its citizens.

J.W.M.
M.C.M.

1
KEYS TO THE KINGDOM: THE LONG STRUGGLE FOR LITERACY

The 1991 film, *Black Robe*, contains a remarkable scene illustrating the power of literacy, a power we frequently take for granted. The story traces the journey of two Catholic priests through the Canadian wilderness of the seventeenth century. While one of the priests writes in his journal, an Algonquin guide asks what he is doing. When the priest explains that words can be written as well as spoken, the Algonquin is clearly skeptical. To prove his point, the priest asks the guide to tell him a fact he cannot possibly know. He writes it down and carries the message to the other priest – well out of earshot – who reads it aloud. The looks of astonishment on the Algonquins' faces reflect the dawning significance of what they have witnessed.[1]

To say that we have lost any sense of astonishment concerning the power of literacy would be an understatement. Though few dispute the importance of becoming literate, the attainment itself is often dismissed as the mere ability to read and write, a technical accomplishment.

We offer an analogy to demonstrate how this tendency is only natural. Literacy's role in society is similar to that of drinking water. It is not an end in itself but enables individuals to achieve the ends that matter to them. Like water, when literacy is widely available it becomes invisible. We use it unconsciously to pursue a better life. And like water, we take literacy for granted, as a given, and the result can be complacency and loss of perspective.

In reality, however, the attainment of widespread literacy is both recent and fragile. In this chapter, we argue that members of literate societies can only understand the true stakes at play by appreciating the sacrifices that many have made in order to become literate. We illustrate how these sacrifices can involve violent conflict, and how a great many individuals nevertheless continue to make them in the present day. The perspective we champion is consequently far different from the everyday notion that literacy is synonymous with instruction and test scores. While these are certainly important considerations in becoming literate, focusing on them risks confusing means with ends. Behaving in literate ways is far more than simply acquiring proficiency. Patronizing bookstores and libraries; reading newspapers, novels, emails, and blogs; broadening our horizons by traveling to unseen places are actions that make us part of the literate community.

The power and value of being literate in a literate society are played out every day around the world. Many individuals, and in fact whole societies, make considerable sacrifices to become literate just as others take it for granted. Societies that do not practice literate behavior are often squalid, undernourished in mind and body, repressive of human rights and dignity, brutal, and harsh. Present-day examples are easy to list, but in fact this has always been the case. As Samuel Johnson observed more than two centuries ago, "The mass of every people must be barbarous where there is no printing." We concede that various forms of "barbarity" can be found in all societies, but they are much more prevalent where literate behavior is absent. Literacy and quality of life go hand-in-hand. With literacy comes the power of belonging to a privileged group and the freedom that derives from that power. Frederick Douglass, who struggled as a slave to learn to read, said it best: "Once you learn to read, you will be forever free."

The ability to read is a necessary, but not a sufficient, prerequisite of being literate. Malcolm X explained the distinction: "I have often reflected upon the new vistas that reading opened to me. I knew right there in prison that reading had changed forever the course of my life." Learning to read must occur in order to become literate, but it does not ensure a literate life. The term *aliterate* refers to those who are able to read but choose not to. A life of aliteracy is little different than that of the illiterate. As Mark Twain incisively remarked, the person who doesn't read has no advantage over the person who can't.

Beyond a cognizance of the sacrifices of resources, time, and effort that many have made to become literate, another means of appreciating the value and power of literacy is to examine the result of depriving a society of its texts. Acts of book burning, or libricide, are a familiar form of forced deprivation, but we must also consider the self-imposed rejection of literacy, which essentially brings about the same end. Joseph Brodsky, the exiled Russian poet, offered a blunt distinction: "There are worse crimes than burning books. One of them is not reading them." And Neil Postman, prolific American author and critic, arrived at a similar judgment: "What Orwell feared were those who would ban books. What Huxley feared was that there would be no reason to ban a book, for there would be no one who wanted to read it."

We suspect that few would take issue with these sentiments, which will ground our examination of nearly every aspect of literacy. They express the importance of not only becoming literate but of subsequently participating in literate communities. Literacy conveys power, confers advantage, and connects us to the living and the dead. As a few examples will show, these qualities are manifested in ways that are often obvious yet sometimes surprising. They have raised teaching to a noble calling yet have occasioned some of the most heinous acts imaginable.

Keys to the Literate Kingdom

Consider the case of two soldiers inserted into a foreign land and charged with preventing armed insurrection. These two men were not officers, nor were they raised in privileged homes. They were not persons of sophistication. They were merely two enlisted men holding the rank of private and doing the dangerous job assigned to them.

Matthew Kilroy and Hugh Montgomery were apprehensive to say the very least, and perhaps intimidated and threatened as well, by the inhabitants, both indigenous and immigrant, of the land they occupied. As with many occupying forces, they were viewed by some as necessary but unwelcome visitors and by others as hated subjugators. The political issues that swirled about them did not concern or even interest them. They were soldiers doing their duty.

Uncertainty traveled with them daily as they completed their tours. Around every corner and behind every door there was the possibility of hostile attack. The disrespect of the locals, expressed in catcalls, jeers, and even isolated attacks, caused these soldiers to be ever alert. They were on edge every moment of every day, not only when they were patrolling the streets, but when they were garrisoned. While they held no preconceived malice toward the locals, they themselves felt increasingly despised. While they viewed their role as one of maintaining the peace and preventing violence – ostensibly noble goals – they were at the same time disrespected. How could this be the case when they were there to help? Why were they so detested?

As time passed, tensions rose among the inhabitants, who increasingly viewed Kilroy and Montgomery as occupiers. Almost daily, stones, chunks of ice, and pieces of coal were hurled at them by both children and adults, sometimes over walls and fences, and at other times thrown by perpetrators in plain sight who then scurried off down King Street. This was not the worst of the affronts, however. Events escalated. Eventually shots rang out.

These events emboldened the locals, who were encouraged by the lack of response. At the same time, Kilroy, Montgomery, and their fellow soldiers felt increasingly frustrated. Though under orders to exercise caution, their training was built on aggression not restraint, on winning battles not keeping the peace, and on conquest not "nation building." As tensions swelled, the protests led to large-scale destruction of property. Armed groups of as many as 60 locals wandered the streets. The pressure on the troops to put down insurrection grew as the escalation involved the destruction of more and more property.

As you may have known (or guessed), Kilroy and Montgomery were British soldiers stationed in Boston shortly before the American Revolution. They were brought to prominence by a signal event that occurred on March 5, 1770, an event now known as the Boston Massacre. On that evening, Hugh Montgomery and Matthew Kilroy found themselves deeply immersed in a confrontation with the colonials. Marching as part of a group to the Custom House to extricate one of their fellow soldiers from a crowd, Montgomery was hit and knocked to the ground with a club. Many believe he was the first to fire. In the altercation that ensued, five colonials were killed. The first was Crispus Attucks.

As a result of the incident, eight British troops and their captain were tried for murder. They were ably defended by John Adams, then a Massachusetts attorney and later the second U.S. president. Only two of the defendants, Kilroy and Montgomery, were convicted – of manslaughter, not murder. Though convicted, Kilroy and Montgomery claimed "benefit of clergy" before sentencing, a centuries-old legal strategy to avoid the death penalty.

Their claim brings us to the point of the story, which is all about literacy. The legal term, *benefit of clergy*, was part of British common law through the eighteenth century, and Kilroy and Montgomery were two of the last people to make use of it. To receive this benefit, one originally had to be of a religious order, as the phrase implies, but in time it meant only that the defendant was literate, a fact demonstrated by reading aloud a Bible passage. If the connection between being literate and avoiding punishment seems unaccountable, remember that literacy was then far from universal. A literate defendant was likely to be well educated and thus to warrant special consideration. Illiterate convicts in time learned to game the system by memorizing a psalm or some other verse and then pretending to read it. Kilroy, for example, is thought to have been illiterate but managed to pass this high-stakes "test" in order to avoid the gallows. Nevertheless, in these two cases, and in thousands of others across centuries and continents, the value of being literate is concretely demonstrated, the merit of entering into a literate society made demonstrable.

The Cost of Literacy

Certainly the benefit of being literate – of holding the "keys to the kingdom" – has always been high. But so has the cost. And because literacy confers power, one way of maintaining a power differential has been to deny literacy to groups with low social standing. Preventing members of these groups from learning to read has repeatedly been a method of ensuring subservience. One example is the plight of women in certain Muslim countries. Others include people of color in South Africa during apartheid, child factory workers in Ireland, and Irish-Catholics in the United States.

There is, however, no more salient example than laws making it illegal to teach slaves to read in the United States. This is not to say that these laws were not occasionally ignored. Circumventing them occurred in a number of ways. Sometimes the master or mistress directly taught slaves in defiance of the law. On other occasions, the few slaves who had learned to read taught others. And an especially poignant method was for slave children to learn alongside the children of their masters, even if it meant sitting outside the schoolhouse and listening in.

As these instances suggest, slave owners were clearly not of one mind on the appropriateness of teaching slaves to read. But fears were fueled as word circulated of slave rebellions. Rebellions led by Denmark Vesey, Gabriel Prosser, and, most famously, Nate Turner all occurred in the early 1800s. Literacy, many reasoned, could only contribute to a rebellious spirit. Some slave owners voiced a more utilitarian objection to literacy instruction. They simply saw no occasion for slaves to utilize literacy in a way that was productive to their work.

For Africans, the motivations to read were clear and numerous. Their families were separated by the slave trade and they wanted to remain connected. They wanted to earn the right to freedom and to gain access to the processes of acquiring that right. They also desired fulfillment as human beings, which meant being vested with membership in the literate community.

A powerful force in favor of literacy instruction was the conservative Protestant belief, held by many slave owners, that it was imperative for blacks to become literate so that they could read the Bible, hymns, and other religious materials as part of their conversion to Christianity. Perhaps the best organized of the campaigns against slave illiteracy was that generated by the Reverend Samuel Davies, who launched a transatlantic crusade. He believed that conversion could only occur if individuals could read religious writings and study the Bible. He initiated an extensive campaign in Europe and raised money to bring books to the slaves of Virginia. Although his success was curtailed by limited resources, his work in the mid-1700s created a corps of literate slaves and free men in Virginia. This initiative became to some extent self-perpetuating as slaves taught other slaves.

In sum, the ambivalence of white Americans, and in particular slaveholders in the South, is clear. The need for slaves to study the Bible afforded a strong impetus for literacy instruction. On the other hand, fears of rebellion militated against these same efforts.[2]

The individual stories of slaves learning to read and of those attempting to teach them are numerous. Many of the best examples derive from the slave narratives, an excellent compilation of the autobiographical stories told by slaves in their own words.[3] These accounts were sometimes written by the slaves themselves, and sometimes dictated to others. None is more relevant than the story of Frederick Douglass.

He wrote of the almost unspeakable atrocities he suffered at the hands of several sets of owners, but then described, with great appreciation, his experience with the wife of one of his masters, Mrs. Hugh Auld. He describes her as "kindly" and explained how she began by teaching him the alphabet and later the spelling of simple words. However, after Mr. Auld discovered his wife's teaching, he forbade her to continue. Douglass quoted Auld as saying,

> "If you give a nigger an inch, he will take an ell.[4] A nigger should know nothing but to obey his master – to do as he is told to do. Learning would spoil the best nigger in the world. Now," said he, "if you teach that nigger (speaking of myself) how to read, there would be no keeping him. It would forever unfit him to be a slave. He would at once become unmanageable, and of no value to his master. As to himself, it could do him no good, but a great deal of harm. It would make him discontented and unhappy."[5]

Douglass went on to explain that these sentiments transformed his life and ironically instilled within him a powerful motivation to learn to read. He wrote that, "What he [Auld] most dreaded . . . I most desired." He further noted that, "In learning to read, I owe almost as much to the bitter opposition of my master as to the kindly aid of my mistress. I acknowledge the benefit of both."

In his moving account, Douglass provided many details of how he continued learning to read, including taking bread from the house and giving it to poor white children in exchange for instruction. He maintained that the more proficient he became, the more he detested being enslaved. He at last noted that the

> very discontent which Master Hugh had predicted would follow my learning to read had already come, to torment and sting my soul to unutterable anguish. As I arrived under it, I would at times feel that learning to read had been a curse rather than a blessing.[6]

Notwithstanding those feelings, Douglass' influence on history, society, his fellow slaves and freemen exemplify the sacrifices made by slaves to hold the "keys to the kingdom."

While Douglass' story of help and self-education is inspiring, it was far from unique. Consider the example of Margaret Douglass, a white woman, who was arrested in Virginia after she opened a free school for black children. She and her husband had been slave owners. After his death in South Carolina she returned to Virginia, committed to the idea of teaching black children to read and write. Although she had not transitioned from slave owner to abolitionist, she nevertheless felt a moral duty to help children read "the word of God." Her work resulted in her arrest and conviction.

What happened next is further evidence of the ambivalence of the times. The jury sympathized with her cause and set the fine at one dollar. She was allowed to leave Virginia to visit her daughter but when she returned for sentencing, the judge ordered that she be imprisoned. In his statement he indicated that he believed that slaves could be converted to Christianity without being able to read, and that he was strongly opposed to "northern incendiaries" and their "outcry against holding our slaves in bondage." He noted that the mail had been "clogged with abolitionist pamphlets and inflammatory documents to induce them [slaves] to cut our throats."

It is tempting to link such prejudicial judgments to antebellum Southern perspectives, but the consequences of educating blacks were not confined to the South. Consider the example of Prudence Crandall. After being educated by Quakers, she formed a school in Canterbury, Connecticut. After a time, she admitted a black girl, a decision that prompted considerable opposition. She refused to compromise her principles, however, and white families began to withdraw their children from her school in 1833. She then opened a school exclusively for black girls in Canterbury. Doing so occasioned still more public outcry, but it also attracted numbers of black female students from throughout the northeast. Local law enforcement persecuted these students, to the point of administering lashes with a whip for "vagrancy." In fact, in 1834 Connecticut passed a law making it illegal to provide free education for black students. Even after successfully challenging the law in court, Crandall was compelled to close the school in response to public outcry.

In Frederick Douglass, Margaret Douglass, and Prudence Crandall we see the cost that many have been willing to pay for their right, and the rights of others, to enter the society of the literate. Beatings, fines, imprisonment, and even death have been the price paid for such opportunities. The public pressure against which they contended was reinforced by laws that forbade such education. Although virtually every state had some form of such laws, they were predominant in the South. The Slave Codes of Georgia, enacted in 1848, made teaching slaves to read expressly illegal and prescribed draconian punishment:

> If any slave, negro, or free person of color, or any white person, shall teach any other slave, negro, or free person of color to read or write either written or printed characters, the said free person of color or slave shall be punished by fine and whipping or fine or whipping at the discretion of the court.

South Carolina, Virginia, and several other states had similar laws, which date back to 1740. Curiously, they lack specific language actually forbidding slaves to read, but specified only that it was illegal to *teach* slaves to read or for slaves to *learn* to read. Apparently legislators of the time felt that preventive measures were sufficient.

After Emancipation, of course, such laws were void, but they were soon replaced with new legislation that preserved their spirit. As part of the Jim Crow Laws of Reconstruction, the ability to read was established as a precondition of exercising the right to vote. For example, the Platform and Resolutions of the People's Party of South Carolina expressly stated that "every person presenting himself for registration shall be able to read and write any section of the Constitution in the English language." Although such requirements were a transparent attempt to prevent blacks from voting, they had the unintended consequence of prompting many of them to learn to read. In fact, during the first 30 years of Reconstruction, literacy rates for blacks rose from 10 to 50 percent. An odd irony, however, arose from the fact that the very literacy tests that disenfranchised many blacks also disenfranchised thousands of illiterate whites across the South. The result was a second unforeseen consequence, that of raising the percentage of blacks in the voting-eligible population.

The plight of African American slaves in the United States is a regrettable chapter in the history of literacy deprivation, but it is not the only one. Instances abound of education, including literacy instruction, being systemically withheld from other targeted groups, or made in effect inaccessible. In parts of the Arab world, the low level of literacy for women is well documented. In some countries, their literacy rate is approximately half the rate for men. Recent events have resulted in some interesting contradictions as well. The literacy rate for Iraqi women was once among the highest in the Arab world. It is now among the lowest. Families fear kidnapping and rape of their daughters if they send them to school, compelling many to give up on schooling for the present. Disruptions brought about by the war have made matters worse. At this writing, more than a million women are displaced and do not have enough money to feed, let alone educate, their families.

The use of violence to prevent access to schools is well documented elsewhere in the Middle East and Africa. In 2007, BBC News reported an attack on a group of girls returning home from school in Afghanistan's Logar Province. The children were aware of the risks, but they traveled in groups and hoped that they would be able to travel safely back and forth to school. Instead, a group of insurgents attacked, firing shots at the girls. Some were able to flee to a farm and escape the attackers. Others were not so fortunate. A 13- and a 10-year-old were shot and killed in the ambush, and three of their friends were wounded. The Afghanistan Education Minister, Mohammad Haneef Atmir, expressed the obvious. "I am very worried that such incidents will make parents very scared to send their children to school," he said. This was undoubtedly the purpose of the attack. Nor was this an isolated incident. In recent years, the Taliban have burned 226 schools, many of which were simply run from tents; 110 teachers and students have been killed by incidents of direct or indirect violence, and another 52 wounded. At this writing, the Taliban have shut down a total of 381 schools.

In neighboring Pakistan, Malala Yousafzai, a 15-year-old girl and vocal advocate of education for girls, was shot in the head by the Taliban for her efforts. Her subsequent nomination for the Nobel Peace Prize in 2013 cast a world spotlight on the issue, at least for a time. The value she ascribed to literacy must give us pause.

These examples confirm not only the potential cost of becoming literate but the fact that many are willing to pay it. Ironically, it is a cost that almost defies empathy on the part of those who belong to a society in which literacy is a given, where one can attend school in relative safety, and where books are available in abundance. Yet the history of these conditions is short and their scope far from universal.

Destroying Literacy, Destroying Cultures

Although acquiring literacy is a milestone of critical importance, it does not necessarily indemnify one against oppression. Perhaps nowhere is the value of literacy more evident than in attempts to destroy cultures, through the destruction of libraries and the burning of books. We find Heinrich Heine's prophetic observation startlingly apt: "Wherever they burn books, sooner or later they will burn human beings." Heine, a German Jew, wrote more than a century before the Holocaust. Despite his eerie prescience, however, it may in fact be easier to kill the members of a society than to obliterate their culture. Destroying a society's books and the repositories of those books is as much a symbolic assault on culture as an effectual means of annihilating it. Such attempts rarely succeed in eradicating all of the texts that embody and transmit a culture. They serve instead as conspicuous acts of terror. And for this purpose there may be no symbol more fitting than fire. In the dystopian world of *Fahrenheit 451*, fire was employed as a public exercise of extermination. But we needn't confine ourselves to fiction. As Manley (2002, p. 196) observes, historical examples abound:

> [I]t's hard to find a stronger image to use than fire. When God revealed himself to Moses, he did so as a burning bush. When Jesus attempted to describe the pain of hell, he conjured up a terrifying portrait of eternal flames. When the white-hooded thugs of the Ku Klux Klan rode menacingly through the rural South to stir up the hatred of racism, they burned crosses on people's front yards. When anti-war dissidents protested U.S. involvement in the Vietnam War, they burned the American flag. When Buddhist monks protested the corrupt Diem regime in South Vietnam, they burned themselves. When the Nazis wanted to rid Germany of dangerous and undesirable ideas, they burned piles and piles of books.

The symbolic destruction of a culture through the burning of its books has long been a method of choice, a fact that provides perverse evidence of its power. The successive Chinese dynasties often burned the books containing the records of their predecessors. In the third century BCE, the Chinese emperor Shin Huang Ti burned all written records so that history could begin anew, with him. He augmented his plan by executing scholars who taught of the past. The last dynasty ended in 1912, but examples of cultural destruction through the burning of books and records have continued in China. The Great Proletarian Cultural Revolution began in May of 1966 with the sixteen-point directive issued by the Chinese Communist Party and its author, Mao Zedong. Education, culture, and literature were all called into question. The work of party loyalists, including student groups and the Red Guard, devastated past culture. Knuth (2003) offers an example of how the act of destroying books so as not be found in possession of them was in some ways worse than having the Red Guard find and destroy them. She recounts a daughter's description of her father:

> [H]e had lit a fire in the big cement sink and was hurling his books into the flames. This was the first time in my life I had seen him weeping. It was agonized, broken, and wild, the weeping of a man not used to shedding tears. Every now and then, in fits of violent sobs, he stamped his feet on the floor and banged his head against the wall ... My father had spent every penny on his books. They were his life. After the bonfire, I could tell that something had happened to his mind.
>
> (Chang, 1991, p. 330)

Yet another attempt to put an end to a culture through the destruction of books and records occurred in Tibet following the Chinese invasion in 1949. The chief target was Buddhist culture. But because the Buddhist tradition included memorizing texts under the leadership of the Dalai Lama, Tibetans succeeded in keeping alive their cultural traditions, including literature. Buddhist monks have a history of memorizing text, a skill that served them well in countering the Chinese onslaught, though the monks were persecuted for their efforts. Avedon (1984, p. 92) describes the forced labor and other hardships they endured:

> *Only 7,000* of Tibet's more than 600,000 monks and a hundred or so of its 4,000 incarnate llamas had escaped. For each scholar who died on a road gang, centuries of learning were lost.

The West has been just as culpable in launching such attacks. Nowhere in history is the progression from destroying books to annihilating those who read them better exemplified than in Nazi Germany. However, the Nazi atrocities were hardly an anomaly. They were long predated by numerous other such attempts to eradicate Jewish culture through the destruction of books and libraries.

One of the more insidious attempts was that of Josef (later Johannes) Pfefferkorn, a German Jew of limited academic background. Imprisoned for burglary, he was ransomed by friends, after which he became a Christian and launched a series of writings against Jews in general and Johann Reuchlin, a German humanist, in particular. In the early 1500s, Pfefferkorn's escalating assaults on Jews, Jewish culture, and religious practices were in keeping with the rising anti-Jewish sentiments of the Dominicans of Frankfort and Cologne. In a 1905 essay, Samuel Hirsch reported the following events that took place on September 28, 1509:

> There appeared in their synagogue three priests, two town councilors, and Johann Pfefferkorn. The latter produced a mandate of the Emperor Maximilian, to the effect that the Jews should deliver to him, Pfefferkorn, all books which contained anything against the Christian faith or against the Pentateuch and the Prophets. By force of this mandate, Pfefferkorn was to be the sole judge of what was to be considered pernicious or otherwise, and his authority in this respect was to extend throughout the German Empire. He entered the synagogue, and in spite of the protests of the Jews, he took away indiscriminately as many books as he could lay hands on, and forbade the Jews, in the name of the Emperor, to pray in their synagogue. The day was too short to search the private houses for books, and he appointed the following day for this purpose.
>
> (pp. 74–75)

Although Pfefferkorn and Reuchlin engaged in a running war of words, the real work of challenging the very existence of a culture involved the destruction of the vessels that preserved and transmitted that culture – books. With events such as these as prelude, it is little wonder that Heinrich Heine warned of how the destruction of books might metastasize into genocide.

The spring of 1933 saw the first burnings of books and libraries that were to become the Holocaust. These were less the direct work of the Nazi regime than of pro-Nazi student groups enflamed by Nazi rhetoric. Book burnings over the course of that spring occurred with frightening zeal and passion. Battles (2004) observes:

> Sigmund Freud, whose name appeared in the *Feuersprüche*, was not impressed. "Only our books?" he reportedly asked. "In earlier times they would have burned us with them." But Freud had evidently forgotten the Heine quote. This was only the beginning, one of the first of thirty university book burnings in the spring of 1933. Over the course of the next twelve years, one hundred million books (according to one estimate) would accompany six million human beings into the flames of the Holocaust.
>
> (p. 167)

The systematic attempts to destroy Jews and their culture are not only infamous but especially well documented. The Nazis "cleansed or aryanized" the books of synagogues, bookstores, lending libraries, schools, and publishers. They dumped books and people in rivers (before choosing to incinerate the latter). In brave, but largely symbolic gestures, Jews hid valuable pieces of literature while burning others to make a show of cooperating with the Nazi cultural destruction.

In April of 1935, Joseph Goebbels, as head of the Reich Chamber of Literature, became the ultimate censoring authority. His attacks on cultures were by no means limited to German Jews. His broad agenda crossed religious and ethnic lines and extended to every country overrun by the Nazis:

> The Nazi agencies in the Soviet Union greedily sought valuable collections, but all of them destroyed more books in the east, because depriving Slavs of education and destroying their culture would make them helots, ripe for ruthless exploitation to extinction. In Ukraine 150 experts working for the ERR stole or destroyed over 51 million books from the central state and university libraries of Kiev, all the regional libraries in other cities, and libraries in palaces, museums, churches, and synagogues.
>
> (Hill, 2001, p. 31)

Although the Dynastic and Maoist Chinese and the Nazis are among the more notorious attempts to destroy spirit and culture through the burning of books, they are not isolated examples. Knuth (2003) explains "libricide" as occurring in one of three patterns. It can occur as part of the overall destruction of conquered cities, either during battle or afterward, as punishment meted out to the vanquished. The second pattern involves the looting of books, which are carried away. The third entails the censorship of offensive and impure thought from the writings of the vanquished.

All three patterns are evident in the centuries-long clashes between Muslims and Christians. The Arab conquest of Egypt was accompanied by the burning of the Great Library of Alexandria in which over 700,000 scrolls were burned, including many original Greek plays now forever lost, allegedly to fuel fires in the bathhouses of the city. Serbs and Croats destroyed repositories of one another's literature faster than librarians could preserve and hide the books. The Croats saw the Serbs as "illiterate barbarians." Yet the Croats were themselves busily at work "cleansing" their society and burning books. In the United States, anti-Muslim flames have lately been fanned by means of Koran burnings carried out by fundamentalist Christians who view such acts as a symbolic strike at the perpetrators of 9/11.

From the Soviet invasion of Afghanistan in 1979, to the response of the Mujahedeen, and continuing through U.S. operations against the Taliban, an extraordinary amount of Afghan literature has been lost. Decades of bombing, strafing, and burning, all part of the ebb and flow of warring parties, have taken their toll on books, libraries, and schools, sometimes intentionally, sometimes as collateral damage.

The list of atrocities committed against human life and the concomitant destruction of cultures through assaults on books and libraries is depressingly long. It is natural to think first of a few high-profile despots, but attempts at cultural annihilation have not been limited to the likes of Hitler, Mao, and Milošević. The Mongols destroyed Baghdad, then filled the Tigris River with books. Joe McCarthy searched actively for pro-communist books to burn. Groups and individuals have often burned particular books that offended them, like Salman Rushdie's *Satanic Verses* and J.K. Rowling's *Harry Potter* series. All are examples of the intent not merely to confront but to extinguish opposing perspectives.

Conclusion

These vignettes are a sobering testament to the power of literacy. They stand as examples of the value of being part of the literate world, of the price some have paid to become literate, and of literature in preserving, and participating in, society and culture. It is profoundly ironic that even the most violent of these examples – and especially the most violent, we argue – validate the claim that the attainment of literacy is vested with inherent power. This is why understanding literacy as a multidimensional concept is so important. This book explores the social, economic, and governmental powers of literacy at a level well beyond test scores.

Why literacy matters at all is a question best explored by examining these dimensions and considering how literacy is indexed in countries around the world. We will use the relationship between literacy and numerous other indicators of a society's well-being to explain numerous world events. We will examine countries that exemplify the correlation between high literacy and extensive human rights, advanced economic development, health care, participatory government, and advanced standing in the world order, but we will present exceptions as well. Anomalies in countries such as Cuba, where literacy and economic development are not commensurate, will be carefully considered.

We will argue that literacy levels are dynamic and subject to change, both in absolute terms and in relative rankings worldwide. We will identify countries that have substantially increased their literacy level relative to others, as well as those that have lost ground. Trends will be explored and trajectories plotted.

We will examine the means of acquiring literacy in a variety of nations. We will pursue how literacy skills are taught and learned and how interest in literate activities develops. Our examination extends beyond the elementary school level, as we explore the crisis of secondary and post-secondary schooling. Learning to apply basic literacy skills in demanding contexts will be examined as will the acquisition of lifelong literate behaviors. We will describe extensive informal networks for developing literacy outside of schools in settings around the world. We will outline the roles of volunteers and agencies other than schools in promoting literacy in societies where schooling is inadequate. We will appraise the nature and effectiveness of governmental support in a variety of countries, and in the process identify policies and initiatives that have shown promise – or have failed. We will test the doctrine that more is better and reach some surprising conclusions.

We will examine what people read and in what format. We will evaluate the evidence behind the frequent assertion that books and newspapers are becoming obsolete, and we will project trends involving the future of libraries, bookstores, newspapers, and face-to-face instruction.

We will describe the range of reading interests and the tension between breadth and depth. We will look in detail at ways of broadening and expanding the topics about which people are willing to read, and how they use a variety of literacy skills while reading for enjoyment and for work.

We will conclude with an examination of the future of knowledge-based economies and changes in the world order. Data from throughout the book concerning different countries and their progress in developing a literate citizenry are presented with detailed analysis. We use this foundation of facts and projections to address questions that are central to the goal of universal literacy. Why is it that some children succeed despite an environment characterized by hardship and failure? Why do certain schools, surrounded by their comparable but failing counterparts, succeed against the odds to instill in their students both the ability and the desire to read? What policy lessons can we distill from these exceptions that can help us make them the rule?

The fact that you are reading this book says a great deal about your preexisting beliefs about literacy. We hope, however, that this chapter has at least resulted in a deepened awareness of the value of literacy, its potential cost, and its role as a conduit of cultural belief and identity. After defining a few key terms, we will turn to an analysis of a broad array of data with the goal of identifying the trends and forces at work within and across countries. We will combine conventional analysis with speculation and hypothesis testing, much in the way that sabermetrics is used in the analysis of baseball, or freakonomics is employed to explain complex relationships between seemingly unrelated events.

Notes

1. View this clip at http://www.youtube.com/watch?v=xoxUto7-sDI
2. For a thorough discussion, see *When I Can Read My Title Clear: Literacy, Slavery, and Religion in the Antebellum South*, by Janet Duitsman Cornelius (1991). Cornelius articulates these two opposing themes.
3. For a compilation of the accounts of 2,300 former slaves, visit http://xroads.virginia.edu/~hyper/wpa/wpahome.html.
4. An approximate unit of length, measuring from the elbow (ell) to the tip of the middle finger.
5. From Chapter 6 of *The Narrative of the Life of Frederick Douglass*.
6. From Chapter 7 of *The Narrative of the Life of Frederick Douglass*.

References

Avedon, J. (1984). *In exile from the land of snows*. New York, NY: Alfred A. Knopf.
Battles, M. (2004). *Library: An unquiet history*. New York, NY: W.W. Norton & Company.
Chang, J. (1991). *Wild swans: Three daughters of China*. Hong Kong: Globalflair, Ltd.
Cornelius, J.D. (1991). *When I can read my title clear: Literacy, slavery, and religion in the antebellum South*. Columbia, SC: University of South Carolina Press.
Douglass, F. (1845). *The narrative of the life of Frederick Douglass, an American slave*. Boston, MA: Anti-Slavery Office.
Hill, L.E. (2001). The Nazi attack on "un-German" literature, 1933–1945. In J. Rose (Ed.), *The Holocaust and the book: Destruction and preservation* (pp. 9–46). Amherst, MA: University of Massachusetts Press.
Hirsch, S.A. (1905). Johann Pfefferkorn and the battle of the books. In *A book of essays* (pp. 73–115). London, U.K.: Macmillan.
Knuth, R. (2003). *Libricide: The regime-sponsored destruction of books and libraries in the twentieth century*. Westport, CT: Praeger.
Manley, W. (2002). In defense of book burning. *American Libraries*, *33*(3), 196.

2

WHAT IS LITERACY? THE CHALLENGE OF FRAMING THE PROBLEM

In describing a literate world, it's important to be clear about the terms we use. This is a time of broadening perspectives, when reading and writing occupy the same conceptual tent as listening, viewing, and browsing. Though we don't wish to undervalue these as modes of communication, we argue in this chapter that clear limits must be set on what counts as literacy. The boundary we've set is a simple one – we define *reading* as any endeavor involving the interpretation of text. We offer reasons we find compelling and that have guided us through the remainder of the book.

Clarifying the Concept

Anyone setting out to write a book about world literacy had better get the definition right. As it happens, that isn't easy. We began the task with the traditional definition of *literacy*, which simply involves reading and producing written language. And in fact, the word *literacy* shares its origin with the words *letter*, *literature*, and *literal*. When we say that a thing is literally true, we mean it's true just as we've spelled it out, word for word and letter by letter. This definition of *literacy*, as entailing the reading and writing of text, is very much standard fare among the educated population. It is the default assumption.

As an example, think about the mental processes you're using to read this page. You are making your way through the text in linear fashion, one sentence after another. There is no question, even in a professional field long known for trenchant debates, that you are engaged in literate activity. And if you are reading this book on a device, no matter. The same cognitive processes are involved. But suppose you come to a chart or diagram. (You soon will.) Is examining a graphic a literate act? The previous chapter began with reference to a YouTube video. Would watching that video constitute literate behavior? Or think of the digital textbooks that have already become a mainstay in many college courses and that are now beginning to find their way into middle and high school classrooms. In these environments, a student can move with a mere finger tap from an anchoring text to an animated graphic or ancillary website, and in some cases even hear a second-language translation or listen to voiceovers. These examples represent the persistent expansion of what counts as literate activity.

You may well be thinking, so what? After all, what they have in common is written text. That's true enough, but for the sake of argument, let's take things a step further. Say you're listening to an audiobook as you drive. Are you engaged in literacy? There's still a text, you might argue, it's just that a third party has converted it to speech so that you can direct your gaze elsewhere. But what if you take in a movie or attend a play? Are these literate acts? In each case, there is a script and the actors are in fact reading their lines to you. So by extending our reasoning, we might categorize plays and movies as literate acts. And even if you'd come across that YouTube video on your own, without this book to anchor and guide you, the characters you'd see are still operating from a script. But imagine there is no text, that there never was. Would engaging in ordinary conversation be an example of literacy? Language is involved but it's not typically written down beforehand. Or what about viewing a painting at a gallery? In this case there's no language whatever, written or oral.

We suspect you might draw the line at this point, if not before. But the trajectory can be logically extended to include any act of communication, even those without language of any kind. Sometimes nonverbal communication even carries the force of law. Make the wrong gesture at Sotheby's and you could wipe out your bank account. Or consider this famous example from contract law. A farmer has an arrangement with a feed store. The storekeeper allows him to run a tab, and the farmer settles at the end of every month. Whenever a purchase is made, the two speak briefly at the counter and the storekeeper records the transaction in a ledger. One day the farmer stops by for a heavy sack of feed and carries it to the counter only to find the storekeeper busy with another customer. The farmer catches the storekeeper's eye and nods at the sack. The storekeeper gives an acknowledging nod in return, and the farmer walks out with the sack. Is this transaction an act of literacy? Legal scholars have in essence ruled that it is by concluding that it constitutes a binding (if wordless) contract.

Our purpose in confronting you with these examples is not to blur the issue but to point out that literate actions must be carefully defined at the outset. If we adopt too narrow a perspective, and consider only the kind of linear reading you are now doing, we risk overlooking a range of activities with clear relevance to any discussion of literacy. On the other hand, if we set the limits too loosely, the original definition can be lost in the disparate array of possibilities that scholars have, almost from necessity, begun referring to in the plural – as *literacies*. In examining how people around the world engage in literate activity, we have taken a middle road by requiring that the activity be grounded in visible written language. Reading a book counts as literacy; listening to the audiobook version does not; reading a play is literacy; watching it performed is not. Examining a labeled diagram is literacy; viewing a Picasso isn't. Texting friends is literacy; phoning them isn't. In short, our line in the sand requires that the individual see written language, either while reading it or writing it. The presence of complementary features (illustrations, videos, podcasts, and like) does not, however, rule out an activity.

What Factors Influence Literate Activity?

Determining the extent to which people engage in various forms of literate behavior can provide the basis for useful cross-country comparisons. Of particular interest is how two countries might differ in the extent to which their citizens engage in a particular activity. Given the right data, we can easily make such comparisons. The challenge lies in how to interpret them. We will argue throughout this book that four major factors are the principal determinants of engagement with literacy: reading and writing proficiency, access to materials, the availability of competing alternatives, and the influence of culture. Any of these four factors is sufficient, in itself, to limit literacy engagement. None, however, is enough to assure it. These factors act in concert, and in ways that are complex and nuanced. In Figure 2.1, we attempt to display the possible interactions among these four factors. A four-way Venn shows all combinations of them, including their individual influence. There are 13 possibilities, making for a complex interplay of the four. Understanding their influence is admittedly challenging, but it is well worth the effort required.

It's important to note that each of these factors is complex. At the very least we must not view them as either-or, all-or-nothing concepts. When we quantify

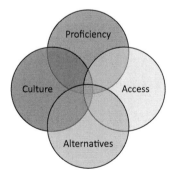

FIGURE 2.1 Interactions among the factors influencing literate activity.

them, we must allow them to vary along a continuum from very negative to very positive. We concede that doing so does not do justice to any of the four, but it nevertheless provides a useful frame of reference.

Proficiency[1]

Our principal interest here is in the ways people of different nations engage in reading, not in how well they read. Of course, it's impossible to completely separate these issues because proficiency is a prerequisite to engagement. Even when there is ready access to books amid a culture conducive to literacy, proficiency can be a barrier that constrains literate activity. So obvious is this constraint that it is easy to become preoccupied with reading proficiency and to overlook the fact that proficiency is necessary but insufficient for literate behavior to occur. Proficiency enables such behavior but it does not cause it. We all know individuals who are perfectly capable of reading but who prefer not to, given a choice. Daniel Boorstin (1984) described this condition as *aliteracy*, proficiency without engagement, as opposed to *illiteracy*, the mere lack of proficiency.

Consequently, thoughtful policies that are implemented to improve reading proficiency should be welcomed, at least as far as they go. To their credit, concern over aliteracy has led the developers of large-scale assessments to include questionnaires about students' attitudes toward reading and about their activities outside school. But the results gain little traction, chiefly because they are overshadowed by the latest findings concerning proficiency. We find it unfortunate that literacy policy is often shaped on the basis of proficiency alone even though the data that might broaden the lens through which literacy is viewed are available. One of our purposes for writing this book is to suggest ways that national policy might be broadened in this regard.

Access

In developing nations, the limited number of print and digital texts clearly constrains the extent to which even proficient readers can participate. Where English is not the indigenous language, the limitation is not just a matter of economics. It involves the mere existence of texts in the first place. Programs such as "book floods," the brainchild of New Zealand researcher Warwick Elley, or Unite for Literacy, the far-reaching enterprise of Michael McGuffee and Mark Condon, have shown success in placing large numbers of books[2] into homes and classrooms.

But the problem of access is hardly limited to developing nations. Neighborhoods underserved by bookstores and libraries, even in an affluent nation, create contexts not unlike those of the developing world. The abundance of digital sources, far from alleviating the shortage, likewise involves differences in access. The "digital divide" refers to this difference as a consequence of economic status.

Although there is evidence that the divide is closing due to the lower cost of devices and their current prevalence in schools, the divide remains a fact of life for many students.

Access is not likely to be uniform across any nation, developed or otherwise, making cross-country comparisons a complex business. This is not to suggest that useful contrasts cannot be made, but the need to carefully qualify them is clear.

Alternatives

A century ago in America, before the advent of electronic media, it was not uncommon for American families to await the arrival of the *Saturday Evening Post* so that they could read it aloud together. Reading was central to engagement with language, supplanting storytelling in the oral tradition during the days before printing. With a more literate populace, access to print permitted reading to compete with leisure alternatives. Ironically, it is now reading that must compete with a new host of alternatives.

As the concept of aliteracy suggests, the powerful combination of proficiency and access does not inevitably lead to engagement. For leisure purposes, reading must compete with the appeal of other options. The range of these options increases with age, eventually including dating and driving.

We would be among the last to argue that children and adolescents should spend every leisure moment with their noses in books, but leisure time is a zero-sum system, and as the alternatives become more sophisticated through technology, and as students are drawn to these alternatives as a result, the time that remains for reading is reduced.

It is cold comfort that some of the most appealing alternatives to conventional reading and writing involve the use of these skills in social media. The laconic, acronym-laden expressions common in texting and the telegraphic compactness of 117-character tweets represent an evolution in literate activity that has proved problematic for teachers. The fear that the low standards for writing in social media environments could spill over, in corrupting ways, into formal writing is understandable. Others counter that such fears have no basis in fact, and indeed we know of no evidence substantiating such an ill effect. The mere fact that adolescents are using literacy for relevant purposes must reinforce their perception of its value.

Culture

With the addition of each new factor into the equation, the possible interactions expand geometrically. Although limited proficiency is enough to discourage or prevent participation in literate activities, adequate proficiency may lead to the same result if access is limited or alternatives are more appealing. Still more possibilities arise when we add a fourth factor, the influence of culture.

We define *culture* broadly to include the language, traditions, and social values of a group. Although cultures may coincide with national borders, they often transcend them, on the one hand, and exist within a national context on the other. However defined, culture influences behavior by creating expectations about what is valued. That influence is conditioned by an individual's tendency to conform to those expectations.

Culture is rarely a singular force. Students move across multiple settings – the home, the classroom, the neighborhood – and each exerts its own influence, setting up its own expectations about conformity. The distinction between in-school and out-of-school literacy is useful in conceptualizing how cultural expectations may conflict with one another, confronting students with an uncomfortable choice during the most vulnerable period of their life.

Consider the influence of one's peers on the decision to engage in literate activities. For many individuals, the need to conform to these social norms is great, and the results can be insidious when literacy is not valued by the peer group. The pressure can be quite subtle. Imagine a middle school boy who is gently mocked by a group of friends who find him reading a book. To the extent the boy desires acceptance by the group, his future as a reader may be in jeopardy.

In the early 1980s, Jaime Escalante, a high school teacher in East LA, finally overcame the resistance of Angel, a Latino student with high social standing among his peers, by persuading him to cooperate. One interchange in the 1988 docudrama starring Edward James Olmos is especially telling:

> **Angel**: I'm gonna fly straight. I got a little problem, though.
> **Escalante**: Yeah, me.
> **Angel**: No, no, no. Seriously, though – books. I can't have the homeys see me haul 'em around.
> **Escalante**: You wouldn't want anyone to think you're intelligent.
> **Angel**: So maybe I can have two books, keep one stashed at home, eh?

This episode does more than illustrate the constraining power of cultural norms. The fact that Escalante's students were juxtaposed in the same school with other groups harboring different values illustrates that cultural influences are not monolithic. Although some of these influences may exercise hegemony, there is an ongoing welter among cultural expectations as they exert their influence in the same space and time.

A Caveat

Describing literate activities, both in degree and kind, is a rather straightforward business. Databases now facilitate quantification and make international comparisons surprisingly easy. In this book, we will offer such comparisons, to be sure, but we will make a point of resisting their superficial interpretation. National contexts, which differ markedly in education, access, culture, and affluence, will be key in offering insights into the status of literacy in the world.

Notes

1 Before you continue reading, take a moment to reflect. We mentioned earlier that when confronted with breaks in the linear flow of text, readers must decide strategically how and when to move between text and graphic. What strategies did you employ? Do they count as "reading"?
2 In the case of Unite for Literacy, the books are available free, in digital form.

Reference

Boorstin, D.J. (1984). *Books in our future: A report from the Librarian of Congress to the Congress.* Washington, DC: Joint Committee on the Library.

3
THE RISE AND DECLINE OF MEASURED READING ABILITY – NATIONAL WINNERS AND LOSERS

If a literate world truly matters, the responsibility for achieving it falls to individual nations. Their policies can hasten or impede progress toward the goal of universal literacy. In this chapter, we argue that the results of international assessments lend themselves to useful comparisons when they are interpreted with care and considered together with other indicators.

We advocate an approach involving five levels of analysis, beginning with a country's current status relative to others. In 2013, Jan Rivkin of the Harvard Business School summarized 2012 findings of the Program for International Student Assessment of 15-year-olds (PISA) this way:

> While our scores in reading are the same as 2009, scores from Belgium, Estonia, Germany, Ireland, Poland and others have improved and now surpass ours.... Other countries that were behind us, like Italy and Portugal, are now catching up. We are in a race in the global economy. The problem is not that we're slowing down. The problem is that the other runners are getting faster.
>
> (Quoted by Chappell, 2013)

Her take is a good first pass at the data. Rivkin views the results at a macro level and clearly sees them as a leading economic indicator.

In order to prompt policy change, however, additional levels of analysis are needed. The next is to compare a country's mean score on an assessment with those from previous points in time. In this way, the achievement of two or more cohorts can be used to index the success of initiatives. The third level is to consider changes in international rankings. Rivkin's track meet analogy illustrates the difference between a nation's progress relative both to its own past and to that of other nations. In other words, it's not merely progress that's important but the *rate* of progress. The fourth level of analysis involves tracking modified cohorts across different assessments. A country that participates in an assessment of fourth graders can follow their progress on PISA and later on an adult assessment. Potential weaknesses in the education system can then be identified by grade and age.[1]

The final level of analysis entails a deeper look at the data to gain a more nuanced perspective on the status of literacy and discover clues that are specific enough to inform policy change. The proportion of individuals at each achievement level can be tracked over time, for example, to determine whether the number of those at risk has fallen. Contextual indicators such as poverty and teacher preparation can also be used to help explain findings and point the way forward.

In short, we contend that the rich data the international assessments provide, analyzed at several levels and considered in the context of a country's social and economic circumstances, can inform meaningful planning and goal setting. We begin by offering the long view of international assessments, which is essential to determining the trajectories of participating nations. We examine findings at the elementary, secondary, and adult levels and use them to track progress in two principal ways – over the course of the past half-century and over the lifespan of a country's citizens. We close with seven suggestions for policymakers who are determined to tilt their national trajectories upward.

The Importance of a Long View

With the release of each new set of findings, current rankings capture headlines but they are not the whole story. Of far greater significance is change over time – change relative to other countries and change within a particular country. A metaphor from photography seems apt. The results of any high-profile assessment represent a still captured from a motion picture. The still provides plenty of useful information, but it is the movie that conveys a sense of change.

It is this series of stills, taken at regular intervals, that drives the fascination with testing and creates a climate of competition. High-stakes testing, long a mainstay in many developed nations, is becoming more commonplace in the developing world, among countries eager for upward mobility. This trend may be due in part to the correlated relationships between reading ability and economic development, health, and human rights; thus, countries may place greater emphasis on test scores in the belief that doing so might improve quality-of-life indicators. Their willingness to participate in international assessments is therefore quite understandable. The results become a vehicle for setting goals and gauging change.

Although international literacy comparisons have achieved a high profile of late, they are far from new. In 1958, William S. Gray, in conjunction with

UNESCO, analyzed comparative reading achievement data across countries. He regarded measures of achievement as a lens through which to arrive at inferences about the quality of teaching and learning on a large scale, inferences he cross-checked by examining national approaches to school reform, methods of teacher preparation, levels of economic development, and other quality-of-life factors. Though his work was seminal, Gray lacked a common metric by which to make comparisons since countries administered a variety of assessments through an assortment of methods. All of that changed with the advent of PISA and its counterpart for younger students, the Progress in International Reading Literacy Study (PIRLS).

These programs can facilitate useful international achievement comparisons, but they are fraught with a number of problems. Stahl et al. (1993) commented on one of the major concerns:

> One of the acceptable uses of comparative literacy investigations is to provide an estimate of the standing of a nation, relative to other countries along specific pedagogical dimensions such as reading levels . . . When used in the appropriate manner these inter-country rankings can point towards special problems and towards areas of needed improvement. Unfortunately, this potentially positive source of information is all too regularly lost to a mentality that promotes a "Literacy Olympics" . . .
>
> (p. 111)

A host of other cautions are well worth noting. Sampling error could lead to skewed and unrepresentative results for a country. Calendar year differences in schooling might advantage some populations and underestimate the performance of others. Major changes in political environment can influence historical trends in complex ways. Translation of items, though closely monitored, can nevertheless result in misinterpretations. Cultural perspectives and experiential differences may alter the perception of some questions across societies. Technical issues likewise abound, such as self-reporting of some information, the equivalency of alternate forms, and item response considerations.

These cautions duly noted, the assessments nonetheless provide valuable information about the status of literacy at a given point in time and about trends across years and age groups. Five series of assessments in particular have shed considerable light on the state of world literacy. One is a major sequence of studies aimed at students in their fourth year of formal instruction (typically 9-year-olds), first known as the IEA[2] Study of Reading Literacy and since 2001 as PIRLS. PISA is a somewhat parallel series targeting 15-year-olds. In addition, three series involve adult literacy: the International Adult Literacy Survey (IALS), the Adult Literacy and Lifeskills Survey (ALL), and the Program for the International Assessment of Adult Competencies (PIAAC). Aside from ALL, which was quite limited, we think it important to discuss these assessments, for each opens a unique window on the status and trajectories of world literacy.

Caveat

We wish to be clear at the outset that our intent in this chapter is not to present a detailed statistical analysis of the various international assessments. There is an extensive scholarly literature that addresses these concerns and it is beyond the scope of this book to describe it in any detail. Instead, our goal is to provide a broad readership with an introduction to the assessments as they have developed over time and to inspect a few of the important trends supported by the results.

IEA[3]

History and Purpose

The IEA General Assembly decided to undertake a study of reading literacy in 1988 and appointed a steering committee and a technical advisory group. An International Coordinating Center (ICC) was established in Germany at the University of Hamburg, and research institutes from 32 systems of education around the world participated in the study. Each system appointed a National Research Coordinator (NRC) responsible for the day-to-day administration of the study.

Between October 1990 and April 1991, IEA assessed students at those grade levels where most 9- and 14-year-olds were found in the 32 national systems. The data were collected from a carefully selected probability sample that included 9,073 schools, 10,518 teachers, and 210,059 students. There were two target populations. Population A included full-time students between the ages of 9 years and 9 years 11 months who took the assessment in two sessions totaling 75 minutes. Population B included full-time students between 14 years and 14 years 11 months and who took the assessment in two sessions totaling 85 minutes. All of the students responded to a background questionnaire about reading at home and at school. Teachers and principals responded to questionnaires about themselves, their teaching, and the school organization.

Funding came from the participating countries, as well as the MacArthur Foundation, the Mellon Foundation, USDOE's National Center for Educational Statistics, the European Community, the Maxwell Family Foundation, and UNESCO.

Literacy Definition

The study defined *reading literacy* as "the ability to understand and use those written language forms required by society and/or valued by the individual" (Elley, 1992, p. 3). Three domains were assessed: (1) narrative prose (both fiction and nonfiction),

(2) expository prose (including both factual information and informed opinion), and (3) documents (in the form of charts, tables, graphs, lists, and so forth).

Measurement

A considerable challenge faced the designers of the study: How to assess the reading achievement of 9- and 14-year-olds in a range of national contexts, where a variety of languages were spoken, and to link the results to voluntary reading activities and to national variations in policies and practices. Professional tensions concerning how best to teach and test reading heightened the challenge but led eventually to workable compromises. National samples of 1,500 to 3,000 pupils per country were systematically selected to be representative of their populations. The test and questionnaires were administered under standardized conditions to the national samples in the eighth month of the 1990–91 school year. Where necessary, these were translated into the local language under the supervision of the NRCs, and the layout, illustrations, instructions, and time limits were standardized though minor cultural adaptations were permitted to allow for more suitable names for people and places, local currencies, and units of measure.

Students read a balanced sample of texts in each of the three domains and answered questions designed to gauge how well they understood them. The texts were drawn from typical home, school, society, or work contexts. A Word Recognition Test was added for the 9-year-old students, requiring them to match words in isolation with corresponding pictures under timed conditions. Scale scores for each of the three domains were computed, with a mean of 500 and a standard deviation of 100. The average scores for each participating country were reported, together with a measure of certain indicators of national development. Six indicators were chosen to highlight national differences in three types of resources (economic, health, and literacy). They included GNP per capita; public expenditure per student on education; life expectancy; percentage of children with low birth weight; newspapers per 1,000 population; and percentage of adult literacy. These indicators were chosen because of their presumed connection with literacy levels in schools and the fact that data were readily available, reasonably accurate, generally stable over time, and useful for interpreting progress in each country. In addition, data for the six factors were aggregated to form a Composite Development Index (CDI).

Questionnaires were designed to obtain contextual information potentially helpful in interpreting test results. Student questionnaires included items about the student's home and school circumstances; teacher questionnaires focused on the teacher's background, instructional practices, and beliefs; school questionnaires sought the principal's perspective on school circumstances and policies. At the national level, National Case Study Questionnaires, completed by NRCs, centered on issues of national policy, enrollment patterns, and economic conditions.

IEA Results for 9-year-olds

Finnish 9-year-olds led the way in all three domains of reading comprehension (see Table 3.1). The Finnish average was more than half a standard deviation above the mean for the 27 participants and 20 points above the average score of the next closest. The United States also performed well and had the second best outcome

TABLE 3.1 IEA Country Means (and Standard Deviations) for 9-year-olds, 1990–91

Country	Grade	Mean age	Overall	Narrative	Expository	Documents
Finland	3	9.7	569 (70)	568 (83)	569 (81)	569 (88)
United States	4	10.0	547 (74)	553 (96)	538 (80)	550 (81)
Sweden	3	9.8	539 (94)	536 (100)	542 (112)	539 (106)
France	4	10.1	531 (74)	532 (93)	533 (84)	527 (81)
Italy	4	9.9	529 (80)	533 (88)	538 (95)	517 (92)
New Zealand	5	10.0	528 (86)	534 (102)	531 (93)	521 (92)
Norway	3	9.8	524 (91)	525 (102)	528 (103)	519 (101)
Iceland	3	9.8	518 (85)	518 (95)	517 (101)	519 (91)
Hong Kong	4	10.0	517 (71)	494 (87)	503 (72)	554 (89)
Singapore	3	9.3	515 (72)	521 (91)	519 (75)	504 (78)
Switzerland	3	9.7	511 (83)	506 (92)	507 (100)	522 (96)
Ireland	4	9.3	509 (79)	518 (94)	514 (89)	495 (84)
Belgium (French)	4	9.8	507 (77)	510 (92)	505 (85)	506 (88)
Greece	4	9.3	504 (75)	514 (88)	511 (85)	488 (85)
Spain	4	10.0	504 (78)	497 (86)	505 (92)	509 (89)
West Germany	3	9.4	503 (84)	491 (93)	497 (104)	520 (94)
Canada (BC)	3	8.9	500 (80)	502 (96)	499 (94)	500 (86)
East Germany	3	9.5	499 (84)	482 (93)	493 (103)	522 (96)
Hungary	3	9.3	499 (78)	496 (80)	493 (101)	509 (89)
Slovenia	3	9.7	498 (78)	502 (94)	489 (93)	503 (82)
The Netherlands	3	9.2	485 (73)	494 (85)	480 (87)	481 (82)
Cyprus	4	9.8	481 (77)	492 (92)	475 (91)	476 (81)
Portugal	4	10.4	478 (74)	483 (81)	480 (84)	471 (92)
Denmark	3	9.8	475 (111)	463 (119)	467 (127)	496 (125)
Trinidad and Tobago	4	9.6	451 (79)	455 (91)	458 (93)	440 (82)
Indonesia	4	10.8	394 (59)	402 (66)	411 (77)	369 (66)
Venezuela	4	10.1	383 (74)	378 (86)	396 (91)	374 (84)

in the Narrative and Expository domains. Youngsters from Sweden, France, and New Zealand also scored well above the international average in each domain. The New Zealanders' performance was especially notable for exceeding predictions based on more limited economic circumstances. Norway, Iceland, and Hong Kong also scored above the international mean (all close to 520 points). Hong Kong presents an interesting case, in that students read the texts in Chinese, an ideographic language well known to present unique difficulties. (We'll examine this issue in the next chapter.)

Children in developing countries performed less well than their peers in the industrialized nations, a finding consistent with economic disadvantage and the lack of long-standing literacy traditions. Included in this list are Venezuela, Indonesia, Trinidad and Tobago, and Cyprus. Nearly a third of the students in each of these countries scored at chance levels or below, indicating virtual non-reader status. Despite some similarities in circumstances, however, it would be a mistake to attribute their performance to the same causes. Each country faced its own unique challenges. For example, nearly 80 percent of Indonesian students took the test in a language other than the one they spoke at home. In Trinidad and Tobago, students were outperformed by those in developed nations, but they did notably better than meager government resources had led researchers to predict.

There were interesting findings among the established nations as well. Portuguese children performed at a level that reflected its history of relatively low funding for schools and low preschool participation. Results from the Netherlands were much lower than anticipated, but the Dutch 9-year-olds were considerably younger than the rest of the sample. These examples underscore the need for nuanced interpretations and for recognizing the complexities that contribute to findings.

IEA Results for 14-year-olds

All 32 countries participated in the assessment of 14-year-olds. Finland again outperformed all others, with the U.S. finishing 9th. A few notable finishers included Sweden, Hungary, Singapore, and Hong Kong. Swedish results were achieved by students with fewer years in school and fewer hours of instruction than children in most other countries. Singapore students employed English as their language of instruction and testing, yet English is the home language for just 26 percent of the sample. Singapore students were also below the international average in age. On the other hand, students in the Hong Kong sample were nearly five months older than the international mean.

Countries with relatively low achievement included Botswana, Nigeria, and Zimbabwe – the only African participants – as well as other developing nations, including Venezuela, the Philippines, Thailand, and Trinidad and Tobago. Each of the African nations had large numbers of students who were below the chance level mark of 25 percent. The majority of students in these countries were tested in a non-native language and the resource levels and traditions of literacy in each case were less than favorable. In both Venezuela and Thailand, low percentages of their 14-year-old populations were still in school – 72 percent and 33 percent, respectively. Belgium, the Netherlands, and Portugal performed more poorly than their status would have predicted. However, Belgium and the Netherlands tested large numbers of students younger than 14.5. The average age of Portuguese students, on the other hand, was 15.6 years at the time of testing.

Results in Context

The IEA study was instrumental in shedding first light on the status of school-age reading literacy in a range of national contexts. The results spurred subsequent assessments and led to oft-cited comparisons, which frequently ignored the nuance needed to interpret the results in meaningful ways. The study also thrust certain countries, most notably Finland, into the role of exemplar – Darling-Hammond has called the country "a poster child for school improvement" (2010, p. 164) – prompting scrutiny of systemic differences that might be emulated.

For most of the participating countries, performance was closely related to national indices of economic development and health. There were likewise many related differences between high- and low-scoring countries, including the size of school and classroom libraries, regularity of book borrowing, frequency of silent reading in class, frequency of reading aloud by teachers, and the number of scheduled hours spent in language instruction. Some of these differences reflect economic disparities and others, we suspect, the level and kind of teacher preparation.

Gender differences, already long documented in the U.S., were observed across borders. Girls achieved at higher levels than boys in all countries at age 9 and in most countries at age 14.[4] Various explanations of this phenomenon have been proposed, among them identification with female teachers. Indeed, in the five countries where 9-year-old girls were found to be furthest ahead of boys, 71 percent of the primary school teachers were female. A competing theory has been that girls tend to mature more quickly than boys, a head start reflected in reading growth, especially when instruction begins early. The IEA results lent some credibility to this argument. In three of the six countries with the largest gender gap in achievement, the start of reading instruction was at age five (New Zealand, Trinidad and Tobago, and Ireland) and in two of these countries, boys were furthest behind at age 14.

The questionnaires used in the IEA study, together with information from other sources such as UNESCO and the World Bank report, deserve closer analysis. General influences of school and community literacy levels included GNP per capita, adult literacy, newspaper circulation (per 1,000 people), public library book circulation (per 1,000 people), economic status of teachers, expenditure on education per student, language homogeneity of the sample, the proportion of low-birth-weight infants, and life expectancy. The countries whose 14-year-olds performed best were the more advantaged on these nine criteria.

In the study of 9-year-olds, 21 educational policy indicators were compared in the 10 highest- and lowest-scoring countries. Many of the same educational policy indicators for 9- and 14-year-olds were the same, with a few notable exceptions. Countries with larger proportions of female teachers exhibited higher literacy achievement relative to other countries with similar economic conditions. Differences in the level of teacher education were positively, but not perfectly, related to achievement. Canada (British Columbia), West Germany, Italy, Norway, the United States, and Venezuela all required more than 17 years of education and training while Botswana, Denmark, the Netherlands, the Philippines, Singapore, Thailand, and Zimbabwe expected 13 years or less. Overall, the extra years of education do suggest a positive influence, both before and after adjustment for economic differences.

Physical facilities were also related to achievement. High school principals were asked to indicate whether their school contained eight features that were hypothesized to be indirect indicators of policies designed to encourage reading growth. These included a library (its size as well as its presence), student reading room, student newspaper, teacher library, drama club, debating club, literature club, and a writing club. Predictably, the higher-scoring countries provided considerably more of these resources for encouraging reading, and the difference was even greater after adjusting for economic differences.

PIRLS

History and Purpose

PIRLS is an international comparative study of the reading ability of students in their fourth year of formal instruction. Plans for the study began in 1999 with a meeting of the IEA Secretariat, the International Student Center (ISC) at Boston College, Statistics Canada, and the National Foundation for Educational Research in England and Wales. The ISC was charged with development and implementation.

PIRLS has obvious roots in earlier IEA studies, such as the Reading Literacy Study in 1991 and 2001. PIRLS was first conducted in 2001 and every five years since then (in 2006 and 2011) to measure trends. Common use of the term *fourth grade* is, of course, not internationally meaningful. The actual policy specifies the "upper of the two grades with the most being nine-year-olds at the time of testing." This age was chosen because of the expectation that children at that point should already have acquired foundational skills and "are now reading to learn" (Kelly, 2003, p. 2).

The number of participating countries has grown steadily. In 2001, 35 countries participated, in 2006, 40 countries, and in 2011, 48. From the outset, the language diversity of the participants presented assessment issues. PIRLS was designed in English and translated into 45 languages. The majority of the participating countries administer PIRLS in one language. Spain, however, administers it in five languages, South Africa in eleven, and Canada together with nine other countries give it in two (Mullis & Martin, 2007).

Literacy Definition

PIRLS began with the IEA definition of literacy but has refined it slightly over the years. At present, reading literacy is defined as:

> the ability to understand and use those written language forms required by society and/or valued by the individual. Readers can construct meaning from texts in a variety of forms. They read to learn, to participate in communities of readers in school and everyday life, and for enjoyment.
> (Mullis, Martin, & Sainsbury, 2013, p. 14)

The study assesses comprehension of two types of texts: literary and informational. Four comprehension strategies were assessed: retrieval of explicitly stated information (20%), arrival at straightforward inferences (40%), interpretation/integration of ideas and information (25%), and examination and evaluation of content, language, and textual elements (15%).

Measurement

PIRLS employs a "two-stage random sample design, with a sample of schools drawn as a first stage and one or more intact classes of students selected from each of the sampled schools as a second stage" (Joncas & Foy, 2013, p. 1). In 2011, national samples ranged from 3,190 to 23,206.

Reading comprehension assessment is based on five informational and five literary passages, each accompanied by twelve questions. For the purpose of tracking trends over time, two of the passages for each area were carried forward from 2001 to 2006 with the remaining six newly developed. In 2011, six of the passages were carried forward from previous studies – one each from 2001 and 2006, four from 2006.

Testing is limited to two passages per student, with additional time allotted for a student questionnaire. Scores above 395 are categorized by four benchmarks with these minimum scores: low (400), median (475), high (550), and advanced (625). It should be noted that from 2001 to 2006 there were changes in the benchmark minimum scores and the 2001 to 2006 comparison reflects these changes. Each benchmark correlates with specific skills the reader exhibits for literary and informational reading (Kennedy & Trong, 2007).

In addition to questions focusing on reading ability, four additional questionnaires are completed to gather further information on factors that may impact literacy. The questionnaires are directed at students, parents/caregivers, teachers, and school principals. The student questionnaire asks about experiences with reading instruction, homework, self-perception and attitude toward reading, out-of-school reading habits, computer usage, resources at home, and basic demographic information.

The second questionnaire, the Learning to Read Home Survey, is completed by the primary caregiver and focuses on home literacy resources, parents'/caregivers' attitudes toward reading and reading habits, home-school connections, basic demographic information and socioeconomic indicators. The third is a teacher questionnaire that gathers information about classroom characteristics, instructional activities to promote literacy development, resources, home-school connections, opportunities for professional development and the teacher's education and background. The fourth questionnaire is completed by school principals. It focuses on enrollment, school characteristics, reading educational resources, instructional time, home-school connections and the atmosphere of the school. The information garnered through these surveys helps to shed contextual light on the proficiency measures and is key to any nuanced interpretation.

PIRLS 2001 Results

Some 35 countries participated in the first administration of PIRLS. The top three finishers were Sweden, the Netherlands, and England. These northern European countries had consistently been near the top of other international assessments. Rounding out the top 25 percent were Bulgaria, Latvia, Canada, Lithuania, Hungary, the United States, and Italy. All of these are economically developed and concentrated in Europe and North America. The bottom 10 percent – Iran, Kuwait, Morocco, and Belize – are harder to characterize, and we will return to this question later in the chapter.

PIRLS 2006 Results

The second PIRLS administration involved 40 countries, including several that took part for the first time. This time a different cast rose to the top: the Russian Federation, Hong Kong, and Singapore. In contrast, the United States fell below the top 30 percent. The bottom 10 percent once again included Iran, Kuwait, and Morocco, plus first-time participant, Qatar.

TABLE 3.2 PIRLS Reading Results, 2001–11

Country	PIRLS 2001 Average Scale Score	PIRLS 2006 Average Scale Score	PIRLS 2011 Average Scale Score	Change since Most Recent Participation*
Argentina	420			
Austria		538	529	**−9**
Azerbaijan			462	
Belgium (Flemish)		547		
Belgium (French)		500	506	6
Belize	327			
Botswana				
Bulgaria	550	547	532	**−15**
Canada (Ontario)	548	555	552	−3
Chinese Taipei		535	553	**18**
Colombia	422		448	**25**
Croatia			553	
Cyprus	494		494	0
Czech Republic	537		545	**9**
Denmark		546	554	**8**
England	553	539	552	**12**
Finland			568	
France	525	522	520	−2
Georgia		471	488	**17**
Germany	539	548	541	**−7**
Greece	524			
Honduras				
Hong Kong SAR	528	564	571	7
Hungary	543	551	539	**−12**
Iceland	512	511		
India				
Indonesia		405	428	**24**
Iran	414	421	457	**36**
Ireland			552	
Israel	509	512	541	
Italy	541	551	541	**−10**

Country	PIRLS 2001 Average Scale Score	PIRLS 2006 Average Scale Score	PIRLS 2011 Average Scale Score	Change since Most Recent Participation*
Kuwait	396	330		
Latvia	545	541	545	
Lithuania	543	537	528	**−9**
Luxemburg		557		
Macedonia	442	442		
Malta			477	
Moldova, Republic of	492	500		
Morocco	350	323	310	
Netherlands	554	547	546	−1
New Zealand	529	532	531	−1
Northern Ireland			558	
Norway	499	498	507	**9**
Oman			391	
Poland		519	526	**6**
Portugal			541	
Qatar		353	425	
Romania	512	489	502	12
Russian Federation	528	565	568	4
Saudi Arabia			430	
Scotland	528	527		
Singapore	528	558	567	**9**
Slovak Republic	518	531	535	4
Slovenia	502	522	530	**9**
South Africa		302		
Spain		513	513	1
Sweden	561	549	542	**−8**
Trinidad & Tobago		436	471	**35**
Turkey	449			
United Arab Emirates			439	
United States	542	540	556	**16**

* Bold face indicates that the difference was significant.

PIRLS 2011 Results

With the third administration in 2011, the average score of all countries combined increased substantially as did the number of participants, from 40 to 48. Finland, which had led the world in the IEA study 20 years previously, reentered the scene and shared second place with the Russian Federation, behind Hong Kong. Finland's performance on PIRLS has again attracted worldwide recognition for its educational system. The United States was able to make up some lost ground, ranking sixth in overall performance and significantly bettering its 2006 performance. The bottom 10 percent included the United Arab Emirates, Indonesia, Qatar, Oman, and Morocco.

On average, 95 percent of the students scored at or above the Low benchmark. This accomplishment, however modest, confirms that basic reading skills are being widely fostered. The medians for the Intermediate, High, and Advanced Benchmarks were 80 percent, 44 percent, and 8 percent, respectively.

Results in Context

Trends from 2001 to 2006. There was a general improvement in PIRLS scores from the first to the second administration, five years later. Russia exhibited an especially notable increase, a development anticipated by researchers due to changes in curriculum and the implementation of new programs. Some 19 percent of Russian students reached the advanced benchmark and 61 percent achieved the high benchmark, compared with only 5 percent and 39 percent, respectively, in 2001. Hong Kong and Singapore made similar gains. Countries such as Sweden, England, and the Netherlands, however, saw a decrease in the percentage of students scoring at the advanced and high levels. In Sweden and England there was a decline in the proportion of students achieving the intermediate benchmark as well. Romania was the only country to have an overall decrease in achievement across all four benchmarks.

Three 10-Year Trends. Decade trends are limited, of course, to countries that participated in both 2001 and 2011. That said, three notable facts emerge. One is that more countries registered statistically significant gains (8) than losses (4). In addition, four countries significantly improved from *both* 2001 to 2006 *and* from 2006 to 2011: Hong Kong, Singapore, Slovenia, and Iran. In contrast, two countries experienced significant declines from 2001 to 2006 and *again* from 2006 to 2011: Lithuania and Sweden. These are significant long-term trajectories that warrant further analysis by policymakers in all six of these nations. Finally, a significant gender gap continued: Girls outperformed boys in all three PIRLS administrations. In no country did the mean for boys exceed that of girls in 2011, although the difference was not significant in five nations. Not surprisingly, girls tended to possess a higher self-concept regarding their reading ability than boys as well as more positive attitudes toward reading as a recreational activity, topics we will return to in Chapter 7.

PISA

History and Purpose

Since its launch in 2000, PISA has targeted the proficiency of 15-year-olds in reading, mathematics, and science literacy. It is conducted in three-year cycles, each administration assessing one of the three subject areas in depth, although all three are assessed in each cycle. PISA 2000 and 2009 included in-depth assessment of reading, and so we review data from these two administrations here. For PISA 2012, reading was not the primary focus, but we include the results for comparisons across years.

PISA is conducted by the Organisation for Economic Co-operation and Development (OECD) and includes member countries and partner countries (and several subnational economies) volunteering to participate. The purpose of the assessment is to measure how well students can apply their knowledge and skills in the three domains to problems within a real-life context. The assessment also gathers information from school principals about school context and from students about their educational experiences and attitudes.

Literacy Definition

PISA attaches the term *literacy* to each subject area to denote its broad focus on the application of knowledge and skills.[5] *Reading literacy* is defined as "an individual's capacity to understand, use, reflect on and engage with written texts, in order to achieve one's goals, to develop one's knowledge and potential, and to participate in society" (OECD, 2009a, p. 14). As with IEA and PIRLS, our primary emphasis is on the reading literacy of 15-year-olds, considered in the light of schooling and contextual factors that might influence performance and help to unpack international comparisons.

Measurement

A target age of 15 allows researchers and policymakers to compare learning outcomes as students are approaching the end of their compulsory school experience. PISA achievement scores are viewed as representing a "yield" of learning at age 15, rather than as a direct measure of attained curriculum knowledge at a particular level. PISA 2009 not only marks the second round during which reading was examined in depth, but also a pivotal point at which the notion of reading was broadened to include digital texts. Like PIRLS, it also examines students' attitudes toward reading and the learning strategies they apply.

38 Measured Reading Ability

In each area of the assessment, tasks were ranked by difficulty and were associated with seven proficiency levels, from 1b (easiest) to 6 (hardest). A student reaches a given proficiency level by demonstrating at least a 50 percent performance on the tasks associated with that level. Students are classified at the highest level at which they are proficient. Baselines were identified as Level 2 in reading, mathematics, and science. If students do not achieve the baseline, they were identified as lacking the essential skills that are needed to participate effectively and productively in society.

PISA 2000 Results

A total of 42 countries or subnational economies participated in the first administration of PISA in 2000 (see Table 3.3). If we consider all three of the assessed domains, the highest scoring students were from Japan, Korea, New Zealand, Finland, and Australia, with Japan scoring the highest in reading and mathematical literacy and Korea taking the top spot in scientific literacy. Brazil, Mexico, Luxembourg, Greece, and Portugal all scored in the bottom 10 percent, with the United States scoring well below the OECD average. When we focus specifically on reading, a slightly different picture emerges. Finland, Canada, New Zealand, and Australia were the top finishers, while Macedonia, Indonesia, Albania, and Peru made up the bottom 10 percent. The United States ranked 16th, and its average of 504 did not differ statistically from the international mean of 500.

PISA 2009 Results

Participation in PISA rose from 42 countries in 2000 to 65 countries in 2009. Top performers in reading included Shanghai,[6] Korea, Finland, Hong Kong, and Singapore. This administration marked a rise in the number of Asian countries performing above the OECD average. The bottom 10 percent included Qatar, Panama, Peru, Azerbaijan, and Kyrgyzstan. In this administration, the United States scored at the international mean (500) and above the OECD average (493), though the difference was not significant.

Across OECD countries, an average of 16.3 percent of 15-year-olds performed at the highest level in at least one area (reading, math, or science). However, only 4.1 percent excelled in all three areas. Two notable exceptions were Shanghai and Singapore, where 14.6 percent and 12.3 percent of students, respectively, performed at the highest level in all three. Given the critical importance of applying a wide range of high-level skills in concert, their acquisition in these two places is laudable, though its rarity elsewhere should occasion concern.

TABLE 3.3 PISA Combined Reading Literacy Mean Scale Scores, 2000, 2009, and 2012*

Nation/Economy	2000	2009	2012	Annualized Change★★	National/Economy	2000	2009	2012	Annualized Change★★
Albania		385	394	**4.1**	Georgia				
Argentina		398	396	−1.6	Germany	484	497	508	**1.8**
Australia	528	515	512	**−1.4**	Greece	474	483	477	0.5
Austria	507	470	490	−0.2	Himachal Pradesh, India				
Azerbaijan		362			Hong Kong, China		533	545	**2.3**
Belgium	507	506	509	0.1	Hungary	480	494	488	**1.0**
Brazil	396	412	410	**1.2**	Iceland	507	500	483	**−1.3**
Bulgaria		429	436	0.4	Indonesia		402	396	**2.3**
Canada	534	524	523	**−0.9**	Ireland	527	496	523	**−0.9**
Chile		449	441	**3.1**	Israel		474	486	**3.7**
Chinese Taipei		495	523	**4.5**	Italy	487	486	490	0.5
Colombia		413	403	**3.0**	Japan	522	520	538	**1.5**
Costa Rica			441	−1.0	Jordan		405	399	−0.3
Croatia		476	485	1.2	Kazakhstan		390	393	0.8
Czech Republic	492	478	493	−0.5	Korea	525	556	536	**0.9**
Denmark	497	495	496	0.1	Kyrgyzstan		314		
Estonia		501	516	**2.4**	Latvia	458	484	489	**1.9**
Finland	546	536	524	**−1.7**	Liechtenstein	483	499	516	**1.3**
France	505	496	505	0.0	Lithuania		468	477	1.1

(*Continued*)

TABLE 3.3 Continued

Nation/Economy	2000	2009	2012	Annualized Change**	National/Economy	2000	2009	2012	Annualized Change**
Luxembourg	441	472	488	**0.7**	Russian Federation	462	459	475	**1.1**
Macao, China		487	509	**0.8**	Serbia		429	446	**7.6**
Macedonia					Shanghai, China		556	570	**4.6**
Malaysia			398	−7.8	Singapore		526	542	**5.4**
Malta					Slovak Republic		477	463	−0.1
Mauritius					Slovenia		483	481	**−2.2**
Mexico	422	425		**1.1**	Spain	493	481	488	−0.3
Miranda, Venezuela					Sweden	516	497	483	**−2.8**
Montenegro		408	422	**5.0**	Switzerland	494	501	509	**1.0**
Netherlands			511	−0.1	Tamil Nadu, India				
Netherlands–Antilles		508			Thailand		421	441	**1.1**
New Zealand	529	521	512	**−1.1**	Trinidad and Tobago		416		
Norway	505	503	504	0.1	Tunisia		404	404	**3.8**
Panama		371			Turkey		464	475	**4.1**
Peru		370	384	**5.2**	United Arab Emirates		459	442	
Poland	479	500	518	**2.8**	United Kingdom		494	499	0.7
Portugal	470	489	488	**1.6**	United States	504	500	498	−0.3
Qatar		372	388	**12.0**	Uruguay		426	411	**−1.8**
Romania		424	438	1.1	Vietnam			508	

* Some countries (or subnational economies) participated but results were not made available for all years.

** Bold face indicates a significant change in annualized score points since the country's (or subnational economy's) first participation in PISA, taking into account the results of all administrations.

Results in Context

PISA confirms that the reading advantage for 9-year-old females, documented by PIRLS, continues throughout schooling. Females outperformed males in every country participating in PISA 2009, and by an average of 39 scale points, the equivalent of more than half a proficiency level, or one year of school. Males, however, outperformed girls in mathematics by an average of 12 points. Not surprisingly, students' expressed interest in these subjects varied by gender, males reporting a greater interest in math, females in reading. Gender differences in science performance tended to be small, both in absolute terms and relative to the large gender gap in reading and math.

PISA has addressed important questions involving the relationship between socioeconomic status and achievement. A long-documented positive correlation between the two has turned out to be rather complex. For example, a PISA 2000 finding was that the relationship of parents' income to their 15-year-old children's reading achievement was far stronger in Germany and the Czech Republic than in Japan or Korea. The reasons for these differences are well beyond the scope of the study to answer, but they are likely to involve policy, cultural, and curricular factors that we take up in the next two chapters.

PISA 2009 addressed the socioeconomic issue in a slightly different way by distinguishing between the status of an individual student and the status of the school that a student attended. Is a student of low socioeconomic status (SES) likely to achieve equally well in a high-SES and a low-SES school? The answer was that, on average, low-SES 15-year-olds did better in reading when enrolled in high-SES schools. In the words of the report, "In the majority of OECD countries, the effect of the school's economic, social and cultural status on students' performance far outweighs the effects of the individual student's socio-economic background" (OECD, 2010, p. 9).

There are important qualifiers regarding the influence of parental income. PISA 2000 confirmed that the level of education attained by parents may be high enough to support their children's learning despite relatively low income. PISA 2009 reported that achievement is related to the presence of two parents in the home, and to the active involvement of parents with their children's schooling. These findings are, at least in part, clear reflections of cultural values transmitted from one generation to the next.

Noted in the PISA 2009 report is the fact that countries of similar prosperity can produce different educational results. Nonetheless, national wealth remains a significant predictor of reading achievement. The 10 countries in which the majority of students scored at Level 1 or below in 2009 all have challenged economies. In stark contrast are the 34 OECD countries, mostly economically advantaged and where, on average, a majority of 15-year-olds attain at least Level 3 proficiency. Still, there are notable counterexamples, such as Shanghai. Although its GDP per capita is well below the OECD average, Shanghai's 15-year-olds finished first in the world. The case of Shanghai demonstrates that a low average income is not incompatible with

PISA 2012 Results

The 2012 administration of PISA centered mainly on mathematics, with reading a "minor" area (OECD, 2014). However, the update provides a useful third point for plotting a country's trajectory. Table 3.3 represents national means over time. Beyond the impulse to appraise a country's status by comparing its ranking with that of others, we suggest that policymakers consider the progress of their own 15-year-olds. Unpacking the need for altered policy is clearly speculative, but the first step is to note whether discernible changes are occurring. The annualized mean change since a country first participated in PISA can be useful. For many countries, this change is not statistically significant, but where the number is bolded, the average yearly rise or fall can be telling.

Some of the trends are surprising. Finland, a perennial high finisher, has lost nearly two points per year from 2000 to 2012, a small but a steady and significant decline. Neighboring Sweden has registered an even sharper drop. In contrast, East Asian countries have all experienced significant yearly increases, as have a number of Eastern European nations. The United States hasn't budged, though it will be interesting to see whether a pipeline effect carries its gain on PIRLS 2011 into PISA 2015. We encourage readers to pursue the more detailed analyses readily available in the research literature. As we have mentioned, our goal is to examine the broad landscape of change.

IALS

History and Purpose

In recent years, the transition from heavy industry to information technologies among the developed nations has occasioned increased awareness of the link between adult literacy and economic health and social cohesion. The threshold of proficiency in these countries has risen accordingly. Literacy has steadily moved to center stage in policy agendas around the globe, as each new phase of globalization brings with it new uncertainties and opportunities related to the workforce. As these changes occur, the mismatch between skill demands and skill attainment is often painfully apparent. Apparent too is the inadequacy of relying on school attendance data as a proxy for literacy assessment.

Countries chose to participate in IALS for four principal reasons: (1) policies to improve literacy need to draw on a strong knowledge base; (2) existing knowledge of educational attainment across countries is scant, especially with regard to objective measures of adults' performance rather than qualifications;

(3) it is crucial to identify differences between groups to help target policy interventions; and (4) literacy is a relative concept that must be studied in the context of economic and social demands. Countries included Canada, Germany, Ireland, the Netherlands, Poland, Sweden, Switzerland, and the United States. In six countries, the survey was administered in the national language, although in Canada and Switzerland, respondents were able to choose the language of the assessment. The survey was coordinated by two agencies in the United States and Canada. Each country was obliged to draw a probability sample representative of the civilian, non-institutionalized population aged 16 to 65.

Literacy Definition

IALS defined literacy as "the ability to understand and employ printed information in daily activities, at home, at work and in the community – to achieve one's goals, and to develop one's knowledge and potential" (OECD, 2000, p. x). This broad skill set was delineated into three domains: prose literacy, document literacy, and quantitative literacy. Prose literacy was defined as "the knowledge and skills needed to understand and use information from texts including editorials, news stories, brochures and instruction manuals" (p. x). Document literacy was defined as "the knowledge and skills required to locate and use information contained in various forms, including job applications, payroll forms, transportation schedules, maps, tables, and charts" (p. x). Finally, quantitative literacy was defined as:

> the knowledge and skills required to apply arithmetic operations, either alone or sequentially, to numbers embedded in printed materials, such as balancing a checkbook, figuring out a tip, completing an order form, or determining the amount of interest on a loan from an advertisement.
>
> (p. x)

Missing from these definitions are references to the ability to apply literacy skills in digital settings or, for that matter, to the existence of additional and distinct skills needed to function in literate ways online. From the definitions just quoted, one might easily impute this intent to the framers of IALS, but the assessment in fact used a paper-and-pencil format. In fairness, the Internet was still in its infancy during the 1990s, but given the present-day importance of digital literacy and the recognized need to adjust our assessments accordingly,[7] the IALS results must be interpreted with this limitation in mind.

Measurement

The assessment comprised a common set of tasks, compiled collaboratively by participating countries and selected according to their relevance across cultures.

In each domain, proficiency was expressed on a scale from 0 to 500. Some of the tasks included in the assessment were at the low end of this scale, some at the high end, but most had values in the 200-to-400 range. Participants were tested in their homes and in the primary language of their country. An interview was conducted first to capture information concerning a respondent's background. This was followed by a 45-minute assessment. Unlike most standardized tests, IALS avoided multiple-choice questions, as it was thought that adults would be more comfortable answering open-ended questions.

Scaling was accomplished by analyzing how people actually performed on the various tasks and then defining proficiency as an 80 percent chance of completing a given task. Tasks on each scale were ordered according to the skills needed to complete them. In prose literacy, 34 tasks of varying difficulty were included in IALS and were measured using various types of textual material and asking the reader to perform tasks requiring information-processing skills. Document literacy, which likewise included 34 tasks of progressive difficulty, required adults to process everyday documents. Quantitative literacy included 33 tasks, each requiring the examinee to comprehend textual information, thus making computational skills inadequate on their own.

Each scale was divided into five levels requiring successively higher skill sets to complete them. For example, at Level 1 of prose literacy, respondents were asked to locate one piece of information in the text that was identical to or synonymous with the information given in the directive. In document literacy, Level 1 involved locating a piece of information based on a literal match. Distracting information, if present, was typically placed away from the correct answer. Some tasks directed the reader to enter personal information onto a form.

IALS described Level 3 as:

> a suitable minimum for coping with the demands of everyday life and work in a complex, advanced society. It denotes roughly the skill level required for successful secondary school completion and college entry. Like higher levels, it requires the ability to integrate several sources of information and solve more complex problems.
>
> (OECD, 2000, p. xi)

In retrospect, Level 3 appears roughly comparable to America's present-day Common Core State Standards' goal of helping "to ensure that all students are college and career ready in literacy no later than the end of high school" (CCSSI, 2010). It is likewise related to the new PISA emphasis on financial literacy.

IALS Results

IALS reported overall 1994–98 means for 20 countries.[8] In prose literacy, three Scandinavian countries led the way: Sweden was first (303.1), followed by

Finland (288.6) and Norway (288.5). The United States ranked 10th (273.7). Portugal (222.6) and Chile (220.8) comprised the bottom 10 percent. There were similar results for document literacy. Scandinavian nations took the top four places: Sweden (305.6), Norway (296.9), Denmark (293.8), and Finland (289.2). The U.S. was 13th (267.9), and Portugal (220.4) and Chile (218.9) again finished last.

The distribution of adults by level of proficiency permits useful illumination of the overall scores. In prose literacy, Chile, Portugal, and Poland had the highest percentages of adults performing at Level 1: 50.1 percent, 48.0 percent, and 42.6 percent, respectively. The U.S. percentage was 20.7. At Levels 4–5, Sweden, Canada, and Finland had the highest percentages: 32.4 percent, 22.7 percent, and 22.4 percent respectively. In the United States, 21.1 percent of adults scored at Levels 4–5.

In document literacy, Chile, Portugal, and Poland once more had the highest percentages of adults performing at Level 1: 51.5 percent, 49.1 percent, and 45.4 percent, respectively. The U.S. percentage was 23.7. Sweden, Norway, and Denmark had the highest percentages at Levels 4–5: 35.5 percent, 29.4 percent, and 25.4 percent, respectively. In the United States, 19.0 percent of adults scored at Levels 4–5.

In quantitative literacy, Chile (56.4%), Portugal (41.6%), and Poland (39.1%) had the highest proportions of adults who performed at Level 1. The U.S. percentage was 21.0. At Levels 4–5, Sweden (35.8%), the Czech Republic (31.9%), and Denmark (28.4%) were the top three countries. In the U.S., 22.5 percent of adults scored at Levels 4–5.

Results in Context

With IALS, the OECD broke important ground in providing a dependable international frame of reference for adult literacy. Because it was carried out in the 1990s, due caution must be exercised in interpreting the relevance of its results to the present. Nevertheless, several conclusions seem well warranted.

First, the headline-grabbing "horse race" rankings of countries by their overall scores, albeit intriguing, are not very useful as drivers of policy. More telling is the proportion of respondents at each proficiency level, and it is here that a different story can emerge. By examining the distribution of its adult population across performance levels – instead of comparing an overall mean with those other countries – policymakers are better positioned to decide where resources can best be focused.

Second, these results enable analyses of the fit between a nation's economy and the literacy levels of its adult citizenry. A country heavily invested in the agricultural sector may argue, not unreasonably, that it can tolerate higher proportions of adults with low-level skills. This is dangerous thinking, however, as future advances will almost certainly raise the threshold of participatory literacy for every sector of the economy. More than ever, predictions based on past assumptions are likely to prove wrong. The national profiles offered by IALS – and its successor, PIAAC – permit not only country-to-country comparisons but within-country examinations of how proficiency is distributed. It is here, we argue, that the real value of the assessment lies.

Third, IALS called attention to how patterns of immigration can affect proficiency. Each participating country had a unique pattern of immigration, which was reflected in the literacy skill distribution of its population. For example, the proportion of immigrants with skills at Levels 3–5 in Sweden and Norway were more than double the proportion in the United States; in contrast, the U.S. proportion at Levels 1 and 2 was nearly double that of these two countries (OECD, 2000).

Finally, IALS delivered a mild surprise by revealing no gender differences. Unlike PIRLS and PISA, women did not consistently outperform men and, in general, the distributions of men and women at each literacy level were similar.

The practice of literacy, within and between countries, and its impact on literacy skills, both inside and outside work was examined by IALS. A key question is how literacy skill and literacy activity reinforce each other. There are some connections between literacy skill and the frequency of engaging in particular activities, such as reading journals, writing letters, calculating prices, and reading directions and manuals. These connections are strongest between the task and the pertinent literacy domain and for tasks with a narrow range of difficulty. Since a person's job influences his/her practices, it also determines how her/his skills develop with predictable occupational differences. For example, with writing, skill level and frequency of practice vary in predictable ways according to occupational requirements. In all countries, for example, respondents at Level 4/5 literacy skills were considerably more likely than those at Level 2 to write letters and memos.

For all the activities surveyed, the clearest differences were between Level 1 literates and the rest. For example, individuals at lower literacy levels reported watching television more frequently, while those scoring at higher levels participated more often in community activities. Most respondents thought that their reading skills served them well not only on the job but in their daily lives, perhaps because the activities they chose were unconsciously constrained by available skills. As for work, people were more confident in their reading skills than in writing or mathematics.

IALS broke new ground by demonstrating that adult literacy can be studied effectively on an international basis. It raised awareness that while cross-national differences must be understood in context, they can potentially be remedied through policy action. And most importantly, it paved the way for PIAAC.

PIAAC[9]

History and Purpose

OECD's most recent attempt to gauge the status of adult skill attainment across borders is the Program for the International Assessment of Adult Competencies (PIAAC), which administers the Survey of Adult Skills. PIAAC data were collected in 2011–12 from adults 16–65 years of age in 24 countries and subnational regions. Results were reported in 2013 (OECD, 2013a, 2013b, 2013c). Although some intentional similarities to IALS permit trend analyses, there are also key differences that must qualify such attempts, beginning with how *literacy* was defined.

Literacy Definition

One of the principal goals of PIAAC was to update the definitions of literacy used in IALS to include digital skill sets. The stated aim was to assess "the proficiency of adults in literacy, numeracy and problem solving in technology-rich environments" (OECD, 2013a, p. 56). Our focus here is on literacy, defined specifically as "the ability to understand, evaluate, use and engage with *written texts* to participate in society, to achieve one's goals, and to develop one's knowledge and potential" (p. 59, original emphasis).

The phrase, *written texts*, was mainly intended to exclude spoken language (see p. 61), but it also established a clear boundary between the conventional notion of a text and the broader notion we discussed in Chapter 2. For example, a video did not qualify as a text in PIAAC. What did qualify were prose texts, documents, and a mixture of the two. In addition, the ability to integrate information across multiple texts was included in the assessment – an ability now recognized as a hallmark of advanced proficiency by the Common Core[10] (see also Chall, 1983/1996).

There were several key differences between the reading components of IALS and PIAAC. In the former, reading literacy was delineated into prose and document scores. PIAAC includes both kinds of tasks but combines performance into a single score. In addition, respondents with very low literacy skills were given a reading "components" test, which included vocabulary, sentence-level comprehension, and fluency. Finally, both print and digital versions were employed, a policy that distanced PIAAC from IALS in important ways. The print version was given, on average, to 21 percent of the adults sampled and the digital version to 74 percent. The print version was provided if a respondent had limited computing experience or simply requested it. It is important to note that the two versions differed in more than format. The digital version, in addition to merely presenting written texts in an online environment, also included tasks unique to the Internet, "such as simulated websites, results pages from search engines and blog posts" (OECD, 2013a, p. 61). Through field testing, OECD concluded that "difficulty and discrimination of most of the test items common to the two versions was largely unaffected by the mode in which the test was taken" (p. 62). This finding enabled PIAAC to collapse the results for the two versions. However, though doing so was psychometrically defensible, it may have masked some important distinctions among the types of online tasks.

Measurement

Like IALS, PIAAC tasks were arranged by difficulty along a 0–500 scale, and the designers established five levels of proficiency. Individuals scoring at Levels 4 and 5 could, for example:

> perform multiple-step operations to integrate, interpret, or synthesize information from complex or lengthy texts that involve conditional and/or competing information; and they can make complex inferences and appropriately apply background knowledge as well as interpret or evaluate subtle truth claims or arguments.
>
> (p. 28)

Further similarities to IALS included the age of respondents, which ranged from 16 to 65, the use of a questionnaire to help contextualize results, and the fact that the assessment was conducted in the home or in an agreed-upon alternative location. These similarities permit useful, though limited, comparisons across the decade and a half between IALS and PIAAC.

Testing began in 2011 and concluded in 2012.[11] In total, approximately 166,000 adults were assessed in 24 countries (or subnational regions). The samples varied from 4,500 to 27,300, depending on the number of respondents needed for representativeness.

PIAAC Results

OECD's 2013 report of the results is highly detailed. Its 461 pages go well beyond overall national rankings and delineate findings by proficiency level and various demographic subgroups. We make no attempt to fully capture the OECD analyses here but encourage close inspection of the report, which can be downloaded at no cost. We will, however, summarize a few of the key findings.

Rankings of the 26 participating countries and subnational regions appear in Table 3.4. We have already characterized overall means as a relatively blunt instrument, signifying little of practical utility for shaping policy. A more useful starting point is to consider the current percentages of a country's adult population at each of the proficiency levels. A cursory inspection of these percentages in Table 3.4 suggests a relatively normal distribution across countries. That is, similar proportions of adults score above and below the middle range (Levels 2 and 3). This observation is

TABLE 3.4 PIAAC Adjusted National Means, Percentages by Level, and IALS Combined Literacy Means*

Country or Subnational Region	IALS1994–98	PIAAC2012	Change	PIAAC Percentages by Level <1	1	2	3	4	5
Japan	–	296	–	0.6	4.3	22.8	48.6	21.4	1.2
Finland	287	288	+1	2.7	8.0	26.5	40.7	20.0	2.2
The Netherlands	286	284	–2	2.6	9.1	26.4	41.5	16.8	1.3
Australia	272	280	+8	3.1	9.4	29.2	39.4	15.7	1.3
Sweden	306	279	–27	3.7	9.6	29.1	41.6	14.9	1.2
Norway	294	278	–16	3.0	9.3	30.2	41.6	13.1	0.6
Estonia	–	276	–	2.0	11.0	34.3	40.6	11.0	0.8
Flanders (Belgium)	277	276	–1	2.7	11.3	29.6	38.8	11.9	0.4
Russian Federation	–	275	–	1.6	11.5	34.9	41.2	10.4	0.4
Czech Republic	277	274	–3	1.5	10.3	37.5	41.4	8.3	0.4
Slovak Republic	–	274	–	1.9	9.7	36.2	44.4	7.3	0.2
Canada	279	274	–5	3.8	12.6	31.7	37.3	12.8	0.9
England (U.K.)	267	273	+6	3.3	13.1	33.1	36.0	12.4	0.8
Korea	–	273	–	2.2	10.6	37.0	41.7	7.9	0.2
England/N. Ireland (U.K.)	–	273	–	3.3	13.1	33.2	35.9	12.3	0.8
Denmark	289	271	–18	3.8	11.9	34.0	39.9	9.6	0.4
Germany	282	270	–12	3.3	14.2	33.9	36.4	10.2	0.5
United States	273	270	–3	3.9	13.6	32.6	34.2	10.9	0.6
Austria	–	270	–	2.5	12.8	37.2	37.3	8.2	0.3
Cyprus	–	269	–	1.6	10.3	33.0	32.1	5.2	0.2
Northern Ireland (U.K.)	264	269	+5	2.5	14.9	36.2	34.3	9.4	0.5
Poland	232	267	+35	3.9	14.8	36.5	35.0	9.0	0.7
Ireland	264	267	+3	4.3	13.2	37.6	36.0	8.1	0.4
France	–	262	–	5.3	16.2	35.9	34.0	7.4	0.3
Spain	–	252	–	7.2	20.3	39.1	27.8	4.6	0.1
Italy	243	251	+8	5.5	22.2	42.0	26.4	3.3	0.1
Averages	–	273	–	3.3	12.2	33.3	32.1	5.2	17.7

*Ordering is by PIAAC means; IALS are rescaled means that combine prose and document literacy for comparison with PIAAC; PIAAC means are rounded.

a fair one, in general terms, but the distributions are not actually normal. They are skewed in one direction or the other, and it is in the nature of these distributions that telling patterns emerge. For example, the proportion of Japanese adults scoring at Levels 4–5 is nearly seven times the proportion in Italy, five times that of Spain, three times that of France, and twice that of the United States. In contrast, the proportion of adults scoring at Level 1 or below in the U.S. is more than three times the proportion in Japan and nearly double that of Finland and the Netherlands.

Results in Context

Efforts to include a wide range of potential correlates occasionally led the authors of the report to confirm the obvious. "Educational attainment," they write at one point, "has a strong positive relationship to proficiency" (OECD, 2013a, p. 137). But this is just good scholarship, and its thoroughness helped to ensure that complex insights could be reached by considering factors in tandem. For example, they found that the relationship between proficiency and educational attainment varies from country to country. Adults with low levels of education in some countries outperformed those with similar education in others. What counts as a basic education has lifelong effects.

In fact, the impact of education is one of the cautionary notes sounded by PIAAC. The overall proficiency means presented in Table 3.4 are for ages 16–65. What they do not reflect is the fact that younger adults consistently outperformed their elders. To some extent, one might attribute this finding to the natural influence of aging, except that the differences varied considerably across countries. The authors attribute these differences to the quality of basic education and to the opportunities for extending subsequent learning.

A similar pattern was evident in the performance of immigrants whose first language differed from that of their new country. Again, we would expect them to be outperformed by native speakers, but there is more to the story. We might also expect that the longer they resided in their adopted country, the better their second language proficiency and the better their performance on the assessment. However, in some countries length of residence made little or no difference in how well they performed. The authors speculate that failure to acquire the language of the host country may be the result of few practical incentives, lack of policies that encourage language acquisition, or both.

Regarding gender, the gap in reading performance was negligible, a finding consistent with IALS. A mean difference of 3.5 points became a mere 0.7 after adjustments for socio-demographic characteristics and practice-oriented factors. Nor were there gender differences when workplace literacy requirements were taken into account.

IALS-PIAAC Trends. There are two important ways of judging literacy trends. One is to test different cohorts of the same age at different points in time using the same (or a highly similar) assessment. The other is to track an age cohort over the years and compare performance at two or more points using different, but age-appropriate, assessments. Each approach has its own advantages and drawbacks, each is worthy of study, and each is made possible through OECD data.

The means for IALS and PIAAC represented in Table 3.4 provide an opportunity to compare different cohorts at two points in time. The differences between them can serve as an overall indicator of the direction in which literacy has moved in a decade and a half. They can also identify national winners and losers at the adult level. For countries registering sizable gains or losses, the differences should provoke careful scrutiny among national policymakers. Their task is to unpack the findings and uncover the likely causes. As we noted with regard to PISA, this is a speculative undertaking, but it is one that is well worth the effort. Topping the list of possible reasons why a national population might grow or regress are policy changes, immigration patterns, economic trends, and tertiary education rates. At the same time, psychometric explanations must also be considered. For example, OECD warns that low response rates can skew results, and it has employed statistical methods of addressing this threat (OECD, 2013b). Indeed, the differences in response rates between IALS and PIAAC are occasionally large, but there appears to have been no systematic relationship with literacy scores (OECD, 2013c).[12] Other changes that might have influenced mean differences between the two assessments were the use of multistage computer-adaptive testing for most PIAAC respondents and an infusion of new items (40%).

IALS-PIAAC Cohorts. Comparing IALS age cohorts with corresponding PIAAC cohorts (older by 16 years), reveals two general trends. One is that literacy proficiency tends to increase during young adulthood. In Australia, for example, 35-year-olds who participated in PIAAC outperformed 19-year-olds who took part in IALS. In other words, roughly speaking, they outperformed themselves at an earlier age. The second trend is not as rosy. Older individuals tended to lose proficiency as time passed. By the time they were 65, Australians did less well on PIAAC than they had done on IALS as 49-year-olds. The aging effect was widespread, and the threshold of the decline ranged from age 33 to 42, depending on the country.

PISA-PIAAC Cohorts. Because PIAAC data included the age of each adult, OECD was able to track students in the four PISA administrations (2000, 2003,[13] 2006, and 2009) forward to their performance on PIAAC. Adults aged 17–28 were compared with the corresponding PISA cohort. These were modified cohorts in that the individuals were not exactly the same. But the authors conclude, and we agree, that comparing these two points in time can offer useful insights into literacy trends. Overall, there was a "reasonably close correlation" between a cohort's PISA scores and their subsequent performance in PIAAC (OECD, 2013a, p. 205).

For countries that run counter to this trend, additional factors may be explanatory. Ireland is a case in point. Irish 15-year-olds placed well above average in

PISA 2000 but as 27-year-olds they performed below average in PIAAC 2012. Did their skills atrophy over time? We think not. A more plausible explanation is the emigration of many well-educated individuals as a result of economic conditions. A recent study conducted by the Émigré Project at University College Cork reported that 62 percent of recent emigrants between the ages of 25 and 34 had at least three years of post-secondary education, compared with 47 percent of their age peers in the general population (Glynn, Kelly, & MacÉinrí, 2013).

This example underscores the importance of viewing trends from a number of angles, using an array of data sources. One general conclusion from the PISA-PIAAC analyses, however, seems warranted:

> [M]uch of the difference in the literacy and numeracy proficiency of young adults today is likely related to the effectiveness of the instruction they received in primary and lower secondary school and their educational experiences outside of school as of age 15.
>
> (OECD, 2013a, p. 205)

Policy efforts directed at improving literacy instruction during schooling are likely to have a pipeline effect.

OECD and Country Profiling

PIRLS and OECD data, then, can provide the foundation of a national literacy profile. Some countries, such as Canada, have devoted considerable energy toward the use of results for this purpose. Space prevents anything approaching a complete national profile here, but we offer thumbnails of three very different countries. Our goal is to illustrate how context can illuminate assessment results.

Finland

Finland's educational status has earned accolades not only in reading but in other subjects. Their math and science scores on PISA, for example, have placed them well above international norms and prompted experts to examine the education system as a whole, not merely how reading is taught. But reading has been the principal source of Finland's fame. Students from Finland had the highest scores for both 9- and 14-year-olds on IEA in 1991. In PIRLS, Finland participated only in the 2011 administration and tied for second with the Russian Federation, just behind Hong Kong. On PISA 2000, Finland was the highest scoring nation and was third in 2009, behind Korea and Shanghai. On PISA 2012, Finland fell to sixth, behind Hong Kong, Japan, Korea, Shanghai, and Singapore (a significant slide since 2000, as we mentioned). The adult population is likewise skewed toward higher proficiency levels. On PIAAC 2012, 22.2 percent scored at Levels

4–5, second only to Japan, at 22.6. Clearly, the momentum of effective schooling is so far being carried forward into adulthood.

Such stunning results might cause one to question the need for any further analysis. One reason for doing so, however, lies in what Meyer and Benavot (2013) have called "the Finnish paradox" (p. 15). "Ironically," they point out, "Finland is the *one* country in the world that most distinctly deviates from the OECD's standard reform package. Finland succeeds not by following the policies recommended by the OECD, but by ignoring them" (p. 15, original emphasis).

Another reason for taking a closer look is the danger of assuming that its place at or near the top of the hill is a given for the foreseeable future. This might not be the case. Finland, like every other nation, serves individuals who struggle. Some 11.3 percent of Finnish 15-year-olds scored below Level 2 on PISA 2012. In addition, Finland's fourth graders had one of the highest gender differences on PIRLS 2011, raising questions about the achievement of boys, and 8 percent of its students failed to reach the Intermediate International Benchmark (Mullis, Martin, Foy, & Drucker, 2012). It is here that deeper analyses might provide specific guidance to Finnish policymakers.

These issues aside, the perennial question asked by outsiders is why Finnish students are so successful. There is no shortage of potential answers. One is that the Finnish language has an unusually transparent (regular) orthography (an issue we take up in the next chapter). Learning to decode words is a straightforward business. Finnish classrooms are largely homogeneous, both linguistically and culturally. Literacy is important to the Finnish people, and represents a cultural value transmitted from one generation to the next. Finnish teachers are well paid, hold graduate degrees, and garner considerable respect (Darling-Hammond, 2010). In addition to these factors, an unusual one has been suggested. Jim Trelease, the champion of reading aloud to children, has speculated that the widespread use of closed-captioning causes children to read while watching television, resulting in a considerable practice effect. "Almost half of all Finnish TV shows are our old sitcoms," he writes. "There are so many shows that the Finns can't afford to dub Finnish into all the sound tracks, so they just run them in English with Finnish closed-captioning" (2013, p. 152).

A number of contextual factors may play a part as well. Though Finland is a sparsely populated country, with slightly fewer than five million residents, it has an advanced economy with a gross national income per capita of just under 48,000USD, based on World Bank statistics in 2011. The average life expectancy is 77 years for men, 83 for women – also well above international averages. In July 2010, Finland became the world's first country to give its citizens a legal right to broadband Internet access. By 2012, Finland had a penetration rate of more than 89 percent for online access.

Ten years of education are compulsory for students in Finland, which, though above international averages, places it at just 55th out of 171 countries, according to UNESCO statistics. However, a completion rate averaging 16.7 years per person (higher for females than males) places Finland second among 110 countries assessed. Tertiary enrollment in Finland was also second out of 151 countries assessed by UNESCO.

It is not possible, of course, to say for certain which of these factors are causally related to Finland's success. We suspect that many of them act in concert to exert an interactive effect, a kind of critical mass for advanced achievement. Unfortunately for those in other countries who would like to emulate Finland, few of these factors are easily exportable. Moreover, the lack of certainty about which of them are really the active ingredients has given rise to a broad range of speculation concerning the secret of Finland's success. Sahlberg (2011), for example, largely dismisses most of the factors we have listed, and instead attributes Finnish preeminence to "improving the teaching force, limiting student testing to a necessary minimum, placing responsibility and trust before accountability, and handing over school- and district-level leadership to education professionals" (p. 5). Teacher preparation in particular is a frequent point of discussion. Finnish teachers hold master's degrees in a selective system, and the success of their students has led to a high level of prestige. "Today," Silander and Välijärvi (2013) observe, "the status of a teacher is largely comparable to that of a doctor or a lawyer" (p. 77). Others point to the decentralization of education, including the lack of high-stakes testing and achievement comparisons among schools (Varjo, Simola, & Rinne, 2013).[14] We can add these to the list of candidate factors that cannot be readily verified.

Morocco

Creating a literacy profile of Morocco is difficult because proficiency data are more limited. There's simply not much of a starting point. Among the OECD assessments, it has participated only in PIRLS, and the results are the polar opposite of Finland's. The nation's fourth graders slid from 350 to 310 across the three administrations. In 2001, only Belize scored lower. In 2006, no country did. Although Morocco has participated in PIRLS since 2001, trend analysis was not conducted because of possible statistical bias.

Girls are underenrolled in Moroccan schools, where the female-to-male ratio is .91. On the other hand, this ratio is better than that of many developing countries, and a key reform took place in 2004, when the Mudawana, the legal code governing family relations, underwent a controversial revision granting more rights to women.

Substantive efforts to improve the quality of education have brought about modest but positive results. One such effort is participation in international literacy assessments, then a rarity among developing countries and a sign of serious intent. There has been a slow, but steady, increase in the completion rates of primary schooling, up from 58 percent to 62 percent during the early part of the first decade of the 2000s. Nevertheless, the adult literacy rate remains in the 50 percent range.

Poverty constrains literacy development both in and beyond the classroom. For example, few learning materials are found in the homes of young children. UNICEF reports that just 21 percent of households contained children's books in 2011.[15] King Mohammed VI has made serious attempts at educational reform and has been leading the fight against poverty, which has earned him the name, "Guardian of the Poor." Still, progress has been limited. The gross national income per capita is just under 3,000USD (compared with 48,000USD in Finland).

To Moroccan policymakers it may seem that any effort is likely to enhance the literacy landscape. This may well be true, but the Moroccan profile presents challenges very different from Finland's, where extensive data can help target abundant resources to sustain high levels of proficiency. In Morocco's case, limited data provide little guidance about how best to employ scarce resources. A reasonable starting point would be to consider responses to the four PIRLS questionnaires (students, parents, teachers, and principals), in an effort to identify useful correspondences. Broadening the country profile to include a richer range of contextual data can likewise be helpful. As an example, Internet usage in Morocco now extends to approximately 50 percent of the population. Consequently, online resources may well be key to the country's literacy growth.

Korea

The rise of the South Korean educational system – concurrent with the blossoming of its economy – has been little short of meteoric. Characterizing its burgeoning economic development as "the great decompression," editors of *The Economist* note that "within the span of a single working life, its [South Korea's] economy has grown 17-fold. Its government has evolved from an austere dictatorship into a rowdy democracy" (October 26, 2013).

Others have noted the parallel between the nation's economy and its education. Marcus Noland, in *Foreign Affairs*, describes South Korea as "the backwater that boomed," observing:

> South Korea's development over the last half century has been nothing short of spectacular. Fifty years ago the country was poorer than Bolivia and Mozambique; today, it is richer than New Zealand and Spain. This is accomplished by general openness of the world economy . . . rapid expansion of the labor force . . . and with a major increase in the educational level of its workforce.
>
> (Jan/Feb 2014)

Viewing its education system through an economic lens, Noland points out that though the cost of a highly educated workforce has been steep, the dividends have justified the expense. By investing over 7 percent of GNP in education, together with an additional 2.8 percent in private investment, South Korea currently outspends all other OECD countries.

There are other ways of indexing the phenomenal growth of education in South Korea. The international comparisons summarized in this chapter have clearly attained the highest profile. A telling but less prominent metric is the percentage of adults with post-secondary associate degrees or higher (OECD, 2009b). In the United States, this percentage hardly varies across four ten-year age groups: 25–34, 35–44, 45–54, and 55–64. Just over 40 percent of the individuals in each of these brackets has earned at least an associate degree. This fact signals a telling stability. It means that Americans who are 25–34 years old are no more likely than those who are 55–64 years of age to have such a degree. In South Korea, however, the situation is strikingly different. Just 10 percent of people between 55 and 64 years of age have an associate degree or higher. Those born in the 1950s earned degrees at about one-fourth the rate of their U.S. age peers. In contrast, well over 60 percent of South Koreans in the 25–34 age group have earned a post-secondary degree – a percentage half again as high as that of Americans in the same age bracket. When one considers that in 1945 less than 5 percent of the population received schooling beyond the elementary level, the transformation is astonishing indeed.

Understanding its causes should be the first order of business for countries seeking to emulate South Korea's success. Surely the financial commitment to education is one, and it is anything but recent. Michael Seth, in his 2002 book, *Education Fever*, traces it back to the end of World War II, when the country gained its independence from Japan and was at last free to develop its policies. But what could have prompted such a commitment? It appears to have been more than a simple cost-benefit analysis on the part of its leaders. Economic promise, Seth argues, was not the sole cause of education fever. The motives behind the postwar policies were complex and included the Confucian tradition of learning, a striving for both personal and international status, and a postwar spirit of egalitarianism inspired by the West. These were (and remain) major cultural influences. The extent to which they are "exportable" is anyone's guess.

Eight General Insights

The OECD findings, together with the results of previous assessments summarized here, now make it possible to view the status of world literacy proficiency through a wide-angle lens. Or rather, two such lenses: one trained on the development of individuals as they move from early schooling to adulthood, the other on the development of proficiency within national contexts over time. The wide array of international data now available presents policymakers with an assortment of riches. Making the best use of them can be a trying experience. We offer here a few takeaway suggestions.

1. Rankings are a poor indicator of literacy growth

A broad but warranted generalization is that literacy, as measured by test scores, has been improving for the majority of countries over the last 20 years. This is a fact that is particularly important to note amidst the periodic frenzy over rankings. Such concerns are an inevitable consequence of comparative assessments, and arguably a healthy one if they help to drive policy in productive directions. But there is a danger that rankings may obscure or devalue positive change. A country might drop substantially in rank while its mean score on a particular assessment holds steady or even improves.

Earlier in this chapter, we listed a number of factors that might skew test scores. Not only are rankings affected by all of these factors, but they are subject to a variety of outside dynamics, such as the number of countries participating at a particular time. For example, Americans might find it heartening to note that U.S. adults ranked fifth in the world in literacy on the Adult Literacy and Lifeskills Survey in 2003. What this factoid ignores is that only six countries took part.[16] PIRLS provides similar examples because the number of countries has continued to grow. When 9-year-olds in Trinidad and Tobago were first assessed in 2006, they achieved a total score of 436 and a ranking of 35th in the world. In 2011 they registered one of the larger mean increases of any country, a gain of 35 points to 471, but their ranking dropped from 35th to 37th. Theirs is an example both of losing ground to overall improvement worldwide and to an extended field of participants. Italy exhibited virtually no change in scores between the PIRLS administration in 2001, when they scored 541 and were ranked 10th in the world, and in 2011 when they scored an identical 541 but tied for 18th place. France dropped minimally in their scores across the three administrations of PIRLS: 525 in 2001, 522 in 2006, and 520 in 2011 – a net decline of only five points. Yet, their rankings fell from 18th to 23rd to 29th. In the 2001 administration, Latvia, with a mean of 545, ranked fifth in the world. In 2011, an identical mean earned them a 14th-place finish internationally. As these examples make clear, rankings are not merely a small part of any country's story, but from time to time they can provoke unwarranted concern.

2. Focus on parallel trends

Concern with rankings may be inevitable, in part because PIRLS and PISA present results in that manner (along with other formats) and in part because of a natural interest in competition with other nations. We suggest that a surer means of informing literacy-related policy begins with studying related trends within one's own country. We recommend participation in all three of the key international assessments (PIRLS, PISA, and PIACC). One reason is that doing so tangibly benefits the participants – especially, as Lockheed (2013) persuasively argues, the developing nations. Another reason is that the achievement trends at all three age levels can be considered together with economic and demographic trends that operate in parallel with achievement.

An important though often neglected factor in gauging a country's status and progress is its prevailing culture. In the opening chapter we described the impact of gender bias as a factor that constrains achievement in certain low-performing countries. But cultural forces also contribute to the outcomes of high-scoring countries, factors that go well beyond the influence of gender. Meyer and Schiller (2013) identify two kinds of national profiles that go far toward characterizing the most successful nations. One is the "relatively egalitarian and individualistic cultures" (p. 207) present in such countries as Canada and Finland; the other is the "relatively collectivist and paternalistic cultures" (p. 207) like those of East Asia. Their point is that success is not exclusively attributable to excellent schools. Policymakers would do well to consider cultural forces as well. Simply improving the quality of literacy education may not bring about the desired results if the cultural context is not sufficiently supportive.

Finally, we also suggest that a new data source, The World's Most Literate Countries study (Miller, 2016) can further complement test results with information about the *practice* of literacy. Multiple data sources, maintained and monitored over time, are the key to obtaining a fine-grained view of literacy growth and enacting policy to foster it.

3. Socioeconomic status isn't a deal breaker

To be sure, the international assessments have substantiated the strong correlation between affluence and achievement. The top finishers in IEA, PISA, PIRLS, IALS, and PIAAC have indeed tended to be the richest. Financial wherewithal bears a reciprocal relationship to literacy proficiency, in that wealth is driven by education in a self-perpetuating cycle. This notion might well discourage the efforts of poorer nations if it were invariably true. Thankfully, it isn't. Researchers at the Center for the Improvement of Early Reading Achievement (CIERA) investigated schools that "beat the odds" – schools that served the poorest children yet still managed to foster high levels of literacy achievement. Findings of these studies have helped to identify key approaches to overcoming the constraints of poverty (see Taylor, Pearson, Clark, & Walpole, 2000). And just as schools can defy the odds, so can countries.

A notable example of a country whose literacy growth has outstripped economic development is Cuba. Although Cuba has not yet taken part in OECD assessments, its national data have documented that efforts to emphasize literacy and health have been productive. Another example is the Russian Federation, which has recently emerged as a top scorer. Russian fourth graders ranked highest in the 2006 administration of PIRLS, and third highest in 2011. Yet, their parents are 55th in the world, as ranked by the International Monetary Fund, in terms of average income – below such countries as Lithuania, Poland, Trinidad and Tobago, Slovenia, and the Czech Republic.

Just as limited wealth need not seal the fate of a country's literacy development, an abundance of wealth does not guarantee it. Perhaps the most persuasive proof of this claim lies in the performance of oil-rich, predominantly Arab countries. The United Arab Emirates generally ranks near the bottom in reading assessment scores but within the top 10 in average individual income. Qatar, where average income ranks number one in the world by a considerable margin, ranked 44th out of 46 countries in PIRLS 2011. Similarly, Kuwait ranked 39th out of 41 countries in PIRLS 2006 and chose not to participate in 2011.

4. Regional shifts in proficiency are occurring

Certain parts of the world have collectively exhibited changes in literacy levels. As we have already noted in this chapter, in northern Europe a number of countries have plateaued or stalled (Sweden and Finland, for example). At the same time, Asian countries have begun to emerge as frontrunners, possibly due to increased emphases on education. Korea, Singapore, Japan, and portions of China have led the way. The apparent push and pull among these competitive countries can be misleading. But make no mistake. Literacy is a not a zero-sum game in which gains in one place necessarily correspond to losses elsewhere. These shifts are the result of national policies and the dynamics they set in motion.

5. There are two gender gaps

Throughout their schooling, girls as a group outperform boys on a worldwide basis. Some countries, particularly but not exclusively in the Arab world, limit the educational opportunities afforded girls, a policy that may contribute to their relatively poor showing on PIRLS and PISA. The two gender gaps – one in achievement, the other in access – are not independent but are likely to exert an interactive effect in countries that proscribe or discourage the education of girls. There can be little doubt that their rankings are adversely affected. IALS and PIAAC results do indicate that the achievement gap dissipates in adulthood, but no Arab country participated in either of these assessments. PISA results have revealed an advantage for girls in every participating country, suggesting that the *potential* proficiency of some countries is not realized when girls do not attend school. This problem extends beyond the Arab world and encompasses countries that have not participated on PIRLS or PISA. For example, in Liberia the ratio of girls to boys in school in 2013 was .89; in the Central African Republic it was .69; in Benin, .79; in Angola, .64.[17] None of these countries is majority Muslim, but school attendance is inequitable nonetheless.

6. Proficiency and motivation are closely related

International assessments have underscored the universality of the connection between the ability to read and the desire to do so. Researchers have described a reciprocal relationship between proficiency and motivation, where one is bootstrapping the other in an upward spiral (see Conradi, Jang, & McKenna, 2014), and international findings do nothing to refute that idea. However, the authors of the PISA report (OECD, 2010) make a causal leap based on the gender gap. Their reasoning is basically this: Girls read better than boys and girls like to read better than boys; therefore, the key to improving the proficiency of boys is to find ways of motivating them. "PISA results," they conclude, "suggest that boys would be predicted to catch up with girls in reading performance if they had higher levels of motivation . . ." (OECD, 2013a, p. 13). This conclusion outstrips the data. It is just as likely that superior instruction in foundational skills would provide boys with the proficiency needed to connect with reading. Of course, neither possibility precludes a two-pronged instructional approach, one that targets both proficiency and motivation. That is the approach we endorse and we will explore it some detail in Chapter 7.

7. Deconstructing national means is imperative

We have already indicated how the proficiency levels established by IALS and later by PIAAC provide a telling first pass at making sense of overall means. But this is just the beginning, or it should be. There is no reason why a participating nation cannot conduct further analyses using the data explorer tools available through OECD.[18] When these are used to conduct secondary and tertiary analyses and when the results are interpreted in the light of factors not captured by the PIRLS and the OECD assessments (such as Ireland's emigration problem), real progress can be made toward uncovering meaningful factors at work in a national context. It is this understanding that must guide the formation of enlightened policy decisions.

8. New policies can have unintended consequences

In the years following World War II, storied mathematician John von Neumann led the way in the use of computers to forecast weather (Harper, 2008). Although he had an intellectual stake in developing accurate computer models of prediction, his ultimate aim was not merely to predict the weather but to control it. A successful model could be used to identify "points of instability–critical points where a small push can have large consequences, as with a ball balanced at the top of a hill" (Gleick, 1988, pp. 18–19). Complexity theorists, however, have pointed to the unintended consequences of these actions. "Von Neumann's mistake," wrote Freeman Dyson, "was to imagine that every unstable motion could be nudged into a stable motion by small pushes and pulls applied at the right places. The same mistake is still frequently made by economists and social planners" (1988, p. 183).

It is in the arena of social planning – especially planning directed at literacy – that von Neumann's example is instructive. It is up to policymakers to look beyond the immediate impact of the changes they enact and do their best to project how those changes might cascade into other factors. There are no crystal balls for viewing the future, but there are wide-angle lenses that from time to time can give us a glimpse.

Notes

1. We might add that statistical software now enables the tracking of true cohorts, those that include exactly the same individuals at each assessment point. The use of true cohorts would lend greater precision to analyses.
2. International Association for the Evaluation of Educational Achievement.
3. For more information and commentary, visit http://www.iea.nl/reading_literacy_study.html
4. Girls showed the largest advantage in the Narrative domain and the smallest in Documents.
5. Financial literacy was added in 2012.
6. Only selected Chinese cities (subnational economies) took part, which were not representative of the entire nation.
7. See, for example, the Online Reading Comprehension Assessment project (ORCA), at the University of Connecticut, conducted by Donald Leu and his colleagues: http://www.orca.uconn.edu/
8. The OECD report included Switzerland as three separate participants, one for each of its official languages, but we have counted it as one country here for the purposes of ranking.
9. Note that the Adult Literacy and Lifeskills Survey (ALL) fell between IALS and PIAAC. It was conducted twice, in 2003 and in 2006–08, targeting individuals ranging in age from 16 to 65. However, because only six countries participated in the first round of ALL and just four in the second, our focus here is on IALS and PIAAC.
10. The two U.S. testing consortia, the Partnership for Assessment of Readiness for College and Careers (PARCC) and Smarter Balanced, which were created to align with the Common Core State Standards, likewise include the ability to comprehend multiple texts. See parcconline.org and smarterbalanced.org.
11. Results of a second assessment, involving nine additional countries, are scheduled for release in 2016.
12. Two of the largest gainers also posted precipitous drops in response rates. The rate for Poland, which recorded the largest score increase from IALS to PIAAC, fell from 75 to 56 percent. Likewise, Australia's response rate for IALS was 96% compared with 71%

for PIAAC. At the same time, the response rate for Sweden, where the largest drop in scores was recorded, declined from 60% to 45%.
13 Reading was not a major focus and "PISA 2003 used a briefer assessment to provide an update" (OECD, 2004, p. 3). Results were largely superseded by PISA 2006.
14 It should be noted that differences among schools are small in any case (Darling-Hammond, 2010).
15 http://www.unicef.org/infobycountry/morocco_statistics.html
16 As you may recall, this is the reason we chose not to discuss the ALL results.
17 World Bank/UNESCO, http://data.worldbank.org/indicator/SE.ENR.PRSC.FM.ZS
18 For example, the International Data Explorer (IDE) for PIAAC begins here: http://www.oecd.org/site/piaac/publicdataandanalysis.htm

References

CCSSI. (2010). *Common Core State Standards Initiative: English language arts standards*. Washington, DC: National Governors Association and the Council of Chief State School Officers. Retrieved from http://www.corestandards.org/ELA-Literacy. Accessed August 1, 2015.

Chall, J.S. (1983/1996). *Stages of reading development*. New York, NY: McGraw-Hill.

Chappell, B. (2013, December 3). U.S. students slide in global ranking on math, reading, science. The Two-Way Blog, National Public Radio. Available: http://www.npr.org/blogs/thetwo-way/2013/12/03/248329823/u-s-high-school-students-slide-in-math-reading-science

Conradi, K., Jang, B.G., & McKenna, M.C. (2014). Motivation terminology in reading research: A conceptual review. *Educational Psychology Review, 26*, 127–164.

Darling-Hammond, L. (2010). *The flat world and education: How America's commitment to equity will determine our future*. New York, NY: Teachers College Press.

Dyson, F. (1988). *Infinite in all directions*. New York, NY: Harper and Row.

Elley, W.B. (1992). *How in the world do students read?: IEA study of reading literacy*. Amsterdam, The Netherlands: International Association for the Evaluation of Educational Achievement.

Gleick, (1988). *Chaos: Making a new science*. New York, NY: Viking Penguin.

Glynn, I., Kelly, T., & MacÉinrí, P. (2013). *Irish emigration in an age of austerity*. Cork, Ireland: University College Cork. Available: https://www.dropbox.com/s/2e7qg1jeuuxujdl/Emigration%20in%20an%20Age%20of%20Austerity_02%2010.pdf

Gray, W.S. (1958). *The teaching of reading and writing: An international survey*. New York, NY: UNESCO/Scott, Foresman.

Harper, K. (2008). *Weather by the numbers: The genesis of modern meteorology*. Cambridge, MA: Massachusetts Institute of Technology. Available: http://mitpress.mit.edu/sites/default/files/titles/content/9780262517355_sch_0001.pdf

Joncas, M., & Foy, P. (2013). Sample design in TIMSS and PIRLS. In M.O. Martin & I.V.S. Mullis (Eds.), *Methods and procedures in TIMSS and PIRLS 2011* (Sample design, pp. 1–21). Available: http://timssandpirls.bc.edu/methods/pdf/TP_Sampling_Design.pdf

Kelly, D.L. (2003). Overview of PIRLS. In M.O. Martin, I.V.S. Mullis, & A.M. Kennedy (Eds.), *PIRLS 2001 technical report* (pp. 1–12). Amsterdam, The Netherlands: International Association for the Evaluation of Educational Achievement (IEA).

Kennedy, A.M., & Trong, K.L. (2007). Reporting student achievement in reading. In I.V.S. Mullis, M.O. Martin, & A.M. Kennedy (Eds.), *PIRLS 2006 technical report* (pp. 173–193). Available: http://timssandpirls.bc.edu/PDF/p06_technical_report.pdf

Lockheed, M. (2013). Causes and consequences of international assessments in developing countries. In H.-D. Meyer & A. Benavot (Eds.), *PISA, power, and policy: The emergence of global educational governance* (pp. 163–183). Oxford, U.K.: Symposium Books.

Meyer, H.-D., & Benavot, A. (2013). PISA and the globalization of education governance: Some puzzles and problems. In H.-D. Meyer & A. Benavot (Eds.), *PISA, power, and policy: The emergence of global educational governance* (pp. 9–26). Oxford, U.K.: Symposium Books.

Meyer, H.-D., & Schiller, K. (2013). Gauging the role of non-educational effects in large-scale assessments: Socio-economics, culture, and PISA outcomes. In H.-D. Meyer & A. Benavot (Eds.), *PISA, power, and policy: The emergence of global educational governance* (pp. 207–224). Oxford, U.K.: Symposium Books.

Miller, J.W. (2016). *World's most literate countries.* Available at http://www.ccsu.edu/globalliteracy

Mullis, I.V.S., & Martin, M.O. (2007). Overview of PIRLS 2006. In I.V.S. Mullis, M.O. Martin, & A.M. Kennedy (Eds.), *PIRLS 2006 technical report* (pp. 1–8). Chestnut Hill, MA: TIMSS & PIRLS International Study Center, Boston College. Available: http://timssandpirls.bc.edu/PDF/p06_technical_report.pdf

Mullis, I.V.S., Martin, M.O., Foy, P., & Drucker, K.T. (2012). *PIRLS 2011 international results in reading.* Chestnut Hill, MA: TIMSS & PIRLS International Study Center, Boston College. Available: http://timssandpirls.bc.edu/pirls2011/international-results-pirls.html

Mullis, I.V.S., Martin, M.O., & Sainsbury, M. (2013). PIRLS 2016 reading framework. In I.V.S. Mullis & M.O. Martin (Eds.), *PIRLS 2016 assessment framework* (pp. 13–31). Chestnut Hill, MA: TIMSS & PIRLS International Study Center, Boston College. Available: http://timssandpirls.bc.edu/pirls2016/downloads/P16_FW_Chap1.pdf

OECD. (2000). *Literacy in the information age: Final report of the International Adult Literacy Survey.* Paris, France: OECD. Available: http://www.oecd.org/education/skills-beyond-school/41529765.pdf

OECD. (2004). *First results from PISA 2003: Executive summary.* Paris, France: OECD. Available: http://www.oecd.org/edu/school/programmeforinternationalstudentassessmentpisa/34002454.pdf

OECD. (2009a). *PISA 2009 assessment framework: Key competencies in reading, mathematics and science.* Paris, France: OECD. Available: http://www.oecd.org/pisa/pisaproducts/44455820.pdf

OECD. (2009b). *Education at a Glance 2009.* Paris, France: OECD. Available: http://www.oecd.org/education/skills-beyond-school/43636332.pdf

OECD. (2010). *PISA 2009 results: Executive summary.* Paris, France: OECD. Available at http://www.oecd.org/pisa/pisaproducts/46619703.pdf

OECD. (2013a). *OECD skills outlook 2013: First results from the survey of adult skills* (Revised version). Paris, France: OECD. Available: http://www.keepeek.com/Digital-Asset-Management/oecd/education/oecd-skills-outlook-2013_9789264204256-en#page1

OECD. (2013b). *The Survey of Adult Skills: Reader's companion.* Paris, France: OECD. Available: http://skills.oecd.org/documents/Survey_of_Adult_Skills_Readers_Companion.pdf

OECD. (2013c). *Technical report of the Survey of Adult Skills (PIAAC).* Paris, France: OECD. Available: http://www.oecd.org/site/piaac/_Technical%20Report_17OCT13.pdf

OECD. (2014). *PISA 2012 results in focus: What 15-year-olds know and what they can do with what they know.* Paris, France: OECD. Available: http://www.oecd.org/pisa/keyfindings/pisa-2012-results-overview.pdf. Retrieved from http://www.oecd.org/pisa/pisaproducts/46619703.pdf

Sahlberg, P. (2011). *Finnish lessons: What can the world learn from educational change in Finland?* New York, NY: Teachers College Press.

Seth, M.J. (2002). *Education fever: Society, politics, and the pursuit of schooling in South Korea.* Honolulu, HI: University of Hawaii Press.

Silander, T., & Välijärvi, J. (2013). The theory and practice of building pedagogical skill in Finnish teacher education. In H.-D. Meyer & A. Benavot (Eds.), *PISA, power, and policy: The emergence of global educational governance* (pp. 77–97). Oxford, U.K.: Symposium Books.

Stahl, N.A., Higginson, B.C., & King, J.R. (1993). Appropriate use of comparative literacy research in the 1990s. *Journal of Reading 37,* 104–113.

Taylor, B.M., Pearson, P.D., Clark, K.F., & Walpole, S. (2000). Effective schools and accomplished teachers: Lessons about primary-grade reading instruction in low-income schools. *Elementary School Journal, 101,* 121–165.

Trelease, J. (2013). *The read-aloud handbook* (7th ed.). New York, NY: Penguin Books.

Varjo, J., Simola, H., & Rinne, R. (2013). Finland's PISA results: An analysis of dynamics in education politics. In H.-D. Meyer & A. Benavot (Eds.), *PISA, power, and policy: The emergence of global educational governance* (pp. 51–76). Oxford, U.K.: Symposium Books.

4
THE CRISIS OF ELEMENTARY SCHOOLING – LITERACY'S TRAINING GROUND

The results of PIRLS document a significant and seemingly intractable problem facing elementary teachers: By fourth grade, in country after country, many have failed to achieve proficiency. The search for root causes leads, quite naturally, to questions concerning the effectiveness of beginning reading instruction. Which methods are likely to yield the best results? One might think that after decades of research this issue would have been put to rest, but the way is tortuous and it is easy to follow it down a rabbit hole of conflicting evidence and confirmation bias.

In this chapter, we argue that the "reading wars" in the English-speaking world over the best methods of teaching children to read were initially caused by too little research and prolonged by too much. These conflicts began in the early eighteenth century and have often involved ad hominem attacks. To the outsider, the more recent exchanges may well have been a source of entertainment, even levity. One prominent researcher has been called a "phonicator" and a "word fetishist" (see Stahl, 1998). Another was described as a "vampire," sucking the life out of learning to read (see Levine, 1994). And we ourselves have been upbraided for "obliviousness" and "paradigm blindness" (Edelsky, 1990, p. 7).

By tracing the history of the debate, we hope to demonstrate that educators now have the knowledge they need to bring all but a small proportion of children to proficiency. Implementing that knowledge in classrooms, however, is no easy task. Practicing teachers frequently resist suggestions that they alter the methods they employ (McKenna & Walpole, 2008), and those in training are sometimes schooled in approaches that are ill suited to meeting the needs of children who struggle. Indeed, as the insults recounted above suggest, teacher educators are sometimes hostile to opposing evidence.

We will discuss the negligible impact of federal initiatives intended to overcome these obstacles as well as the recent advent of tough new standards, the coaching movement, and promising alternatives to traditional special education. We also hope to dispel a few of the misconceptions about reform by considering how children are taught to read in other nations. These include the ideal age at which instruction should begin, the optimal amount of instruction children should receive, and whether English orthography is an unavoidable impediment. However, in order to place these issues in perspective and better appreciate the shrill history of reform, it is important to begin with an understanding of how reading normally develops.

How Reading Develops

The goal of elementary reading instruction the world over is simple enough: to instill in children a level of proficiency needed for success in secondary school. The devil, however, is in the details. If we examine the trajectory along which normally developing readers progress, we find many ways to go wrong. Let's begin by considering what *should* happen.

In the primary grades, children pass through discernible stages toward adultlike patterns of oral reading. They begin by gaining an awareness of phonemes – the units of sound that make up all spoken words (*cat* has three, *the* has two). They then learn how letters (individually and in clusters) are used to represent these sounds. Practice leads to faster and faster application of this knowledge until eventually word recognition becomes automatic.

That is just how it happened for you. The vast majority of words you encounter in print are recognized without conscious effort, allowing you to devote nearly all of your attention to comprehension, where it belongs. As you read this page, you are applying a host of strategies and skills you undoubtedly take for granted. And in fact, the very point of the instruction you received in elementary school was to enable you to do just that – take them for granted. For a proficient reader like yourself, the process is very much like breathing. Most of the time you are unaware that you are breathing, although if necessary you can seize control of the process for a short time – when the doctor tells you to take a deep breath or when you jump into a pool. Likewise, if you encounter an unfamiliar word (no longer an everyday occurrence), you can momentarily marshal the skills you learned long ago in order to pronounce it. Test yourself with *bandiferous*, a made-up word used at the Center for the Study of Reading as an illustration some years ago. To pronounce it, you probably used a combination of letter-sound knowledge plus some larger "chunks" you've seen in other words (like *band*, *different*, and *ponderous*).

Automatic decoding of nearly every word is the hallmark of the fluent reader. But fluency is only part of the equation. Children must also have adequate vocabulary and experiential knowledge on which to draw, and they need to be able to approach reading tasks strategically. (This means reading a short story with a different mindset than reading a textbook or a Wikipedia entry.) Unlike fluency, vocabulary, prior knowledge, and comprehension ability do not develop in stages. They gradually accrue as children learn new words, have more experience in the world, and encounter a variety of texts that range in type and difficulty. In the upper elementary grades, children should be able to read and learn from appropriate texts independently.

How do they get to that point? The old wisdom was that the elementary teacher's first order of business was to develop fluency (usually by the end of second grade) and then to worry about vocabulary and comprehension. The new wisdom is that we cannot afford to wait. Vocabulary and comprehension are too important for later reading to be put off. Consequently, interactive teacher readalouds are now a staple of many primary classrooms as a way to build vocabulary, share vicarious experiences, and give youngsters a chance to stretch their comprehension muscles.

So what can go wrong? For some children, learning the code can be a protracted source of frustration, particularly when the instruction they receive is less than explicit. Cognitive psychologists now agree that humans are hard-wired for oral language but not for reading. Written words superimpose an arbitrary code onto spoken language, and for some children it may just as well be a code hatched by the CIA. Because their efforts to crack it fall short, fluency is delayed and the vocabulary and knowledge they might have acquired through wide reading are limited. It's the beginning of a vicious cycle.

Even when decoding is not a problem, proficiency is far from assured. Children raised in poverty, by parents with limited education, exist in an environment that is not conducive to oral language development. In America, a common estimate is that children begin kindergarten with vocabularies ranging from 1,500 to 5,000 words (Adams, 1990) – a sobering gap that only widens with age. To say that schools are not successfully addressing this problem would be an understatement. Andrew Biemiller, a Canadian researcher, puts it bluntly. "Vocabulary levels diverge greatly during the primary years," he writes, "and virtually nothing effective is done about this in schools" (2012, p. 36).

Framing the Problem: How Is Reading Taught?

As the PIRLS results document, every country contends with a significant portion of their elementary population who have difficulty acquiring proficiency. The percent varies, but the problem is universal. To understand how countries respond we need to view their efforts in the context of their overall system of literacy education.

It should come as no surprise that elementary reading instruction varies from country to country in the developed world, but the differences are less prominent than one might expect. Variations in language, culture, and tradition have led to systems that, while distinct, are nevertheless remarkably similar. We suspect that the similarities are due to the simple fact that educators everywhere are faced with the same goals and tasks in teaching children to read. To provide some perspective, let's consider the approaches used by five developed countries: the United States, South Korea, Australia, Denmark, and China.

The United States

In the U.S., formal reading instruction begins in kindergarten, around age 5. Although now the rule, this hasn't always been the case. Until the last few decades of the twentieth century, formal instruction began in first grade while kindergarten was devoted to socialization and oral language development. In many places kindergarten was not compulsory or was offered for only half a day. Nowadays, kindergarten teachers serve every child, and they must provide systematic instruction in beginning word recognition. This work is organized sequentially and progresses through several stages during the primary years, from learning letter-sound associations in kindergarten, to mastery of a full range of decoding skills in first grade, to near-effortless fluent reading by the end of second. Throughout the elementary years, the children are exposed to new vocabulary and receive instruction in comprehension strategies. During the primary grades, teachers are expected to split their time between teaching the whole class and providing differentiated instruction to small groups of students with similar needs. Students who fall behind may receive additional instruction from a reading specialist or special educator. Persistent problems may lead to classifying a student as learning disabled, after which an individualized education program, or IEP, is developed. This document has the force of law in compelling instructional approaches and accommodations.

Most U.S. schools rely on a commercial "core program" that provides a reading anthology, support materials, assessments, and an organizational structure to help teachers plan and deliver instruction. The use of core programs was once nearly universal, but times have changed. They are now more prevalent in some states than others. In New York, for example, adoption of commercial cores has declined considerably in recent years.

The driving force behind instructional methods and materials is not whether they come from a particular source but whether they reflect an official set of standards. Until recently, these standards were developed by each state, although a good deal of overlap was evident. However, a recent push for new standards was prompted not because of inconsistencies across state lines but by the perception that the standards were too low. This concern led to the development of the

Common Core State Standards, a project of the National Governors Association and the Council of Chief State School Officers.[1] Since their release in 2010, all but a handful of states have adopted the Common Core as their official standards for the English language arts.

South Korea[2]

As in the U.S., formal reading instruction in South Korea also begins in kindergarten, but children are 6 rather than 5. The difference does not result in lost time, however. This is because most Korean children start learning to read at home when they are 3 years old. They are taught either by their mothers or by private home-school tutors hired by parents. In addition, since the Korean alphabet, *Hangul*, has regular letter-sound correspondences, most Korean children are able to decode words more easily than children in English-speaking countries (Yoon, Bolger, Kwon, & Perfetti, 2002). This is the reason they can usually read and write the Korean alphabet and even decode basic sentences before entering elementary school.

Reading instruction for children in most public schools relies heavily on textbooks based on the Korean National Curriculum and Standards of Language Arts. The language arts textbooks consist of three separate books – Reading, Writing, and Listening/Speaking – per semester. Students who fall behind are encouraged to participate in after-school programs. For those requiring additional help, most elementary schools maintain self-contained special education classes at each grade level.

The compact geography of South Korea, together with its linguistic and ethnic homogeneity, has led to a uniform system of education throughout the country. At first blush, the situation would seem to be altogether unlike the U.S., where state and local control of education is a time-honored tradition and where independent systems have developed in all 50 states. But when we compare these state systems, we find far more similarities than differences.

Australia[3]

This is likewise true of Australia, where there has been a similar impetus to craft (perhaps *clone* is a better word) the same system in every state. The Australian Curriculum, Assessment and Reporting Authority (ACARA) has been charged with developing a national curriculum, and it is left largely to each state to determine how to implement it. ACARA is on par with America's Common Core State Standards and with South Korea's National Curriculum and Standards.

Let's examine Queensland as an example that represents the nation in many respects but that retains an individual identity. Formal reading instruction has traditionally begun during Year One, when children are 5–6 years old. Many Year One children have attended a noncompulsory "Prep Year," which is called Reception or Kindergarten in other Australian states. The Prep Year was reconfigured in 2012 to be the official start of reading instruction. Once again, this development closely mirrors the American trend. The same is true for instruction, which follows the established skills progression and is often couched in a commercial core program.

Students who struggle are often "caught" in the Year Two "Net," which involves benchmark assessments. These children receive interventions from specialists. The idea of monitoring each student's progress in order to intervene when appropriate is comparable to the Response to Intervention initiative in America, which is designed to serve the same function but with different timelines and terminology.

Denmark[4]

In Denmark, kindergarten is almost universal and includes a much wider age range (from 2.5 through 5). In American terms, this amounts to a combination of preschool and kindergarten. It is during the following year, called grade 0, however, that children master the 29-letter alphabet. Until 2009, formal reading instruction began in grade 1, but Denmark has followed a common pattern by mandating that it begin a year earlier.

The method of instruction varies considerably because Danish policy embraces the "principle of free choice of teaching method." This policy has perpetuated the familiar rift between teachers who prefer explicit instruction in letter-sound relationships and those whose instruction is more implicit. Danish research supporting explicit teaching has not altered official policy but has resulted in hybrid approaches that aim to preserve the best of both orientations. Not surprisingly, a variety of commercial materials has arisen. Most teachers make use of these products but they frequently adapt and supplement them as well.

Denmark has followed another international trend by adopting a set of Common Objectives in all subjects. Although mandated, these are somewhat broad, but they are sharpened considerably in the Guiding Curriculum, which is specific about how the Objectives are to be attained. The Guiding Curriculum is not mandated but has been adopted in nearly all of Denmark's 99 councils (school districts). Since 2009, the attainment of the Common Objectives in reading is determined through a national test administered in grades 2, 4, 6, and 8 (corresponding to U.S. grades 3, 5, 7, and 9). This pattern of standards and tests, though similar to developments in many other developed countries, has not had the often-punitive impact on teachers and schools in the interest of accountability. The Danes appear largely content with their schools, and their above-average PIRLS results certainly offer little cause for alarm. As a Danish colleague shared with us, "Most parents are more concerned with how their children feel about going to school than about their test scores."

China

Because of its long political isolation and a challenging nonalphabetic written language, one might expect reading instruction in China to differ markedly from that of other countries. This is not the case. Like the U.S., South Korea, Denmark, and Australia, schooling for Chinese students begins with You er Yuan (kindergarten). Although not required, kindergarten is nearly universal. It is a three-year experience (introductory, intermediate, and advanced), serving children aged 3–6. Six-year-olds then move to a graded system, in which a national literacy curriculum is implemented, and supported by benchmark testing.

Differentiated instruction and special education are nonexistent. Beyond receiving some limited after-school instruction, students who struggle receive little additional assistance. China is similar to South Korea in that parents often hire tutors to assist their children or enroll them in weekend academic training centers. The combination of private tutoring and limited support at school helps perpetuate a stratified system that favors the affluent. Western educators will no doubt find it surprising that this is not viewed as a problem in China, but merely as a reflection of the Chinese core value of "elite education."

As in other countries, reading instruction proceeds from basic skills taught during the first two years after kindergarten (called the fundamental stage) to more sophisticated instruction during grades 3 and 4 (the intermediate stage) to a focus on independent application of literacy skills during grades 5 and 6 (the advanced stage).

The complex ideographic writing system is understandably a source of difficulty for many Chinese youngsters, and teachers cannot rely on the consistent progression of skills that grounds the curriculum in countries where children learn to read alphabetic languages. Since the 1950s, the approach to this dilemma has involved the use of pinyin, a phonetic spelling system that uses the Roman alphabet plus diacritical markings.[5] Most of the books read by children in grades 1 and 2 are written in pinyin, but at the end of grade 2 they face a demanding transition to reading books that employ conventional Chinese orthography. The changeover doesn't amount to going cold turkey, however. Instruction in Chinese characters and high-frequency words proceeds in parallel with reading in pinyin. This instruction is similar to the decoding activities used by teachers in English-speaking countries, except that the focus is visual rather than auditory. For example, an American teacher might highlight the sound patterns in rhyming words by replacing the initial consonant (*cat* becomes *fat*, which becomes *hat*, and so forth). A Chinese teacher would use a similar approach to introducing characters. The word 口 (meaning "mouth" in Chinese) can be changed into different characters by adding different strokes, such as 中 ("middle"), 日 ("sun"), and 白 ("white").[6] By the end of grade 2, children are expected to know 1,200 characters and 1,800 high-frequency words. By the end of grade 4, these benchmarks rise to 2,000 characters and 2,500 words, and by the end of grade 6, they must know 2,500 characters and 3,000 words.

From Country to Country: What's the Difference?

Although we have by no means undertaken a comprehensive analysis of all 65 OECD countries, the five developed nations we chose represent a variety of cultures, languages, and educational traditions. Despite these differences, a few parallels are striking. All have implemented a graded system and all have some form of kindergarten. All have adopted national standards and use, to varying extents, commercial teaching materials. All begin by stressing letter-sound correspondences even when, in China's case, the alphabet had to be borrowed.

At the same time telling distinctions emerge. Four of the countries have safety nets for children who struggle, but in China extra support is left up to parents, and the idea of universal literacy runs counter to an elitist tradition. Parental support figures prominently in China and Korea, where parents promote early development by working directly with their children or hiring tutors. In the U.S., Denmark, and Australia, parental influences vary but are generally less prominent.

Perhaps the most important difference concerns the sense of urgency to increase literacy achievement and reduce the number of children who struggle. In the U.S. and Australia, these have become policy issues of central importance. But in Denmark, buoyed by high achievement and a tradition of teacher autonomy, there is little of the angst that drives the accountability pressures of No Child Left Behind (NCLB). In the two Asian countries, there is plenty of concern but it is largely the kind felt by parents for their own children rather than something resembling collective apprehension.

The Reading Wars: Does It Matter How Children Are Taught?

The challenge of serving readers who struggle has led to a variety of reform efforts in the U.S. and elsewhere. In this section, we focus primarily on those undertaken in the United States. Underlying reforms is the assumption that improved instruction is the key. Although it may seem obvious that the choice of methods will influence reading growth, research aimed at identifying the best methods has tended to divide rather than unite educators. Academics have been notoriously divided into camps that espouse either explicit instruction in foundational skills or meaning-based approaches in which acquiring skills is viewed as largely a byproduct of meaningful encounters with print. The "reading wars," as they have been called, have occasioned spirited exchanges over the years, and we have contributed to these from time to time.

It is common to assume that the debate over methods of instruction began in the twentieth century. In reality, barbs have been traded for hundreds of years.

In the early eighteenth century, Jean-Jacques Rousseau attacked John Locke (by then conveniently dead) for espousing a phonics-oriented approach. A century later, Horace Mann attacked William Holmes McGuffey (creator of the McGuffey readers) for the same reason. Of course, these famous individuals were arguing on the basis of virtually no research whatever. And so one would think that the abundance of research evidence available during the past 50 years would have put these issues to rest and put an end to the reading wars. But findings are disputed, evidence is cited selectively, and philosophy sometimes trumps science (McKenna, Robinson, & Miller, 1990; Pressley, 2006).

Since the middle of the twentieth century, research findings, though abundant, have done little to build consensus about how best to teach reading. On the contrary, the dominant orientation of American reading instruction has moved from one extreme to another, like a pendulum (Slavin, 1989; Stahl, 1998). To illustrate these pendulum swings, Table 4.1 presents a history of key events from midcentury forward.

TABLE 4.1 Key Events in American Reading Instruction

Time	Events
1940s & 50s	Whole-word instruction is prevalent; phonics is minimized
1955	Rudolph Flesch publishes pro-phonics book, *Why Johnny Can't Read*
1957	Russians launch Sputnik, first artificial satellite, engendering fears
1960s	Phonics emphasis gains momentum
1964	NAEP is launched to monitor achievement in reading and other subjects
1965	Federal government creates Title I, targeting children in poverty
1967	Jeanne Chall publishes pro-phonics *Learning to Read: The Great Debate*
1969	First set of NAEP results released
1970s	Emphasis shifts to comprehension
1976	Center for the Study of Reading is founded to investigate comprehension
1983	National Commission on Excellence in Educ. publishes *A Nation at Risk*
1985	CSR publishes *Becoming a Nation of Readers*, stressing balance
Late 1980s	Whole language movement gains momentum, fueling "reading wars"
1990	Marilyn Adams publishes pro-phonics *Beginning Reading Instruction*
1992	NAEP begins reporting state-level data, thus weakening whole language
1998	Federal report, *Preventing Reading Difficulties in Young Children*, appears
1998	Reading Excellence Act is passed, requiring scientifically based reading instruction (SBRI)
2000	National Reading Panel Report stresses phonics

(*Continued*)

74 The Crisis of Elementary Schooling

TABLE 4.1 Continued

Time	Events
2001	Reading First initiative launched in K-3, requiring SBRI
2002	USDOE creates Institute for Education Sciences to further SBRI
2004	IDEA permits RTI as a process for identifying special education students
2005	Striving Readers initiative for middle and high schools
2008	Reading First evaluation released; though flawed, it is unimpressive
2009	Race to the Top begins, funding contingent on a state's adoption of CCSS
2010	Common Core Standards released
2010	Reading First ends
2011	Striving Readers is newly funded

During the 1940s and 50s, educators believed that decoding instruction should be minimized in favor of whole-word instruction. This was the era of Dick and Jane. For example, this text from a Scott Foresman primer illustrates how the words were deliberately repeated as built-in drill despite the unnatural language that resulted.

> Dick said, "Look, look.
> Look up.
> Look up, up, up."
>
> (Gray et al., 1951, p. 6)

In the mid-1950s, however, two trends began to steer American instruction in a different direction. One was the growing suspicion that a limited emphasis on phonics was mistaken. In 1955, Rudolph Flesch took establishment researchers to task in *Why Johnny Can't Read*, a book that challenged the idea that phonics should have only a limited role in reading instruction. His grass-roots approach encouraged parents to sidestep schools and provide phonics instruction at home.

The other trend was the paranoia unleashed by the Cold War. Although Cold War fears extended into many aspects of American life, they included the conjecture that American schools were performing at levels below their Soviet counterparts. In what now appears a bizarre development, the National Defense Education Act (NDEA) of 1958 allocated defense funds for (among other things) reading instruction. In the confluence of these two trends was the belief that American children received too little instruction and lagged behind Russian children as a result. The need for a greater emphasis on phonics attained growing acceptance as a means of closing the perceived gap with Russian children.

"Can Ivan read better than Johnny?" was the title of an influential article appearing in *The Saturday Evening Post* (Trace, 1961). Its author claimed that Russia's presumed scientific superiority was related to inadequate phonics instruction in America. These developments made the 1960s and early 70s the heyday of phonics instruction, furthered in part by Jeanne Chall's 1967 book, *Learning to Read: The Great Debate*. On the basis of a comprehensive review of the available research, Chall concluded that a greater emphasis on phonics was indeed desirable.

The 1960s saw two more federal initiatives as well. In 1964, NAEP was launched in an effort to gauge longitudinal achievement trends using its own (presumably unbiased) assessments. (The first results were not available until 1969.) In 1965, Congress established Title I, a massive funding program, still very much in force, directed at reading and math in impoverished schools.

The Soviets, meanwhile, did not turn a blind eye toward these developments. Tröhler (2013) has suggested that the Soviet Union was simultaneously taking steps to keep pace and that "many of its means and measures – especially in the field of education – were surprisingly similar" to those being implemented in the U.S. (p. 141). These Cold War developments, he asserts, were essentially the genesis of PISA.

In America, the result of the phonics movement was that children as a group did in fact learn to decode more proficiently (Stahl, 1998). However, comprehension assessments documented a persistent problem, suggesting that phonics alone was not the irresistible force that some had claimed (Stahl, 1998). During the 1970s, momentum shifted away from phonics and in the direction of comprehension. In 1976, the Center for the Study of Reading was established to investigate comprehension instruction. In 1985, the Center produced the bestselling book, *Becoming a Nation of Readers* (Anderson, Hiebert, Scott, & Wilkinson, 1985), which did not oppose phonics instruction but advocated a balanced approach that included both decoding and comprehension. This moderate position did not, however, have the effect of bringing the warring parties together. In the mid-to-late 1980s, the whole language movement, imported from British Commonwealth countries, gained extraordinary popularity. Its central premise was that decoding knowledge should not be explicitly taught in decontextualized lessons but should instead be indirectly fostered through meaningful encounters with whole texts (hence the term, *whole language*). This notion ran precisely counter to the stance taken by advocates of phonics instruction – and by the federal government.

Fueled in part by concerns raised by the publication of the alarmist *A Nation at Risk* (National Commission on Excellence in Education, 1983), the government funded a new review of research on beginning reading. In this 1990 review, *Beginning to Read: Thinking and Learning about Print*, Marilyn Adams underscored the need for systematic decoding instruction and argued persuasively for its implementation in beginning reading curricula. Not all were persuaded, however. Advocates of whole language immediately attacked the review (and Adams personally). What the federal government perceived as a winning strategy to convince teachers of the need for systematic decoding instruction had backfired.

Their next move was far more successful. In 1992, for the first time in its history, NAEP released achievement results for individual states. Previously, results had been reported only for major geographic regions and for the nation as a whole, so that state accountability was not an issue. California, the leader in whole language advocacy, was the lowest of all the states, and its superintendent resigned. The influence of whole language diminished rapidly thereafter.

But the government was just getting started. It empanelled a group of prominent researchers to produce yet another research review, this time limited to experimental and quasi-experimental studies – the gold standard of scientific inquiry. The National Reading Panel (NICHHD, 2000) used a narrow lens in its endeavor to identify effective practices, but its findings, predictably, were immediately controversial. However, the government had learned from the earlier reviews of Chall and Adams that research alone was not likely to be effective in advancing its agenda of skill-based instruction. Consequently, financial incentives were used to ensure the implementation of evidence-based instruction. Anticipating the National Reading Panel's report, Congress passed the Reading Excellence Act of 1998. Extensive funding was provided to participating states, but only if they pledged to implement instruction and use materials aligned with the findings of the Panel. Most, but not all, states participated. In 2001, the Bush administration picked up the mantle of early reading intervention, signaling the bipartisan nature of the concern. A new initiative, Reading First, was far more extensively funded than Reading Excellence and reached all 50 states.

Impact of Reading Initiatives

As Reading First drew to a close, educators awaited the results of an effectiveness study designed to gauge its impact. The report was released in 2008 and offered little evidence that substantive improvements had been realized. Despite success stories reported at the state level, and despite a badly flawed design (McKenna & Walpole, 2010), policymakers took the results of the evaluation at face value and terminated the program.

Where, then, does all of this leave us? A sizable proportion of American students who lack proficiency remains. It is clearly true that two powerful forces – research findings and financial incentives – have had little impact on the problem. The egalitarian ethic that underlies American exceptionalism may well necessitate a belief that all children can succeed – that we can actually accomplish the goal of leaving none of them behind. The idealism reflected in this goal seems at best a naïve hope (George Will has described it as "loopy") and at worst a political contrivance built around a target date so distant that legislators could not be held accountable.[7] But discarding this perspective would mean condemning innumerable children to an illiterate fate.

The Standards Movement. Policymakers have no power to directly influence learning. Students are unresponsive to fiats. Teachers and administrators, however, are on the receiving end of mandates designed to influence students indirectly. An example is the move toward state standards, squarely based on the assumption that teachers may not be adequately challenging their students. NCLB exerted federal pressure on teachers by denying funding to states unless they first established standards approved by Washington and then developed and administered high-stakes assessments designed to measure the attainment of those standards.

But tests can be murky indicators of achievement. The pressure to demonstrate that growing percentages of children are meeting the standards has led some states to game the system by adjusting difficulty and easing the criteria for passing. The federal response has been to embrace the Common Core State Standards.[8] Federal carrots, such as Race to the Top funding, were made contingent on adopting these standards, and at this writing nearly all states have done so. Proponents of the Common Core insist that the standards do not constitute a national curriculum, but the distinction is largely semantic. We will surely see relatively uniform curricula intended to achieve the standards, and uniform assessments intended to gauge their attainment, developments that may occasion teacher pushback (Zancanella & Moore, 2014).

But will using standards to raise the achievement bar actually reach the quarter to a third of students who struggle? Putting into place more rigorous standards does not, in itself, guarantee that achievement will rise, and critics have charged that the new standards are window dressing that ignores an implacable reality. In 2012, Tom Loveless, Senior Fellow at the Brookings Institution, wrote that "The empirical evidence suggests that the Common Core will have little effect on American students' achievement. The nation will have to look elsewhere for ways to improve its schools." In 2015, however, he walked back this prediction a bit by conceding that recent NAEP gains were related to how strongly a state had implemented the CCSS (Loveless, 2015).

Research Centers. Over the past half century, research centers, funded federally or through foundations, have played an important role in conducting investigations and distilling the lessons of research for practitioners. The Center for the Study of Reading, established in 1976, is a principal example of a federal center. During a time when nearly all research was quantitative in nature, the work of the centers was noncontroversial. However, the rise to prominence of qualitative inquiry and a focus on sociocultural issues has resulted in a new use of federal centers, as weapons in support of scientifically based instruction. A consequence of the Reading First and Reading Excellence initiatives has been federally sponsored, easy-to-read reports that presume to distill important lessons for practitioners. Sources include the Center on Instruction and the Florida Center for Reading Research, which complement the work of the What Works Clearinghouse.[9] Such organizations operate in parallel with traditional universities, and in our view they were intended as a means of bypassing the objections of academics who oppose scientific research in literacy. Make no mistake – we have found many of the products of such organizations to be extremely useful and we are in sympathy with their methods. Our reservation is that such reports, and their executive summaries, may become a resource through which the nuances of research into complex issues are sacrificed for the sake of convenience. There is an unfortunate tendency for teachers, administrators, and policymakers to read a few bulleted findings and derive from them the false confidence that they deeply understand how to apply them in schools.

The Coaching Movement. Another residual effect of Reading First and Reading Excellence is the proliferation of literacy coaches. The rationale for coaching is that improving instructional practice is not likely to result from "drive-by" professional development delivered by itinerant experts. What's needed is someone on site to observe and conference with teachers as they attempt to implement more effective practices (e.g., McKenna & Walpole, 2008; Walpole & McKenna, 2013). We are hopeful about the potential of coaching to alter, first, teachers' beliefs, then their instruction, and finally the achievement of their students. The research evidence for the impact of coaching on achievement is growing (e.g., Walpole & McKenna, 2009; Walpole, McKenna, Uribe-Zarain, & Lamitina, 2010), although the nature of the coaching provided to teachers is an important factor. Because coaching is now a part of the International Literacy Association's Standards for Reading Professionals, the future of coaching seems promising. However, demonstrating a causal link between coaching and achievement is fundamental to the case for coaching. Only when policymakers acknowledge such a link are they likely to make coaching a standard line item in instructional budgets.

Response to Intervention. Traditionally, American students have been identified for special education services on a "wait to fail" basis. After experiencing a prolonged period of little growth, children are first tested for general intellectual capacity and then, if the results are within normal limits, they may be categorized as reading disabled. In 2004, a revision of federal law permitted a different route to special education. Rather than waiting passively for a child to fail, a school may now implement one or more intervention strategies, either in small groups or individually. Records kept of the child's responsiveness to these interventions may reveal effective approaches that preclude the need for special services. RTI is still evolving and takes many forms. It has only begun to be rigorously investigated. What seems clear is that RTI will transform the nature of special education and bring about greater collaboration between special educators and classroom teachers. Far less clear is whether RTI will significantly reduce the proportion of students who struggle.

Forces and Horses

These developments have been heralded as hopeful trends and hyped as the long-awaited remedy to the nation's literacy woes. But in the midst of so much hope, history suggests a different outcome. In our previous work (McKenna, 2011), we have likened literacy initiatives to an old riddle: What happens when an irresistible force meets an immovable object? The "immovable object" – the stubborn presence of so many struggling readers – has remained unmoved by the best efforts of researchers, teachers, and policymakers. To the lengthy list of "irresistible forces" we are tempted to add all of these new American initiatives – Race to the Top, the Common Core Standards, research centers, coaching, and RTI. All have clear links to the past, and to outcomes that are not encouraging.

A wild card in the future of literacy – one that lacks a discouraging connection to the past – is technology. Although its advocates have long promised just-around-the-corner breakthroughs, the reality has been less than spectacular. On the other hand, the sheer pace of change compels us to keep an open mind. Already its development has led to complex trends that defy prediction. In a time of shifting ground, when our very notion of what counts as literacy is challenged, one certainty is that technology does not reduce the need for reading proficiency – it accentuates it. The Internet is replete with text and requires navigational strategies with few counterparts in the world of print. But technology offers support as well. Social networking has the potential to facilitate collaboration. Assistive technology offers supports to struggling readers in the form of on-demand pronunciations, definitions, translations, simplified text, and other aids. E-books on devices appear poised to revolutionize how we think about text. And at the same time, the hardware needed to house such applications grows ever faster, smaller, and cheaper. These trends are driven by business, not education, and they are inevitable. How they will play out as educators attempt to harness technology's potential is unclear, and whether technology will prove to be the irresistible force needed to achieve near-universal literacy remains to be seen.

A different metaphor also seems apropos, one that may better characterize technology as a means of fostering literacy growth. The recurrent initiatives aimed at the problem of limited reading proficiency are reminiscent of the siege of Troy. After ten years of resisting direct assault, the Trojans were ultimately defeated by an unnoticed invasion they unwittingly welcomed. Our hope is that technology will prove to be a Trojan horse, freely admitted into the everyday actions of all students but requiring and fostering literacy levels that the world of print did not.

The efforts of educators are ever constrained by what has been called the 91–9 problem. From the moment of birth until high school graduation, a student will spend just nine minutes in school for every 91 minutes spent outside. A major determinant of school success is what happens during those 91 minutes.

In settings where literacy is not highly valued, the work of teachers can be passively undermined. If technology can claim a larger space for literate activity during those 91 minutes, the work of teachers during their scant nine minutes might be reinforced and expanded.

Just to be clear, we borrowed the Trojan horse metaphor from the technology industry itself, where the motive has been, first, to find ways of getting into homes and then to become part of the everyday life of consumers. This metaphor has a downside both in the industry (where it is sometimes used to describe worms and viruses) and in literacy. The problem is this: What if the literacy we admit into our homes is a pale image of the academic literacy needed for career success? What if it discourages prolonged engagement with text and fosters nonstandard expression? Critics of social media have already sounded the alarm. In *The Dumbest Generation*, Mark Bauerlein (2009) warns of the "stupefying" effect that digital technologies have had. Nicholas Carr (2011), in his book, *The Shallows*, has gone even further, suggesting (controversially) an adverse neurological impact. We will return to these issues in Chapter 8.

What Can Comparing Countries Teach Us?

Comparing countries is risky business. For every point of comparison, we're forced to trivialize or ignore factors that may help explain a difference. A good example of this pitfall occurred during the Cold War. It seemed at the time that the two Germanys presented a textbook experiment in which a single country had been divided more or less randomly into two parts, distinguished mainly by the economic system in place. The fact that West Germany thrived while East Germany languished might have been taken as hard evidence that the capitalist system is superior to communism. Not so fast, a colleague of ours in the U.S. State Department remarked. The fact is, the partition had not resulted in two roughly equivalent parts. Rather, the West had the advantage of a well-developed industrial base, a landmass two and a half times as large, and far easier access to Western trade partners. These factors rigged the scales, making comparisons of the economic systems problematic.

We do not believe, however, that such a pitfall automatically precludes comparisons across countries. Instead we argue that our Cold War example teaches two lessons. The first is that we must exercise due caution in examining differences and that it's likely our conclusions will never be more than a starting point. The second is that comparisons made by others need to be qualified in the same manner and that critiques based on contextual factors are justified. Given these caveats, we believe it's possible to reach a few tentative conclusions about when reading instruction should begin, how much instruction children should receive, and whether the spelling system matters. These are issues of both instruction and policy.

Does Earlier Mean Better?

The best time to begin reading instruction has been debated for hundreds of years. The issue centers around the following conundrum: The longer we wait, the more children will be prepared to learn, but in the meantime those who are already prepared will be left cooling their heels. The idea of waiting has been advocated by key figures in the history of education. John Dewey recommended waiting until third grade. Jean-Jacques Rousseau suggested waiting until children reach adolescence, reasoning that childhood is filled with enough problems. Such ideas strike us as outlandish today, but there is evidence that "jamming down" the reading curriculum may come at a cost. A quarter century ago, New Zealand researcher Warwick Elley (1992) cautioned against the drive to begin instruction at ever-earlier points in time. To support his case, he used IEA data to compare national achievement levels with the age of beginning instruction. He concluded that children who begin their instruction later can usually catch up. A present-day example is Finland, where, as we have seen, children typically rank near the top in international comparisons like PIRLS, but where formal instruction does not commence until age 7. In contrast, the United States has gone in the opposite direction, reducing the onset of reading instruction from age 6 to 5.

Does More Mean Better?

The question of how much instruction children should receive requires a Hobson's choice among several imperfect metrics. One of the more popular is length of the school year, a measure often used to explain the mediocre performance of American children and argue for an extended year. To be sure, children in the United States attend school fewer days than children in a number of other countries. The difference between America and several of these nations is especially striking: Japan and South Korea (40 days), Australia and the Netherlands (20 days). But such comparisons can be misleading. For example, a recent study revealed that South Korean elementary students receive just 143 hours of literacy instruction in an entire school year (Park, Min, & Oh, 2010). In contrast, American students, even by the most conservative estimate, receive 270 hours of instruction yearly despite attending school 40 fewer days. Again, however, the amount of private tutoring South Korean students receive suggests that days in the school year can be a surprisingly weak measure of how much instruction children may actually receive. Common sense tells us that the quantity of instruction, at least up to a point, is clearly important, but we believe that what occurs during that time may be more telling. And what occurs is the net effect of national policy, local implementation, cultural factors, and teacher variance.

Is Spelling to Blame?

The complexity of a language's orthography is often maligned as a source of relative difficulty in learning to read. In all languages, as we have mentioned, spoken words comprise sequences of phonemes, the building blocks of every word we say and hear. In alphabetic languages, letters represent these phonemes, and learning to map letters to sounds is a milestone of word recognition. The rub lies in the match between letters and phonemes. Some languages, such as Finnish and Dutch, have a one-to-one correspondence between the two, making learning to decode fast and straightforward. Such orthographies are said to be "transparent" or "shallow." But in "deep" spelling systems like that of English, there are more phonemes (44 by most counts) than letters. This means that many letters are overworked and children must learn a perplexing variety of letter-sound associations. Proponents of simplified spelling, have long argued that deep orthography can be a barrier to reading development.

This problem was once thought to be so grave that artificial alphabets were created, words were printed with color-coding, and diacritical markings were placed over letters (similar to the approach used to teach Hebrew). The most famous initiative was the initial teaching alphabet, or i/t/a, introduced in the British Commonwealth by Sir James Pittman. In i/t/a, 44 symbols were used to create a one-to-one match between letters and phonemes. We suspect that most readers of this book have never heard of i/t/a, and for good reason – it didn't work. Although children did make early gains relative to their peers who were taught with traditional materials, they inevitably lost ground (and probably suffered considerable confusion) during the transition to regular spelling.

Making orthography the heavy, however, is not an easy argument. Most English-speaking children eventually learn to decode well (even those who struggle), and three Canadian provinces were among the top seven PIRLS finishers in 2006. Moreover, fourth graders in these provinces, the U.S., and England outscored children in countries such as Norway and Spain, where the languages children learn to read have shallow spelling systems. By the same token, students in the U.S. and England were outperformed by children who were learning to read languages with simpler orthographies, such as Swedish, German, and Dutch. All this proves is that the spelling system, in itself, explains very little. When nations like Korea and Finland rise to the top of international studies, the shallow orthography of their written language is not likely to be the active ingredient in their success. The fact that their populations are highly homogeneous in terms of demographics, language, and culture is the elephant in a room of probable causes.

In the case of Finland, Darling-Hammond has pointed out that schools have so far maintained their high international status despite having to contend with increasing numbers of non-Finnish-speaking immigrants. This is certainly true, but at approximately 5%, the overall proportion is still far smaller than in the public schools of most Western nations, and these students perform significantly worse than their Finnish-speaking classmates on the reading component of PIRLS (Hansen et al., 2014).

It is nevertheless notable that spelling has sometimes become a matter of national policy. We have mentioned the formal adoption of pinyin in China as a means of forestalling the complex system of ideographs used in written language. However, this was not the first time that national policy was altered to address the problems posed by Chinese orthography. Chinese characters were used in Korea well into the fifteenth century, and their proper use had long conferred prestige. But it was also a maddening and unnecessarily complicated system, a fact that prompted Sejong, a fifteenth-century monarch, to convene a group of scholars and charge them with inventing a new alphabet. The result was Hangul, unveiled in 1446 and used to this day. Hangul comprises just 24 letters, one for each phoneme in spoken Korean.

What Are the Lessons for Policy?

The answer to this question may depend on which metrics you value. If your primary concern is for children who struggle, you can take heart in the fact that in most developed countries, only a handful of fourth graders fail to reach the Low benchmark for PIRLS, which involves the ability to comprehend explicit facts and make simple inferences. In the U.S., such readers make up only 4% of the population. On the other hand, if you believe that children with high levels of proficiency are key to international competiveness, you may find reassuring the fact that 12% of American fourth graders meet the Advanced benchmark. This is, after all, not so different from the 19% reported for Singapore and Russia.

One difficulty with this reasoning, attractive though it is, lies in the fact that the NAEP results paint a much gloomier picture. How can it be that only 14% of U.S. fourth graders fail to reach the Intermediate PIRLS benchmark while 36% fall below the Basic level on the NAEP? To answer this question, the U.S. Department of Education funded a comparison of the two assessments (Binkley & Kelly, 2003). The short answer: PIRLS is easier. It is at the middle school where the NAEP comes into much better alignment with its international counterpart, PISA. Here the picture is less confused and it offers little comfort. In the next chapter, we examine the implications for adolescent literacy instruction.

Notes

1 The Standards and related materials may be downloaded at no cost by visiting www.corestandards.org.
2 We are indebted to Bong Gee Jang of Oakland University for his insights into Korean reading instruction.

3 We appreciate the assistance of Kylie Meyer of Queensland University of Technology in summarizing Australian reading instruction and the Queensland experience in particular.
4 We are indebted to Bettina Buch of Aarhus University for her insights into Danish reading instruction.
5 For a musical example of how Chinese children are introduced to Pinyin, visit http://www.youtube.com/watch?v=b9Ayvjy-Dgs
6 We are indebted to Huijing Wen, of the University of Delaware, for these examples and for her insights into Chinese reading instruction.
7 NCLB was enacted in 2001, with the goal of universal literacy in third grade by 2014.
8 There is a common misconception that the CCSS were the product of the U.S. Department of Education. As we noted earlier, they were actually developed jointly by the National Governors Association and the Council of Chief State School Officers.
9 In recent years, this agency has in effect consolidated the work of a number of federally funded centers.

References

Adams, M.J. (1990). *Beginning to read: Thinking and learning about print.* Cambridge, MA: MIT Press.

Anderson, R.C., Hiebert, E.H., Scott, J.A., & Wilkinson, I.A.G. (1985). *Becoming a nation of readers: The report of the Commission on Reading.* Washington, DC: National Academy of Education.

Bauerlein, M. (2009). *The dumbest generation: How the digital age stupefies young Americans and jeopardizes our future.* New York, NY: Tarcher.

Biemiller, A. (2012). Teaching vocabulary in the primary grades. In J.F. Baumann & E.J. Kame'enui (Eds.), *Vocabulary instruction: Research to practice* (2nd ed., pp. 34–50). New York, NY: Guilford Press.

Binkley, M., & Kelly, D.L. (2003). *A content comparison of the NAEP and PIRLS fourth-grade reading assessments.* Washington, DC: U.S. Department of Education.

Carr, N. (2011). *The shallows: What the internet is doing to our brains.* New York, NY: W.W. Norton.

Chall, J.S. (1967). *Learning to read: The great debate.* Columbus, OH: McGraw-Hill.

Edelsky, C. (1990). Whose agenda is this anyway? A response to McKenna, Robinson, and Miller. *Educational Researcher, 19*(8), 7–11.

Elley, W.B. (1992). *How in the world do students read?: IEA study of reading literacy.* Amsterdam, The Netherlands: International Association for the Evaluation of Educational Achievement.

Flesch, R. (1955). *Why Johnny can't read – And what you can do about it.* New York, NY: Harper & Brothers.

Gray, W.S., Artley, A.S., Arbuthnot, M.H., & Gray, L., (1951). *The new fun with Dick and Jane: Guidebook.* Chicago, IL: Scott, Foresman and Company.

Hansen, K.Y., Gustafsson, J.-E., Rosén, M., Sulkunen, S., Nissinen, K., Kupari, P., et al. (2014). *Northern lights on TIMSS and PIRLS 2011: Differences and similarities in the Nordic countries.* Copenhagen, Denmark: Nordic Council of Ministers.

Levine, A. (1994, December). The great debate revisited. *The Atlantic Online.* Available: http://www.theatlantic.com/past/politics/educatio/levine.htm

Loveless, T. (2012). *2012 Brown Center report on American education: How well are American students learning?* Washington, DC: Brookings Institution, Brown Center on Education

Policy. Available: http://www.brookings.edu/~/media/newsletters/0216_brown_education_loveless.pdf

Loveless, T. (2015). *2015 Brown Center report on American education: How well are American students learning?* Washington, DC: Brookings Institution, Brown Center on Education Policy. Available: http://www.ewa.org/sites/main/files/file-attachments/brown_ctr_2015_v2.pdf

McKenna, M.C. (2011). Issues and trends in American literacy education: When irresistible forces meet an immovable object. *Korean Literature & Language Education, 8,* 23–43.

McKenna, M.C., Robinson, R.D., & Miller, J.W. (1990). Whole language: A research agenda for the nineties. *Educational Researcher, 19*(8), 3–6.

McKenna, M.C., & Walpole, S. (2008). *The literacy coaching challenge: Models and methods for grades K-8.* New York: Guilford.

McKenna, M.C., & Walpole, S. (2010). Planning and evaluating change at scale: Lessons from Reading First. *Educational Researcher, 39,* 478–483.

National Commission on Excellence in Education. (1983). *A nation at risk: The imperative for educational reform.* Washington, DC: Author.

National Institute of Child Health and Human Development. (2000). *Report of the National Reading Panel. Teaching children to read: An evidence-based assessment of the scientific research literature on reading and its implications for reading instruction* (NIH Publication No. 00–4769). Washington, DC: U.S. Government Printing Office.

Park, C., Min, Y., & Oh, E. (2010). The comparative study on the instruction time in the elementary school systems. *Journal of Learner-Centered Curriculum and Instruction, 10*(1), 127–151.

Pressley, M. (2006). *Reading instruction that works: The case for balanced teaching* (3rd ed). New York, NY: Guilford Press.

Slavin, R.E. (1989). PET and the pendulum: Faddism in education and how to stop it. *Phi Delta Kappan, 70,* 752–775.

Stahl, S.A. (1998). Understanding shifts in reading and its instruction. *Peabody Journal of Education, 73*(3&4), 31–67.

Trace, A.S., Jr. (1961, May 27). Can Ivan read better than Johnny? *Saturday Evening Post, 234,* pp. 30+.

Tröhler, D. (2013). The OECD and Cold War culture: Thinking historically about PISA. In H.-D. Meyer & A. Benavot (Eds.), *PISA, power, and policy: The emergence of global educational governance* (pp. 141–161). Oxford, U.K.: Symposium Books.

Walpole, S., & McKenna, M.C. (2009). Everything you've always wanted to know about literacy coaching but were afraid to ask: A review of policy and research. In K.M. Leander, D.W. Rowe, D.K. Dickinson, R.T. Jimenez, M.K. Hundley, & V.J. Risko (Eds.), *Fifty-ninth yearbook of the National Reading Conference* (pp. 23–33). Milwaukee: NRC.

Walpole, S., & McKenna, M.C. (2013). *The literacy coach's handbook* (2nd ed.). New York, NY: Guilford Press.

Walpole, S., McKenna, M.C., Uribe-Zarain, X., & Lamitina, D. (2010). The relationships between coaching and instruction in the primary grades: Evidence from high-poverty schools. *Elementary School Journal, 111,* 115–140.

Yoon, H.K., Bolger, D.J., Kwon, O.-S., & Perfetti, C.A. (2002). Subsyllabic units in reading: A difference between Korean and English. *Precursors of Functional Literacy, 11,* 139–163.

Zancanella, D., & Moore, M. (2014). The origins and ominous future of the U.S. Common Core Standards in English language arts. In A. Goodwyn, L. Reid, & C. Durrant (Eds.), *International perspectives on teaching English in a globalized world* (pp. 199–209). London, UK: Routledge.

5

THE CRISIS OF SECONDARY AND POST-SECONDARY SCHOOLING – LITERACY'S PRACTICE FIELD AND PROVING GROUND

The half-century of NAEP results for grades 8 and 12 mirror those for grade 4. About 1 in 4 high school seniors falls below the Basic level, defined as the minimum proficiency needed for 12th-grade work. At first blush, this statistic may seem just a logical extension of the dismal trajectory for younger students. The real story is far worse, however. For one thing, many of the least-able readers have dropped out of school before reaching 12th grade and are not available for NAEP testing. And *Basic* has always been an optimistic term. We might find consolation in the glass-half-full conclusion that 3 out of 4 high school seniors read at the Basic level or higher. The fact is, however, Basic has never been good enough. Authors of the Carnegie report, *Reading Next*, lend perspective to the matter by pointing out that 70 percent of American adolescents require remedial services in reading (Biancarosa & Snow, 2004).

No doubt the situation would have seemed less dire, perhaps even tolerable, in past eras when heavy industry dominated the U.S. economy. The accelerated transformation to an IT world, however, has raised the stakes for literacy, a matter we will take up in Chapter 10. These higher stakes have brought Americans the Common Core and a parade of federal initiatives. Standing in the way are three formidable problems: the natural tendency of weak students to become disaffected, the compounding of their difficulties over time, and the structure of secondary schools.

Here, a bit of history may be helpful. During the twentieth century, U.S. secondary schooling underwent a vast transformation in both attendance and mission. In 1910, just 8.8 percent of 17-year-olds were enrolled and the curriculum was largely academic (Mintz, 2003). The Progressive movement led to a number of sweeping changes. For example, 1910 was also the year junior high schools were introduced, replacing the 8–4 organizational pattern (an eight-year elementary school followed by a four-year high school) with a 6–3–3 arrangement. There was a concurrent push to broaden the focus of high schools to include vocational preparation as well as liberal arts education. During the 1970s and 80s, middle schools rapidly replaced junior highs. Their focus on adolescent development differed considerably from the subject-centered junior high school. By serving a younger age range than the junior high, their near-universal use has led to today's typical grade structure of K–5, 6–8, and 9–12.

The structural evolution of U.S. secondary schools has, to say the least, not been associated with improved achievement. The flat NAEP trajectories bear stark testimony to the intractability of the problem. In 1983, *A Nation at Risk*, the report of the National Commission on Excellence in Education, pointed to a "rising tide of mediocrity" and employed the bluntest language in its call for change. Most notably:

> If an unfriendly foreign power had attempted to impose on America the mediocre educational performance that exists today, we might well have viewed it as an act of war.

Mintz (2003) credits the report with single-handedly initiating the standards movement. Certainly it is easy to see forerunners of the Common Core in recommendations like this one:

> The teaching of *English* in high school should equip graduates to: (a) comprehend, interpret, evaluate, and use what they read; (b) write well-organized, effective papers; (c) listen effectively and discuss ideas intelligently; and (d) know our literary heritage and how it enhances imagination and ethical understanding, and how it relates to the customs, ideas, and values of today's life and culture.

The standards movement is grounded in the assumption that schooling has, up to the present, sought to achieve standards that are too low to prepare students for post-secondary success. Bringing standards into alignment with college and career expectations would compel teachers and curriculum developers to make the changes necessary to achieve the more aggressive standards. We depict this top-down logic in Figure 5.1. In brief, increasing the rigor of standards necessitates tests that are correspondingly more rigorous. The pressures the new tests are sure to exert will cause educators and curriculum developers to adopt new approaches that will ultimately lead to higher student performance.

This logic is not without its skeptics. They are quick to point out how previous attempts to raise standards have not had the hoped-for trickle-down effect. Ultimately, of course, this is an empirical question.

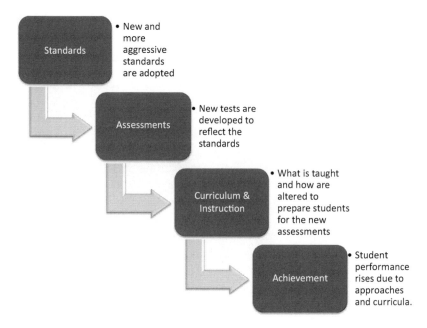

FIGURE 5.1 Rationale for the new standards.

Addressing the Right Achievement Gap

If there is any issue on which educators are likely to agree it is the desirability of reducing the "achievement gap." The consensus begins to erode, however, when we sharpen our definition of what that phrase denotes. A common – and we think wrongheaded – take is that the achievement gap is the distance between the highest- and lowest-performing students. The goal of eliminating this gap runs counter to a pair of inconvenient truths – that such a gap is natural and that it increases over time. We are not arguing that the proficiency of weaker readers can't be improved – far from it. But the idea that the gap can be closed in such a way that every student reads as well as the ablest among them is indefensible from the start. And in our view, this is not the achievement gap that matters. It is the difference between where struggling readers are and where they need to be for successful entry into either the workforce or post-secondary education. (Figure 5.2 offers a schematic for conceptualizing these two gaps.)

The idea of intervening in order to close, or at least narrow, this gap in middle and high schools has proved elusive. Unfortunately, with each passing year the window for successful intervention closes a little. Opportunities to acquire knowledge and vocabulary through reading have been lost. By the time the students leave elementary school, the cumulative impact is enormous. At the same time, academic self-concept erodes and with it the value adolescents ascribe to

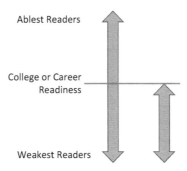

FIGURE 5.2 Two views of the achievement gap.

reading. Many are locked in a downward spiral of diminishing skill and will – or rather, a holding pattern until they can drop out. We will address this issue in some detail in Chapter 7.

The challenge of meeting the needs of these students would be difficult under the best of circumstances, but the design of secondary schools can act as a constraint on the help they receive. In the next section we provide a bit of history concerning how this came to be, together with comparisons of the U.S. with three other key countries.

Why Do So Many Students Experience Difficulty?

One reason is that the bar is raised with each cycle of assessment. In the case of NAEP, for example, the skills required to score at the Basic level become more sophisticated as students move from grade 4 to grade 8 to grade 12. These skills are selected based on what students need to be able to do in order to succeed at these grades. Consequently, if a student were to score below the Basic level at all three points in time, it would not mean that there was no improvement, just that there was not enough to keep pace with the demands of increasingly challenging material. In the U.S., the extent of the problem is likely to be magnified in coming years. This is because the new and more challenging tests brought about by the Common Core are certain to identify a larger percentage of students who lack proficiency. It is tempting to argue that the new standards artificially magnify the problem, in much the same way that reducing the cholesterol threshold from 300 to 200 put a large number of people at risk with the stroke of a pen. Yet this change in standards was not arbitrary. It reflected new findings concerning actual levels of risk. Likewise, the challenges presented by the reading of more complex texts reflect the changing reality of a world beyond high school.

Most students eventually attain fluency during elementary school. The main problem faced by those who struggle is that they lack the vocabulary and background knowledge to succeed in middle and high school (Lewis, Walpole, & McKenna, 2014). As we noted in the previous chapter, building vocabulary is not an aggressive priority in elementary schools, and much depends on incidental encounters with new words during reading. For this reason, children who experience reading difficulties in the early grades are at a disadvantage because of the time lost as they slowly improve. They simply have fewer chances to encounter new words through reading and their vocabulary growth suffers as a result. In middle school, they face teachers who are content specialists and who often lack the expertise and time to help them. Language arts teachers, to whom they might expect to look for assistance, are primarily concerned with literature, grammar, and composition. Reading specialists are few in number and historically have not worked closely with special educators.

In any case, most of the adolescents who struggle suffer from inadequate vocabulary and prior knowledge, gaps that by this point are not easily addressed by specialized instruction. By the time students reach high school, they are shunted into courses designed to separate the wheat from the chaff – general and basic at one extreme, advanced, honors, and Advanced Placement (AP) at the other. Students experiencing difficulties (more than a quarter) often find even the basic courses daunting, and they begin to consider dropping out as soon as they are old enough. At this late date, it is nearly impossible to cross the line from basic to college-bound courses. For many who struggle, open admission policies make a post-secondary education possible, but remedial coursework is often required.

Why Does the Problem Persist?

Our take on the available evidence is that there are two reasons. One is structural, the other pedagogical.

From a structural standpoint, middle and high schools are not designed to address the problems of struggling readers. We know that such a statement is likely to rankle dedicated secondary teachers, and although their efforts are laudable the data suggest that those efforts have been largely unsuccessful. Students facing the course requirements of high school have little time to take advantage of remedial opportunities, even when they are available. There are few reading specialists employed in middle or high school, too few to address a problem so extensive. Special educators are likewise spread thin. What about English teachers? Surely their close connection with reading places them in a good position to work with students who are struggling. Through our involvement with high schools, however, we have witnessed the greatest pushback from English teachers. Many are disinclined to take the steps necessary to provide real assistance, arguing that to do so would mean reducing their standards.

High schools have long relied on one structural component, however. This is the differentiation possible by means of leveled coursework. These alternatives provide a mechanism for matching reading materials with reading levels. Up to a point, this system works, especially for abler students. For those who struggle, course requirements can still present considerable difficulties.

A second reason for the stubborn persistence of the problem is the fact that by this point academic deficits are not easily addressed by teaching. We are by no means arguing that the problem is insoluble for all students. The unfortunate reality, however, is that secondary students with good foundational skills are likely to experience difficulties due to inadequate background knowledge and limited exposure to reading academic text. These problems have a cumulative effect. Through reading, students are exposed to academic language, and at the same time they acquire the knowledge they will need to comprehend in further reading. This doesn't happen for those who struggle. By the time they reach middle and high school, the gap between what they know and what they need to know has widened into a chasm. We don't deny that good teaching can narrow that gap to some degree, but it can't be eliminated. And, of course, the assumption of good teaching begs the question of who will provide it and when.

What Has Been Done to Address the Problem?

Since the enormity of the problem was first documented during the 1960s, there has been no shortage of attempts to solve it. Title I funding provided secondary school reading specialists. Easier (that is to say, "dumbed down") versions of texts were published. Programs to boost vocabulary were created. Computer-assisted instruction was implemented (and continues to be, in more and more sophisticated incarnations).

Possibly the boldest solution, however, was to head off the problem entirely by focusing on early intervention, as early as the primary grades. The rationale for early intervention is indeed compelling. A parable told by Robert Slavin and his colleagues embodies the argument. It bears reading in full:

> Once upon a time there was a town that was having a serious health problem. Approximately 30 percent of the children in the town were coming down with typhoid and other diseases because of contaminated drinking water. The town council allocated millions to medical care for the typhoid victims, yet some of them died or were permanently disabled. One day, an engineer proposed to the town council that they install a water treatment plant, which would prevent nearly all cases of the disease. "Ridiculous!" fumed the mayor. "We can't afford it!" The engineer pointed out that they were already paying millions for treatment of a preventable disease. "But if we bought a water treatment plant," the mayor responded, "how could we afford to treat the children who already have the disease?" "Besides," added a councilman, "most of our children don't get the disease. The money we

spend now is targeted to exactly the children who need it!" After a brief debate, the town council rejected the engineer's suggestion.

The town council's decision in the parable is, of course, a foolish one. From a purely economic point of view, the costs of providing medical services to large numbers of children over a long time were greater than the cost of the water treatment plant. What is more important, children were being permanently damaged by a preventable disease.

(Slavin et al., 1991, p. 404)

This analogy makes a powerful case for early intervention. Though reasonable people will differ as to what an effective intervention might look like, few would any longer support a wait-to-fail approach. Given the disappointing history of remedial and intervention efforts described in the previous chapter, it appears unlikely that elementary schools will ever be able to provide their middle school counterparts with universally literate sixth graders. This is not to say that the proportion of entering middle schoolers with reading difficulties can't be reduced. We firmly believe that it can. But middle and secondary schools serving high-poverty populations with limited parental education will have literacy problems to contend with for the foreseeable future.

The shortcoming of all these approaches is that, for the most part, they haven't worked, at least not on a large scale. There are a great many success stories, scattered here and there like so many "points of light," as a former president might have described them. But bottling their essence and distributing it broadly is not likely to happen.

What Can We Learn From Other Countries?

As students pass from elementary to secondary school, their formal reading instruction is largely behind them. Most have acquired the basic skills needed for reasonably fluent reading. In light of these facts, one might well wonder if any additional instruction were needed. The problem, however, is that a significant proportion of students in grades 8 and 12 are incapable of reading assigned materials. In the United States, the extent of the problem has been clearly documented for nearly half a century. Nor is it limited to America. Analyses of the PIRLS-to-PISA cohorts, which we summarized in Chapter 3, have demonstrated that every participating country faces a similar problem, though the extent of the problem varies.

At the school level, researchers have long pursued a particular Golden Fleece – namely, the secret of schools that have succeeded despite demographic probabilities. These schools, variously described as "against-the-odds" or "turnaround" schools, have been the subject of intense scrutiny in an effort to distill their secrets. What if the same idea were applied at the country level? Might those countries in which the percentage of readers at risk fell substantially between PIRLS and PISA have important lessons to tell? To answer this question, we returned to the cohort comparisons described in Chapter 3 in search of countries where the percentage of 9-year-olds scoring below the Low International Benchmark was at least 10 percent higher than the later percentage of 15-year-olds. We concede that this was not the ideal approach to the problem because strict cohorts could not be tracked between the two assessments. Nonetheless, we believed that a robust against-the-odds secondary system would reveal itself through the analysis we undertook. It did not. Not a single nation exhibited such a pattern.

This is not to say that important insights cannot be distilled from other countries. We have selected three that have led the industrialized world despite differences in language and culture.

Korea[1]

One of the most remarkable changes in education in South Korea is the incredible advancement in secondary education. South Korea was a country where the majority of the adult population had no secondary or higher education in the 1950s. Today, however, according to a 2011 OECD report, 94 percent of Korean adolescents obtain a high school diploma, one of the highest proportions in the world.

In secondary schools, instruction for adolescents in most public schools relies heavily on textbooks based on the *Korean National Curriculum and Standards of Language Arts,* consisting of seven sub-categories: listening, speaking, reading, writing, literature, grammar, and media. Several revisions have appeared since the standards were introduced in 1945. Notably, in the latest revision media literacy is incorporated into one of the seven strands, requiring Korean adolescents to view and represent digital texts.

Teachers mostly use two different textbooks: *Korean Language*, which includes reading and literature, and *Korean Language Communication*, which targets listening, speaking, writing, grammar, and media. In middle schools, language arts teachers use different types of supplementary texts with multiple content-area literacy strategies, such as literature circles and reciprocal teaching. This trend has been strongly influenced by American methods textbooks that have been translated into Korean and are now widely used in undergraduate literacy methods courses and professional development workshops.

In high schools, teachers usually restrict their teaching and assessments to the content in their textbooks in order to prepare students for the National Standards Test. Because students' scores on the Korean Scholastic Aptitude Test (KSAT) are by far the most important factor in college admissions, reading instruction in most high schools emphasizes testing skills and speed-reading to prepare their students for the KSAT.

Ironically, the number of places in higher education exceeds the number of high school graduates. So getting into college is not a problem Korean high school students face. The problem is getting into the *right* college. Higher education in Korea serves as a prerequisite for upward social and professional mobility. One can argue that this is true elsewhere as well, of course, but the cachet of certain institutions is remarkable in Korea – in particular the so-called SKY universities: Seoul National University, Korea University, and Yonsei University.

The pressure to follow a trajectory leading to an influential college undoubtedly contributes to Korea's high standing on international literacy assessments. One consequence, suggested by Korean researchers, may be a decline in recreational reading (e.g., Jang & Kim, 2013). This finding is quite understandable. A heavy diet of reading for academic purposes doesn't exactly set the stage for still more reading after hours, no matter how engaging the material. (We'll return to this phenomenon in Chapter 7.)

China[2]

Chinese secondary schools include junior and senior middle schools, each spanning three years. An entrance exam is required for the latter. In some places, specialized secondary schools are available, with programs typically ranging from 3 to 7 years depending on the area of specialization. A comparatively small proportion of those who complete secondary school go on to college, though in recent years the Chinese government has increased its support, and the percentage has risen from 10 (in 1980s and early 90s) to about 50 today.

Vocational schools were stressed as an alternative to college in the reforms that began in 1978. They enroll students who have failed or are unwilling to go on to senior high schools, and their popularity has risen in both urban and rural areas because of the job-related professional training they provide. Efforts are now underway to develop a tiered vocational system of increasing skill sophistication.

In China, the language arts curriculum is somewhat less centralized than in Korea. However, the Ministry of Education has set standards for middle schools throughout the country, and most use the standards-based curricula published by the People's Press. Schools in higher-performing areas are permitted to implement regional curricula if they choose, such as the Shanghai and Jiangsu versions.

Like the elementary school, the teacher-student ratio varies from region to region. In the less-developed inland cities and remote areas, the students in each class can number as many as 60. Somewhat surprisingly, similar ratios often exist in exclusive middle schools because of demand. Generally speaking, however, the ratio is less than 30 students per teacher and frequently less than 20.

Classroom instruction attempts to cultivate independent study, focusing on the development of good study habits and building on existing interests. Motivation has been especially emphasized over the past few years. For example, a district in Shanghai initiated a "Reading Journey" program that replaces the traditional approach that a Chinese colleague has described as spoon-feeding. There are now more group discussions in a climate that is largely student-centered.

Junior middle school is divided into two stages: the fundamental stage (grades 6 and 7) and the advanced stage (grades 8 and 9). For grades 6 and 7, reading instruction centers on the study of well-crafted sentences and passages as well as cultivation of students' reading interests. For grades 8 and 9, reading instruction focuses on genres, broadly defined as expository, persuasive, and narrative.

Instruction during the advanced stage is geared specifically toward preparing students for the national high school entrance examination. In many respects, this test is even more crucial than in Korea, because spaces are limited. Like Korea and, we would argue, the U.S., scores ultimately relegate applicants first to a few key universities, next to less-discriminating regular universities, and finally to provincial universities.

Efforts to differentiate instruction vary widely. Some schools reserve the last class each day for small-group instruction based on needs, and it is notable that the instruction provided is for all students, not just those who struggle. For example, there are three groupings in a well-known middle school in Shanghai, corresponding roughly to proficiency below, at, and above grade level.

As in Korea, recreational reading is more the exception than the rule for adolescents. Chinese students are heavily burdened with homework and their education is exam-oriented. Though teachers provide reading lists at the beginning of each semester, many of the titles go unread. Exceptions include the classics, which might be tested, plus kung fu novels or cyber novels. There are signs that changes may be in the wind, however. Recent years have witnessed a middle school enthusiasm for web-based serial stories and novels. Overall, however, changes and innovations have been minimal in China due to the overriding influence of the national standards.

Germany[3]

Germany is similar to the United States – and unlike many of its European neighbors – in its decentralized stance regarding education. Its 16 states have extensive autonomy in developing policy, though in reality there are more similarities than differences (also like the U.S.). Elementary schooling beyond kindergarten lasts four years in 14 of the states and six years in Berlin and Brandenburg. At the end of elementary school (*Grundschule*), several types of secondary schools are possible, but, at the risk of oversimplifying, these options basically involve a bifurcated choice between college preparatory and vocational programs. The overall approach is consequently described as the German dual, or binary, system.

The more academic path begins with enrollment in the *Gymnasium*, likely a perplexing term for Americans unfamiliar with the system. In most states, entrance is determined largely on the basis of the *Grundschule*'s recommendation, which in turn depends largely on grades in core subjects. In 10 states, however, parents can overrule a negative recommendation and have their child placed in the *Gymnasium* on a probationary basis for six months to a year. In six states, parents have no such prerogative. During the first two years of *Gymnasium*, many students falter and opt for the more vocationally oriented *Realschule*.

Following a vocational path is arguably better suited to some. It is linked to business placements during part of the day for older students, a partnership that often works well. Because study depends on a limited number of business apprenticeships, however, there is competition for the available places, intensified by the fact that high school graduates and college dropouts are also eligible to apply.

A defining distinction between the German and American systems is the age at which the academic-vocational decision is made. In the German system, this point is reached much earlier. Critics might call it too early for still-developing students who might realize their potential later than others. There is, for example, virtually no chance of a student's moving from *Realschule* to *Gymnasium*. On the other hand, defenders of earlier identification argue that enough evidence has accrued by the end of *Grundschule* to make a reasonable judgment. They also point out that U.S. middle schools, though ostensibly comprehensive, quickly begin to categorize students through course selection.

What Are the Lessons for Policy?

One difficulty with implementing an approach developed abroad is that, much like an organ transplant, it might well be rejected by the recipient. In place of antibodies, political and cultural contexts can exert enormous negative influence on educational policy. In this case, one can easily imagine the pushback resulting from an attempt to widely institute an admission test to enter certain middle schools, as in China, or to develop a German-like dual system of middle schools. We do not think it prudent to dismiss these possibilities out of hand, however, and indeed versions of each have been successfully piloted in the U.S. In fact, the lack of uniformity among American school contexts suggests that no one-size-fits-all approach to reform can ever be widely successful. The variety of approaches among the German states affirms this idea. However, the lack of a foreign model that successfully points the way toward the rescue of a sizable proportion of struggling adolescents must continue to give one pause.

Structural Change

Efforts to extend the time devoted to literacy instruction at the secondary level have taken several forms, including extending the school year, extending the school day, and restructuring time within the existing school day. The last and cheapest of these has been implemented in many forms, some of them more successful than others. An example with great face appeal has been one in which daily time is apportioned for recreational reading. Every teacher supervises a group, thus ostensibly showing solidarity in support of literacy. We strongly suspect, however, that a more targeted use of such time will yield better results as it has at William Penn High School in New Castle, Delaware. There, teachers of specific subjects and at certain grade levels can reserve such time for extra work in content literacy. This plan is similar to the Chinese approach we have described. The key lies in the development of a coherent plan through which professional learning is provided to teachers so that they can help their students accomplish content objectives through reading and writing. In other words, it may not be necessary to add minutes to the school day or days to the school year. Success may lie in better use of the minutes already available.

Instructional Change

Making better use of available time naturally involves the instructional approaches teachers choose to employ. This amounts to a two-part problem. The first involves convincing teachers to make reading a central part of content area instruction. Many teachers choose to circumvent literacy difficulties by eliminating the expectation that students read in order to acquire content knowledge. The idea is simply to tell them what they need to know in order to achieve the standards. A good example is the trend beginning in the 1990s to minimize the use of science textbooks in preference for inquiry materials, an era we might call the Age of Kits. The rationale was that students might become more actively engaged through hands-on activities. It had clear appeal but ignored the reality that scientists do far more than conduct experiments using equipment. They read. A lot. This is not to say that inquiry materials are ineffective. The danger lies in creating an imbalance in which reading is relegated to a peripheral role. As Yarden, Norris, and Phillips (2015) have recently reported, the demands of scientific literacy are central to success in college, and they are unlikely to be met without conscious attention by secondary school teachers.

The second part of the problem is that when teachers at the secondary level do attempt to make reading and writing a part of their instruction, they tend not to use evidence-based approaches. Molly Ness (2007) observed science and social studies teachers at both the middle and high school levels for an extended period in an effort to see how frequently they employed the most effective instructional strategies. She was astonished to discover that virtually none of the strategies on her short list were used by any of the teachers. When asked why, the teachers responded that they were too busy preparing their students for the high-stakes tests that were to come. No matter that the students would be required to read in order to pass those tests.

Just to be clear, research has clearly identified the sort of instruction likely to advance content literacy, defined as "the ability to use reading and writing for the acquisition of new content in a given discipline" (McKenna & Robinson, 1990, p. 184). The International Literacy Association has endorsed such instruction in a position statement (Moore, Bean, Birdyshaw, & Rycik, 1999). In addition, several landmark reports have reconfirmed reading and writing strategies that can be used effectively in content literacy instruction. Four of these reports are *Reading Next* (Biancarosa & Snow, 2004), *Writing Next* (Graham & Perin, 2007), *Literacy Instruction in the Content Areas* (Heller & Greenleaf, 2007), and *Writing to Read* (Graham & Hebert, 2010). But are these strategies enough? The idea of content literacy is now being broadened to include sociocultural interaction and the new literacies of the Internet as well as conventional instructional strategies. Our concern is that content-area teachers, who have long resisted the conventional approaches, will resist these new approaches as well.

Early Intervention

We have already stated the case for early intervention, and it is an elegant one. The fact that efforts have not yet significantly reduced the number of struggling readers arriving in middle school is no reason to stop trying. Machiavelli observed that in their early stages political problems are easy to address but difficult to detect. As time passes, however, they become easy to detect but difficult to address. The same might be said about reading problems. A K-12 policy that begins with prevention and progresses to intervention is the most likely way forward.

Notes

1 We are indebted to Bong Gee Jang of Oakland University for his insights into Korean reading instruction.
2 We are indebted to Huijing Wen, of the University of Delaware, for her insights into Chinese reading instruction.
3 We are indebted to Gisela Beste of the National Institute for School and Media in Berlin-Brandenburg (LISUM) and to Andrea Aker, former senior official of the Baden-Württemberg government, for their contributions to this overview.

References

Biancarosa, G., & Snow, C.E. (2004). *Reading next – A vision for action and research in middle and high school literacy: A report to Carnegie Corporation of New York*. Washington, DC: Alliance for Excellent Education. Available: http://www.all4ed.org/files/ReadingNext.pdf

Graham, S., & Hebert, M. (2010). *Writing to read: Evidence for how writing can improve reading. Carnegie Corporation Time to Act Report*. Washington, DC: Alliance for Excellent Education.

Graham, S., & Perrin, D. (2007). *Writing next: Effective strategies to improve writing of adolescent middle and high school.* Washington, DC: Alliance for Excellent Education. Available: http://www.all4ed.org/files/WritingNext.pdf

Heller, R., & Greenleaf, C.L. (2007). *Literacy instruction in the content areas: Getting to the core of middle and high school improvement.* Washington, DC: Alliance for Excellent Education.

Jang, B.G., & Kim, J.-Y. (2013, April). *Comparing structural differences in reading amount, reading attitudes, and reading achievement between U.S. and Korean adolescents: Findings from PISA 2009.* Poster presented at the annual meeting of the American Educational Research Association, San Francisco, CA.

Lewis, W., Walpole, S., & McKenna, M.C. (2014). *Cracking the Common Core: Choosing and using texts in grades 6–12.* New York, NY: Guilford Press.

McKenna, M. C., & Robinson, R. D. (1990). Content literacy: A definition and implications. *Journal of Reading, 34,* 184–186.

Mintz, S.L. (2003). Secondary education. In J.W. Guthrie (Ed.), *Encyclopedia of Education* (2nd ed.). New York, NY: Macmillan.

Moore, D.W., Bean, T.W., Birdyshaw, D., & Rycik, J.A. (1999). *Adolescent literacy: A position statement for the Commission on Adolescent Literacy of the International Reading Association.* Newark, DE: International Reading Association.

National Commission on Excellence in Education. (1983). *A nation at risk: The imperative for educational reform.* Washington, DC: Author.

Ness, M. (2007). Reading comprehension strategies in secondary content-area classrooms. *Phi Delta Kappan, 89,* 229.

Slavin, R.E., Madden, N.A., Karweit, N.L., Dolan, L.J., & Wasik, B.A. (1991). Success for all: Ending reading failure from the beginning. *Language Arts, 68,* 404–409.

Yarden, A., Norris, S.P., & Phillips, L.M. (2015). Teaching scientific reading. *Innovations in Science and Technology Education, 22,* 109–124.

6

SUPPORTING LITERATE CULTURES – THE PAST, PRESENT, AND FUTURE OF LIBRARIES, NEWSPAPERS, AND BOOKSTORES

Collecting, organizing, and dispensing the written word have long been the central roles played by libraries, newspapers, and bookstores. Libraries and to a certain extent newspapers have also served an archival function, storing information and facilitating its retrieval. Each is an indisputable sine qua non of a literate society, a fact that warrants careful consideration of their trajectories.

In this chapter, we examine the evolution of all three, guided by two critical considerations. We first review historical influences, both positive and negative, that have shaped the development of each over time. Next we consider the role of technology in the near term as a factor with little historical precedent. As we intend to make clear, the pace of change has rendered past assumptions increasingly problematic. Libraries are no longer large box repositories for print books only. The circulation of print newspapers continues its decline over the last 70 years, but expands in online delivery, circulation of free dailies, and even in paid circulation in some countries. Brick-and-mortar bookstores are now coffee shops, public meeting places, purveyors of both print and digital media, and anchors of urban renewal. This chapter documents these changing histories and examines the relative effects across nations, races, genders, and ages.

Libraries

Since information began to be communicated through visible symbols, the need to collect and preserve "writings" has fallen to institutions presently known as libraries. Michael Harris (1995) notes that though the origin of the library is unknown, we can define its present-day incarnation as "a collection of graphic material arranged for relatively easy use, cared for by an individual or individuals familiar with that arrangement, and accessible to at least a limited number of persons..." (p. 3).

These elements are common to all libraries, but their specific form varies with patronage and funding. This variation is indeed broad. There are, for example, public libraries (Boston Public Library), university libraries (University of Illinois Library), privately held collection libraries (J. Walker's Private Library), special purpose libraries (Missouri Botanical Garden Library), government libraries (Library of Congress), and religious libraries (the Vatican Library), to name a few.

Regardless of form and origin, libraries have always played a critical role in the practice of literate behaviors. Herbert Samuel's observation that a library is "thought in cold storage" may underplay the importance of what happens when individuals discover and thaw out what they need. The writer of a recent blog post observes that libraries have "developed into important social structures that facilitate not just the reading of books but a meeting point of different people, different ideas, discussion and debate" (*Ten Best Libraries in the World*, 2011).

Though their archival value cannot be overstated, libraries are far more than receptacles of knowledge. They provide people from a wide expanse of socioeconomic strata, ages, races, and genders with access to information. Just as libraries facilitate the literate practice of individuals, they simultaneously facilitate greater equality of access. However, this breadth of access has not always been the case. It has evolved over time.

Libraries of the Past

Libraries have probably been with us as long as writing systems. In *The Memory of Mankind*, Tolzmann et al. (2001) note that a common theme through history is that as a society or culture becomes wealthier, it places a higher value on literacy. One reflection of its ascension has been in the building of libraries.

In their early development, libraries served not only as repositories but as publishing houses, complete with scribes who copied text and others (librarians) who made decisions about which books would be copied and, thus, which would survive for later generations. Storage was a singular problem for the earliest libraries due to the sheer volume required to house tablets. Obviously, this problem was attenuated over the centuries as more convenient methods of storage emerged, such as books.

Lerner (2009) notes that some of the first true libraries were developed by the Assyrians, who had a gift for organization and efficiency. More importantly, Assyrian libraries were open to any individual who could read, a policy that provided an early precedent for equality of access. King Assurbanipal (seventh century BCE), for example, developed the palace library at Nineveh, which not only became one of the most extensive in the world but was open to both official and unofficial scholars. Later, Egyptian libraries, which began in temples, soon expanded to include secular writings, many of which were oriented toward medicine and astronomy. The evolution of the libraries of antiquity culminated in the creation of the library at Alexandria in the third century BCE, and its destruction marked one of the greatest setbacks in their development.

Fast forward to the late Middle Ages, when libraries had long been reserved for use by the literate elite. They were poised, however, to recapture their role in the more egalitarian dissemination of knowledge. As the humanist writers in Italy were helping to usher in the Renaissance, they also contributed to the rebirth of open libraries. Tolzmann et al. (2001) note that "the principle that libraries should be open to the public may well serve as one characteristic differentiating the Renaissance library from the library of the Middle Ages" (p. 59).

Lerner (2009) thoroughly documents the role of what he refers to as Gutenberg's Legacy, the advent of the printing press, "a machine that combined flexibility, rapidity, and economy to allow the production of books that the increasingly literate, increasingly numerous European city-dweller could afford to buy and read" (p. 83). Lerner observes that:

> to ensure that the Greek and Latin classics were published in complete, accurate editions, editors and printers searched the libraries of Europe for the best available manuscripts. These were purchased, exchanged, borrowed, or sometimes stolen, and turned over to the printers to serve as copy.
>
> (p. 84)

He states that this period of time also gave rise to the greatest progress in the establishment of libraries through private collections. Kings and princes, "motivated by ostentation or piety" (pp. 86–87), had historically collected books. With the greater prevalence of books, however, collecting became a passion of others, including successful business people.

Prior to Gutenberg's invention, few Europeans could read and few books were available to those who could. Of these volumes, only a small number were written in languages other than Latin. Lerner notes that "by 1800, at least in the Protestant countries of Northern Europe, over half the adult population could read simple vernacular texts. . . . As both the number of readers and the taste for reading increased, the book trade grew likewise" (2009, pp. 126, 129). Beyond the obvious effect of extending the availability of books, the printing press also raised the need for organizing them in ways that allowed them to be retrieved and shared. It was out of these needs that the origins of library science arose.

Esdaile (1934) discusses the growth and expansion of the national libraries from a period that roughly extended from the invention of the printing press through the nineteenth century. The Bibliothèque Nationale, in Paris, became one of the first libraries to house broad-based collections funded by, and for, an entire country. During roughly the same period, the University of Vienna founded a collection (transferred to the Town of Vienna in 1466) through the patronage of the Imperial House of Hapsburg. This collection eventually became the National Library of Vienna. The Antiques Division of the British Museum's Library of National History was similarly formed by the collection of a number of influential individuals, and it was opened to the public in 1759 as a national library. The Library of Leningrad, formed from the collections of Catherine the Great and others, opened in 1776 in St. Petersburg.

Such libraries profoundly influenced the fledgling United States. The Library of Congress was launched when Congress moved to Washington, DC, in order to serve both houses of Congress. After the British destroyed it during the War of 1812, it was rebuilt under Jefferson's leadership, and partially on the basis of his own collection.

In the mid-1800s, booksellers and magazines devoted to book reviewing emerged. And though books were expensive, the cost was mitigated by the formation of reading societies, reading clubs, reading rooms, and subscription libraries, where for a relatively modest fee people could borrow and return books. These organizations were forerunners of the great public lending libraries, which first developed in Britain around 1850. The Industrial Revolution and the congregation of individuals in urban areas created a critical mass of potential readers in places that could be served by a single institution. Book circulation grew substantially. The Boston Public Library became one of the leading public libraries in the United States and exerted considerable influence as a social and intellectual center of the time.

The number of public libraries likewise continued to grow in many countries. Lerner (2009) observes that in 1768 the Japanese, under the Meiji Restoration, attempted to catch up to European technology, establish comparable educational institutions, and develop Japanese as a literary language replacing Chinese. And so the change facilitated by literacy and libraries began to spread well beyond Europe and the United States. Access was also expanded to females, and by the middle of the nineteenth century women represented a significant proportion of library users. This development was due in part to the limited educational opportunities available to women through other institutions. By 1869, 46 percent of the Boston Public Library's 11,000 users were women (Lerner, 2009). Gender is yet another example of the equalizing effect of libraries.

Children were also a target of expansion. In Great Britain, providing library services for children was seen as a way to reduce poverty. In America, as free public education spread across the country in the late nineteenth and early twentieth century, children's material in libraries became an important segment of their holdings. As Henry Barnard stated, "Without such books the instruction of the school-room does not become practically useful, and the art of printing is not made available to the poor as well as the rich" (1849, p. 61).

In sum, the long history of libraries, from Alexandria to the present day, has proceeded in the general direction of greater accessibility. Notwithstanding a few setbacks, they have transitioned from serving the elite few to a diverse literate public. With their transformation has come considerable responsibility. Just as the printing press played a vital role in this progress, there can be little doubt, as Harris (1995) observed, that "every aspect of human existence was being influenced by the new information technology. All those charged with management of libraries have been forced to pay close attention to these developments" (p. 294). This insight is critical as we consider the current reformation in availability and equality of access to the printed word.

Current Libraries

Given the long history of change for libraries, it is not surprising that their evolution continues. What *is* surprising is the rate of change. We define "current" as a period of time extending from the late twentieth century to the present, a period characterized by rapidly accelerating developments. Some have projected an end to the conventional notion of a library as a physical receptacle. They argue that technology has offered new storage and retrieval systems that make the value of a repository less critical. (We can only speculate about the first U.S. president to declare a presidential library unnecessary!)

When we compare large libraries with big box stores, we see at once a major flaw in such an analogy. Box stores dispense physical goods, and though their virtual forms (such as walmart.com) have gained some traction, it is hard to imagine a time when consumers will reject the conventional option of pay-and-carry shopping. Libraries, however, dispense products that have digital forms that are essentially equivalent to their print forerunners, a fact that raises questions about the need for physical storage.

But sounding the knell for libraries may be premature. Norman (2012), an Australian librarian, refers to the "frail, fatal, fundamental: the future of public libraries." He observes that "public libraries will survive and thrive . . . by recognizing their changing roles with the digital world of content, the role of shifting to that of content aggregators, access managers, and educators of digital literacy." He goes on to observe that "people crave knowledge and a sense of belonging to a community so the future of libraries is sound and a physical building should reflect those very human desires." The physical presence of libraries is transforming from looming floors of "stacks" and daunting wooden card files, catalogued through strict adherence to the Library of Congress classification system, to social "learning places" with coffee shops, classes for children and adults, and places to listen to books. Consequently, even as the need for storage declines, the need for space continues.

Behind the scenes, ever-expanding content has hastened library interdependence. Piper (2013) points to the need for inter-library cooperation as huge digital collections become intertwined. He observes that:

> by the beginning of the 21st century, several trends in the evolution of libraries had emerged – collaboration was the key to survival; technology would play an integral role; library as 'place' would supersede a warehouse function; and digitalization would prevail.

As is the case with change in any field, there are those who decry what others perceive as monumental advancements. In an article titled, "The New York Public Library Must Be Saved from Itself," Lewis (2013) took a cautionary stance in discussing the wisdom of changes such as moving most bound volumes to storage locations and transforming the use of physical space. And so the debate continues between those who want to see the library as a place for researchers (and the very quietest of readers) and others who want to see the library as an important part of the social fabric. In any event, time marches on and some change is both inevitable and needed.

Three of the major facets of such change include usage and accessibility of materials, the role of libraries as centers for urban revitalization, and their role as technology instructor and online service provider. As the nature of the library evolves, questions always arise as to whether or not utilization of these services is increasing, decreasing, or remaining constant. It is difficult, however, to accurately index library use over time as the nature of the usage changes. One conclusion does seem relatively clear from the analysis of available data: Libraries are not dwindling in the same ways as brick-and-mortar bookstores and print newspapers. In some respects, usage is flat; in others, it has increased; and in still other respects, it has declined. Galbi (2008) discusses book circulation in public libraries since 1856. He observes that "library book circulation, per user, has no strong long-run trend, neither up nor down. From 1856 to 1978, library users borrowed about 15 books per year. From 1978 to 2004, book circulation decreased by approximately 50 percent" (p. 352). However, he further notes that about half of this decline has been made up by usage of "audio-visual" materials. The ability to index other types of usage including readings of summaries, synopses, and abstracts online creates different issues in assessing usage. An additional consideration is that while during the period from 1856 to 2004 the circulation of books *per user* may have gone down precipitously, the number of users, per library, has gone up dramatically. The greatest increases occurred during the years from 1978 to 2004.

Similarly, the number of volumes held per library has increased. A U.S. public library survey revealed that "Public library buildings had 1.57 billion visits during FY10. Although this was down by . . . 1.1 percent from FY2009," it was "the first time visitation had decreased since FY 2001" (Swan et al., 2013, p. 14).

During the 10-year period from 2000 to 2010, visitation showed a 10-year increase of 32.7 percent. Similarly, "public libraries circulated 2.46 billion materials in FY2010; a one-year increase of 2.1 percent, and a 10-year increase of 38 percent" (p. 26). All this is to say that while fewer people visited the library, they made use of more information.

Further, "circulation of children's material comprised 34 percent of the total circulation ... This reflects an increase of 2.7 percent in one year and 28.3 percent in 10 years" (p. 12). While the collections have included more and more digital media, print books still constituted 87 percent of the total collection in FY2010, although this percentage decreased over the previous 10 years. Finally, and perhaps most importantly, the survey revealed that 171 million people were registered to borrow materials from public libraries in FY2010. This number marked an *increase* over FY2009.

In summary, while there may be a lower circulation of some types of materials and annual fluctuations in the number of users, overall library usage remains strong in the United States, with well over half the population being registered users, and circulation continues to increase. Even as libraries face changes in the nature of the materials they house and the patrons they serve, libraries continue to play an important, if shifting, function. Van der Werf (2010), writing about the future of libraries in the Netherlands, states that:

> knowledge is information, whether it is hardcore data or a poetic narrative. In order for it to exist, it must be compounded by communication. An ideal egalitarian agent for this task is the public library. For knowledge is the library's commodity, and as a result, it attracts producers and consumers of knowledge.
>
> (pp. 18–19)

As accessibility and usage create opportunities for the people of the world to interface with the rapidly exploding knowledge base, their ability to locate and read that information online becomes critical. An important study issued by Zickuhr and Rainie (2014) clarifies the differences of older and younger library users. Younger Americans – ages 16–29 – exhibit a fascinating mix of habits and preferences when it comes to reading, libraries, and technology. Almost all Americans under the age of 30 function online, and they are more likely than older patrons to use libraries' computer and Internet connections; however, they are also still closely bound to print, as 75 percent of younger Americans say they have read at least one book in print in the past year, compared with 64 percent of adults 30 and older. We will return to these trends in Chapter 8.

Similarly, younger Americans' library usage reflects a blend of traditional and technical services. Americans under the age of 30 are just as likely as older adults to visit the library, and once there they borrow print books and browse the shelves at similar rates. Large majorities of those under age 30 say it is "very important" for libraries to have librarians as well as books for borrowing, and relatively few think that libraries should automate most library services, move most services online, or move print books out of public areas.

At the same time, younger library visitors are more likely than older patrons to access the Internet or use the library's research resources, such as databases. And younger patrons are also significantly more likely than those 30 and older to use the library as a study or "hang out" space:

> Significantly more younger than older patrons say they go to the library to study, sit and read, or watch or listen to media. And a majority of Americans of all age groups say libraries should have more comfortable spaces for reading, working, and relaxing.
>
> (Zickuhr & Rainie, 2014)

The growth of libraries as technological service providers, though recent, extends back well over a decade. "Survey data show that in 1994 just 12 percent of American libraries offered patrons access to online databases. In just two years, that number tripled to 36 percent" (Rogers, 1996, p. 27). Since then, the situation has changed considerably. In a study of Internet connectivity in U.S. public libraries, the American Library Association (2008) reported that

> nearly all of America's 16,543 public library buildings offer free public access to computers, to the Internet, and to trained staff equipped to help library users gain technology skills and find the information they need for school, work, and more. This public service provides a critical source for millions of Americans, as nearly three-quarters of public libraries reported that they are the ONLY provider of free access to the Internet in their communities.

The study further noted that most of these libraries provided subscriptions for free access to databases.

So while today's libraries are used extensively and technology occupies a much bigger portion of their product base, they are also serving an interesting new role, or perhaps a role resurrected after many years. They are becoming centers of urban revitalization. Vallet (2013) does an excellent job of examining and categorizing some of the important roles that both Flemish and Dutch public libraries play. She identifies the roles of "urban landmark, area oriented herald, and target group patron" (p. 654). As examples of the role of urban landmark, Vallet cites the cities of Ghent and Delft, noting that "the public library reinforces the overall profile, image, and identity of the city (the public library is our new cathedral)" (p. 656). The examples of the area oriented herald are Antwerp and the Haig:

> the first located its central library at the "DeConinck plein," a former impoverished neighborhood near the central station of the city. The latter invested in tailor-made branch libraries that each fit the specific features of different neighborhoods all over the city.
>
> (p. 656)

In describing the role of target group patron, she characterizes the library as "liaison or personal coach of the urban citizens with special social, cultural, informational and knowledge needs" (p. 656). Ostend, Roeselare, and Roosendaal are three public libraries that have exemplified this public responsibility.

Urban revitalization in Italy, in cities such as Bologna and Sala Borsa, fits not only the new roles of the library, but also aligns with the long history of their cities.

> The library's success in terms of public services and its impact on the social life of the city are strictly linked to its central location and the comprehensive cultural role of this area. This happened despite the fact that the library is scarcely visible from the outside due to concerns regarding the older building's façade.
>
> (Galluzi, 2009, p. 53)

This was an important success in Sala Borsa as they attempted to "promote their historical value and, at the same time, integrate them into the urban area in which they are located" (Galluzi, 2009, p. 53). The new library in Bologna was

> meant to be not only a traditional library, but also a multi-media center; a place not only for studying and professional activities, but also for activities as a meeting place. Moreover, it intended to offer distance services, taking advantage of new technologies.
>
> (Galluzzi, 2009, pp. 53–54).

Overall, building and sustaining public libraries may be somewhat difficult because of significant challenges such as the increasing costs of all public services. Hopper (2013) observes that both visitation and circulation per capita have increased in public libraries over the past ten years, extending the trends observed in data from the previously cited studies. The availability of Internet-ready computer terminals in public libraries has doubled over the past ten years, and librarians expect an 85 percent increase in the use of online library services in the near future. So, just as libraries in other parts of the world, including Belgium, Holland, Italy, and many other countries, have become important in the building of communities, Hopper explains that community must be thought of in a much broader way than the narrow, regional, physical sense. "We must increasingly be outside the library building where the people are and actively engaging our communities for the library to be seen as integral to the community infrastructure" (p. 27).

Amid such a welter of change, are there exemplars among the libraries of today comparable to the great libraries of the past? Two interesting examinations of the best libraries in the world offer insights. The libraries are not statistically analyzed for a level of technical excellence or the amount of holdings. They are instead afforded broadly based judgments rendered by two organizations. In *Ten Best Libraries in the World* (2011), it is noted:

> Libraries represent man's most successful attempt in democratizing knowledge in the Modern Age. The magnificent institutions have also developed into important social structures and facilitate not just the reading of books, but a meeting point of different people, different ideas, discussion and debate. Libraries, especially the ones featured on this list, tend to be the epicenter of activity in the neighborhoods in which they are located.

Thirty-five libraries in the world are rated "best" in another survey. We think it important to note that the first list is a subset of the second, offering some concurrent validity to these informal assessments. In other words, all 10 of the libraries listed as the best in the world are contained in the 35 listed in the other study.

Some important comparisons and contrasts can be formed from those libraries identified as the 35 best. They represent a wide range of places, origins, and architecture. Although the United States has nine of the 35, 19 countries are represented and seven have more than one library on the list. There are libraries with connections to internationally famous universities, such as the Bodleian Library at Oxford and the Trinity College Library in Dublin. There is even one high school library on the list, the Exeter School Library in Exeter, New Hampshire, a school long noted for its ties to Harvard. There are others that belong to individual states, such as the State of Victoria Library in Melbourne. Further, there are multiple examples of city libraries, including the Boston and New York Public Libraries, and the City Library of Stockholm. There are several libraries with religious origins. The most obvious example is the Vatican Library in Rome. The Monastery Library in Ulm, Germany, and the Library of the Abbe of St. Gall in St. Gallen, Switzerland, are also included. There are libraries that owe their beginnings to patrons; for example, the Herzog August Library in Wolfenbüttel, Germany, and the Morgan Library and Museum in New York City, the latter originating from the private collection of J.P. Morgan. There are libraries that are part of larger museum collections such as the Rijksmuseum Library in Amsterdam and the Reading Room at the British Museum in London. Finally, there are libraries with origins in government, such as the Canadian Parliamentary Library in Ottawa and the Library of Congress in Washington.

Miller (2016), synthesizing data primarily from the Online Computer Library Center (OCLC), identifies countries with the greatest number of libraries and library users. Variables include library holdings, number of academic libraries, number of public libraries, number of school libraries, number of library users, and number of certified/degreed librarians – all based on per capita analysis. Considering some of these variables and looking at more developed countries, those with the highest library ratings include Finland, Iceland, Norway, and Australia; India and China are among the lowest rated.

Libraries of the Future

Forecasting change is invariably risky business, but we believe that current trends offer a reasonable basis for a few near-term projections. A classic example concerning the future of libraries was made in 1961 by Dartmouth Professor John G. Kemeny, back in the days of card catalogues and stacks and long before emails, iPads, and the Internet:

> Each page of each "book" in this library (of the future) ... will be stored on possibly a square millimeter of tape. The patrons will never go to the library, see the master tapes, or find that a book is "out." Copies will be made for them to read conveniently and enlarged on the screens of viewing devices in their own offices or homes ... Even our richest universities will not be able to afford building, cataloging and keeping up with the kind of libraries they have now.
> (Future Library, 1961)

Kemeny's prescience emboldens us to offer a few of our own projections. We expect to see the functions performed by the library, and the services offered by librarians, continuing to evolve very quickly. The function of the library as a downloading station, accessed either physically or remotely, will become even more critical. For example, most libraries have acquired large catalogues of audio books over the last 20 years. These were first available in cassette form and later as CDs. Today, the vast majority of public libraries provide opportunities for registered patrons to download the content digitally – without ever physically "checking out" anything from the library.

New roles for librarians are also emerging, and they are likely to differ in developing countries, where much of their time will be spent not merely in helping patrons find materials, but in teaching them how to use archival digital databases by which the patrons can easily find their own materials. In the developed world, populated by digital natives, we envision their customary roles as brokers and facilitators to continue.

We suspect that the library as a physical place will not vanish in the future, but changes are apt to occur in location and interior design. We foresee locations changing in two ways. The role we previously discussed – as urban revitalization centers – will grow in importance. As it does, some library locations will become even more centralized. At the same time, many cities throughout the world are expanding the number of smaller, remote, or "branch" libraries in an effort to provide their services at closer proximity to suburban patrons.

Just as the location of the library changes physically, so will its interior. Less and less space is likely to be allocated to shelving hardcover books, an increasing number of which will go the way of the card catalogue. Rooms will be redeployed as space for social clubs, book clubs, author signings, coffee shops, listening centers, and rooms full of bays for computer terminals and remote device recharging. All will occupy much of the space previously allocated to print storage.

Finally, the borders of the library will continue to blur as digital technology extends its reach to off-site patrons. In the future, people in remote African villages, Muslim girls in restrictive learning environments, Laplanders, Inuits, Pacific Islanders, and many others will be able to access the same information as those with direct physical access to the world's libraries. This trajectory is already evident in developments such as "The World Digital Library," "The World Public Library," and the "www.virtuallibary." Verschaffel (2010), summarizes these changes well:

> The entire history of intellectual culture can – in principle – easily and cheaply be digitized and stored and made available virtually everywhere . . . we will download and read any text on the book device we carry with us, such as our mobile phone. So, the end of the book is near, but what about the library? Most libraries have adapted to the new developments and have transformed themselves . . .
>
> (p. 85)

Consequently, libraries will survive and even thrive in the years to come. But their look, feel, and function will be different.

Newspapers

If there is one overall notion that captures the trend in newspapers, it is that sales, circulation, readership, and revenue are in decline. This is not a recent phenomenon. Although it can be argued that readership and sales revenue for printed papers are down due to self-competition with their own online versions of the same papers, this would be a major oversimplification capturing only one cause of decline.

Clearly, print readership has diminished, largely due to the emergence of paperless technologies for the delivery of news and the changing lifestyles of potential readers. This trend has proceeded for some time and it is certainly not solely attributable to the online availability of newspapers or to cable news outlets. Butler (1945), in an edited book concerning the role of books and libraries in wartime, commented on newspaper readership at a time well before the emergence of online news or cable television:

> . . . the gravity of the status of reading in the United States should be emphasized by the fact that the number of newspapers, particularly daily newspapers, is gradually but surely decreasing, and, among the newspapers remaining, individual ownership is beginning to yield to the pressure of chain ownership.
>
> (p. 90)

The Golden Age of Journalism, an era when print journalism was at its zenith, began with the penny daily papers in the 1830s and continued until the emergence of varying news delivery technologies beginning in the 1930s (Douglas, 1999). The days of the great newspaper battles, in cities such as Chicago and New York, are gone. In retrospect, it is hard to imagine that each of these cities had five to ten daily newspapers – with both morning and afternoon editions. And the influence of the iconic newspaper ownership, including Hearst, Pulitzer, and Scripps, has given way. All this did not happen yesterday. Newspaper circulation began to give way to movie theater newsreels, then radio, then television broadcast news, then cable television news, and now to online, customizable news tailored to the individual and with video accompanying the text.

It is important to recognize, however, that the decline in newspaper readership is not uniform around the world. In some areas, such as Japan, sales have moderated slightly, but remain very strong, while in other areas, such as India, growth has been explosive in recent years, despite subsiding somewhat. Print journalism is more successful as emerging economies develop. As they become more mature and established, expanded technologies are accessed and other news forms tend to take over. So, worldwide data on newspaper circulation is not as revealing in the aggregate as specific national and regional data.

Notwithstanding the occasional spottiness of this transformation, major declines are prominent in most advanced economies. The evidence is visible from various perspectives. It is hard to ignore that *The Boston Globe* was sold in 2013 for less than 10 percent of the price just over a decade earlier.

The history of newspapers is an interesting one, which reveals much about changes in literate practices in developed, developing, and underdeveloped nations. The circulation of newspapers worldwide, in both print and online forms, is also revealing. Challenges to newspapers are prevalent in terms of competing technologies and pricing of print papers, from expensive to inexpensive to free. Without question, the future of newspapers will be intriguing to watch, perhaps with a scorecard, to note the survivors and their survival strategies.

Newspapers of the Past

The issuance of the first newspaper in history is a point of contention. Some say the newspaper first appeared as the proceedings of Parliament in the seventeenth century. Others argue that the first newspapers were printed in Germany at about the same time. There is agreement, however, that among the first newspapers was a monthly published in the Republic of Venice. It was called *A Gazetta*, a name that likely was taken from a Venetian coin and may have been the price of a copy. The first newspaper in North America was printed in Boston in 1690. By the time of the Revolution, 87 newspapers were in operation, and their content was becoming increasingly diversified and their reporting of events differed significantly.

Early newspapers were expensive to publish and to purchase, and for more than two centuries after Gutenberg, printing presses were largely reserved for books. By the middle of the nineteenth century, however, presses had become far more plentiful and cheaper to operate. It was then that the Penny Press was born. Most journalistic historians cite the emergence of the "penny papers" as the beginning of a century-long heyday of print journalism, both in the United States and elsewhere in the world. War correspondence, investigative reporting, muckraking, and serialized fiction all became part of an expanding product.

In the twentieth century, the emergence of new technologies for the delivery of news signaled the downturn of print news. Richard Gengras, Senior Director of News and Social Products at Google, identifies one of these technologies as particularly instrumental in the decline of print journalism: "something happened in the late 40s that changed the world of newspapering, and that change was the introduction of television" (Warsh, 2013).

While television was the largest single contributor to declines in newspaper circulation, certainly its forerunners – first newsreels shown in serial form in movie theaters and then radio with the emergence of journalistic personalities such as Edward R. Murrow – had already brought about declines in print circulation. Major U.S. newspapers lost on the order of 90 percent of their market valuation. Papers and newspaper chains, which had sold for literally billions, were drastically devalued. Later, the appearance of 24/7 cable news television, designed to be able to meet smaller niche audiences with a more personalized editorial point of view, provided stiff competition. Blogs became omnipresent and names like Huffington Post, Buzz Feed, Mashable, and Deadspin appeared, tailored to ideologically specific readerships.

With all of these developments, and with journalism in general, is the importance of time. From the beginning of print journalism, a goal has always been to reduce the time between the occurrence of an event and the reporting of it. Mott (1941) cites an illustrative example:

> The War of 1812 did something to waken the newspapers to the inconvenience of tardy news reports; and a growing feeling for timeliness as a

quality of news caused some eastern papers to employ express riders, or firms which hired such riders, to carry dispatches more swiftly than the mails could travel. At first this was done only for special events, such as the delivery of President Monroe's message to Congress, but by the mid-thirties such enterprise was fairly common.

(p. 193)

As telegraph and then telephone communications came of age, the lag time from event to print was further reduced. Changes in printing methods such as the linotype, more mechanized distribution systems, and the growth of newsgathering agencies all contributed.

Current Newspapers

The decline in newspaper circulation in the United States, Western Europe, and several other parts of the world warrants further analysis. Hargrove, Miller, and Stempel (2011) in a study of city and community newspapers, report a decline "of 10.6 percent in daily circulation from 2008 to 2009" (p. 84). Although they report that newspapers serving smaller communities have declined less in readership than those in large cities, the overall trend cannot be escaped. Only 5.7 percent of people living in big cities, and 4.4 percent of the people in smaller communities regularly read both print and online newspapers, and well over half of the people in both cities and smaller communities regularly read neither online nor print versions of a newspaper.

In a 30-year examination, dating from 1977 to 2007, Preston (2009) provides a frank perspective on evening papers in the U.K.:

> Thirty years ago – in June 1977 – the Daily Mirror sold 3,879,000. This June (2007), that figure was 1,565,711. In June 1977, the Daily Express sold 2,312,152. Make that just 770,403. The Telegraph sold over 1.3 million 30 years back. Make that now 892,000. – Hugely bolstered by cheap subscriptions, foreign sales and a word I barely remember from the 70s . . . bulks . . . Why are national daily sales down to 11.6 million when those with not so long memories can recall 14 million?
>
> (p. 13)

He notes, however, that "Internet advertising continues apace" (Preston, 2008, p. 319). He also observes that while increases have occurred in advertising revenue online, they are not producing the profitability that has been expected based on past performance. His takeaway point concerns the consequences of failing to adapt:

> Simply life changed but evening newspapers didn't or couldn't . . . human living patterns changing, moving on, have done that. Complain about the

dying years of evening journalism and all you're doing is complaining about life. These enemies of the evenings were inertia, fatalism, and cost-cutting.

(p. 319)

Further inspection of newspaper circulation worldwide shows that, while the decline in major city daily newspapers has been pervasive, this is not true in all corners of the globe. Clearly, many of the great dailies have declined. Beyond the U.K. and the United States, in the Czech Republic, *Blesk* went from 435,000 to 305,000 in four years. For Germany's *Bild*, circulation dropped from over 3.1 million to 2.9 million in the two years from 2008 to 2010. In the same two years, *Neues Deutschland* fell from 460,000 to 430,000. *Metro* in Hungary dropped from 314,000 to 278,000 while Poland's *Fakt Gazeta* plummeted from 495,000 to 373,000 and its *Gazeta Wyborcza* shrank from 411,000 to 255,000. In Sweden, *Aftonbladet Dagens*, *Nyheter*, and *Svenska Bagbladet* all went from a circulation of well over 300,000 to between 175,000 and 290,000.

As we have suggested, however, the international numbers are not all negative. Over the five-year period from 2008 to 2012, the *Times* of India increased its circulation from 2.9 to 3.3 million, although the 2012 figure does represent a decrease over 2011. While circulation of the major dailies in Korea, including *Shosun ILBO*, *Donga ILBO*, and *Joongang ILBO*, have decreased slightly, the decline is not as precipitous as in other countries. A growth picture exists in Malaysia, where circulation of papers such as *Harian Metro* went from 324,000 to 386,000, and the *Metro Ahad* rose from 363,000 to 420,000. *Zaman* in Turkey increased its circulation from 753,000 to 888,000 over a four-year period. In summary, a generally downward trend in circulation is far from universal, with many regional counterexamples, particularly in the developing world.

MarketingCharts.com (2013) provides relevant data on both newspaper circulation and advertising trends by region. We summarize some of these data in Table 6.1. They confirm both an overall decline in circulation and revenues but also the presence of considerable regional differences.

The same conclusion was reached by the authors of a report from World Press Trends, which collects newspaper circulation and revenue data from over 70 countries. They noted that although overall circulation fell modestly, from 537 million in 2008 to 530 million in 2012, the decline "masks huge regional variations" (*The Economist*, 2013). In the United States, during the same period, circulation fell by 15 percent but advertising revenues plummeted by 42 percent. This drop alone accounted for almost three-quarters of the world decline in advertising revenue. In Europe, circulation and advertising revenues have both fallen by 25 percent. Circulation in Asia has risen by 10 percent, offsetting declines elsewhere in the world. China has surpassed India to become the world's biggest newspaper market.

Data from the International Federation of Audit Bureaus of Circulation (IFABC) reveal disturbing trends after 2011, and Jackson (2013) notes that some of the most severe circulation declines between 2010 and 2011 were in Romania,

TABLE 6.1 Newspaper Circulation and Advertising Revenue, 2008–12

Region	Circulation		Advertising Revenue	
	One Year (2011–12)	Five years (2008–12)	One Year (2011–12)	Five Years (2008–12)
North America	−6%	−13%	−7.6%	−42.1%
Western Europe	−5.3%	−24.8%	−3.4%	−23.3%
Eastern Europe	−8.2%	−27.4%	−5.6%	−30.2%
North Africa	−1.4%	+10.5%	+2.3%	−22.0%
Asia	+1.2%	+9.8%	+3.6%	+6.2%
Australia and New Zealand	+3.5%	+1.0	−8.3	−24.9%
Latin America	+<0.1%	+9.1%	+9.1%	+37.6%

where three papers saw circulation drop by more than 40 percent, five others by more than 20 percent, and where only one paper witnessed a decline of less than 10 percent. Spain's leading paper experienced a circulation drop of 1.3 percent, but the next three largest papers all declined by more than 10 percent.

Consider the examples of Germany, India, and China to see how explosively change can occur. In *Bloomberg Business Week*, Ewing (2008) reported that "Germany's newspapers are doing fine despite the ad flight to the web." He went on to explain how German papers took advantage of and embraced the web in novel ways, and that *Bild* "hasn't been hit by the same problems as U.S. papers, including advertisers lost to the web." Just five years later, the news was completely different. Mueller (2013) summarized the change:

> Axel Springer, Europe's largest newspaper publisher, appears to be losing faith in its core business. The company has scenarios for cutting millions in spending and slashing hundreds of jobs at the tabloid, Bild, a cash cow that still generates sensational returns, despite a fast sinking circulation.

"It came to Germany almost a decade later than America," Schnibben (2013) observes, "but the newspaper crisis is sweeping the country with plummeting circulations and revenues. The German news media must reinvent itself in order to retain readers." He further notes:

> Daily newspapers are threatened economically by the internet, but journalistically, even more so ... Organizations that have been successful online are those that satisfy their readers' needs for information and classification more quickly, in a more differentiated way and, above all, at a lower cost.

An irony of the Internet is that it can allow the news to reach a wide audience, but that audience does not need a particular paper's website to get that paper's news. By trying to reach everyone, a paper is actually competing with every other paper that is trying to do just that, and sites like Google, which don't actually do any of the journalistic work behind the news (and thus have lower costs) are better at reaching a large audience. As Schnibben reports in *Der Spiegel* (2013), "Google sucks up four times as much advertising money as the websites of all print media organizations combined." The emphasis, according to these articles, has to be on attracting paid subscribers to their websites.

India and Japan face challenges similar to Germany's. That is, imminent declines are challenging what used to be considered some of the most positive newspaper circulation and revenue figures in the world. Now, for the first time in recent years, circulation in both these countries appears to have stabilized.

Japanese newspaper readership has begun an all-but-inevitable decline for the simple reason that new readers are not being created. The thinking has been that, because newspaper readers are older, the readership would remain steady as younger people aged and naturally became newspaper readers. The problem with this reasoning is that the basic issue isn't age but the changing cultural and social landscape. The society that created a newspaper culture in Japan no longer exists. The factors that contributed to creating a newspaper culture in the past don't have the same effect on a new generation of readers (Nippon. com, 2014).

There are also other obstacles in Japan, such as the distribution network. Japanese newspapers are largely sold by agents. The papers are delivered by the same agents who collect the circulation fee. In order for Japanese papers to fully embrace the Internet, they will have to change their business model, and that means addressing that distribution network (VandeKlippe, 2014).

Japanese newspapers, like those in the West, compete with digital sources for advertising revenue and do their best to take advantage of digital platforms. The difference between Japan and the West is that the Japanese press does not rely on advertising revenue to the extent that Western papers do, so that they face a more gradual decline, but a decline nonetheless. If they cannot convince a new generation to read newspapers, whether print or digital, the decline will continue and likely accelerate.

Indian newspapers, until very recently, were the fastest growing in the world. Between the years 2005 and 2009, paid circulation grew by over 40 percent (Myers, 2011). But the situation is beginning to change. Indian newspapers needn't worry about digital competition – at least not yet. According to Mallet (2013), it will be another 15 years before that inevitable "tsunami" strikes the subcontinent. The major Indian papers face a more pressing problem, however. The biggest hurdle for outside news sources is not just their lack of regional coverage, but lack of regional coverage in the local vernacular. It seems that a common theme in the newspaper industry, in general, is that local newspapers are suffering far less than the larger, nationally distributed papers (*The Economist*, 2009).

Indian newspapers are similar to those in Japan, as far as home delivery is concerned, but there are telling differences. Japanese newspapers get the majority of their revenue from paid subscriptions. This makes them less vulnerable to economic downturns that affect advertising, but it requires that they be able to replace aging readers with those from younger generations. Indian newspapers are very inexpensive, an important factor in a context of high poverty, and rely almost solely on advertising revenue. There is also virtually no digital competition in India, because of limited access.

Clearly, newspaper paid circulation has declined, but not for all papers and not in all places. The unevenness can be partly ascribed to newspapers where the editorial policies have been more agile. Another reason may be the method of distribution and collection. Still another lies in the fact that emerging economies have a greater interest in news from around the world. It remains to be seen how long print journalism can hold out against the tide of technology in these places, but the overall trend seems not only clear but inevitable.

The Japanese hope that an aging population will come to realize the benefits of newspapers ignores the fact that technology innovations have usurped one function of a conventional paper after another. Checked the classifieds lately? Online auto, real estate, and job markets have met that demand in quicker and more comprehensive ways. Care to rant? Letters to the editor can be sent off and sometimes even posted while you're still hot. Enjoy political cartoons? Binge view an entire gallery rather than only those your local editor selects.

Technology also serves the journalistic goal of reducing the time between an event and coverage of it, and it does so far better than print. Even though newspapers have greatly reduced the lag time, they can never compete with the near-instantaneous turnaround of electronic news sources. The accelerated pace also applies to shopping. News sites now feature point-of-purchase advertising through which we can shop online so seamlessly that we hardly need break our train of thought. Timing the appearance of ads has also been adjusted. Advertising for a Labor Day sale occurs not during the week before, as print requires, but on Labor Day. And coupons are just as successful online as they are in print, perhaps more so.

The distribution of print papers is also costly and simply cannot be sustained competitively. Consider the Indian circulation model described by Auletta (2012):

> Dadar Railway Station is the largest of 65 newspaper delivery depots in Mumbai. At 4:00 a.m., 40 trucks and vans packed with newspapers and magazines have parked and slid open their back doors. During the next few hours 231,000 newspapers will be unloaded ... vendors cluster around the back of each truck ... they pass the bundles on to deliverymen – there

are some 8,300 in Mumbai, who pack as many papers as they can on their motorbikes, rickshaws, bicycles, and shoulders and set out to slip them one by one under or beside the door of the city residents.

This model is only possible with large amounts of cheap labor and lack of widespread digital competition. Auletta explains:

> One reason that Indian newspapers thrive is the absence of digital competition. Less than 10% of the population has access to the internet, and, with two-thirds of the population surviving on less than two dollars per day, expensive smart phones and tablets aren't about to replace print media as the reading platform of choice.

In the near term, this contention is certainly true. However, improved resources will confront Indian print publishers with the same challenges faced by their peers abroad. No doubt they will be able to observe some survival strategies from the examples they witness, but we suspect that none will sustain them against the displacement they fear.

A related challenge to the newspaper industry, and a major one, is finding a sustainable financial model. As Warsh (2013) observes about Amazon's takeover of the *Washington Post*, "It is easy to doubt Bezos' intuition – that nobody will be reading printed newspapers 20 years from now . . . Radio didn't disappear and it seems highly likely . . . that neither will newsprint, though surely it will be transformed."

Given declining circulation and ad revenues, at least in the developed world, what is a sustainable financial model for newspapers? There are questions of both distribution and pricing, and countries have answered them differently. The Japanese model of distribution, which includes agents actually going from door to door delivering and collecting, is a model that has proved sustainable in the past but that seems oddly anachronistic in an era of evolving reader habits. In India, where Internet penetration has been far lower, the digital competition is likely to emerge gradually but will eventually gather strength.

In the developed world, lost revenue on the print front is being somewhat mitigated by increased earnings from online subscribers, but not at a rate that is currently sustainable. This problem is clearly articulated in a recent report from the Pew Research Center (Jurkowitz, 2014).

> For all the expansion, it is far from clear that there is a digital news business model to sustain these outlets. First Look Media founder and funder, Peter Omidyar, has acknowledged that solvency is at least five years away. The Huffington Post has 575 editorial employees but are still only flirting with profitability according to analyst Ken Doctor. Global Post, which recently

signed NBC as a content partner but has never operated in the black. Asked if the explosion of hiring suggested digital news has figured out a successful business model to sustain those jobs, one veteran industry observer responded simply, "No, that's the irony."

(p. 1)

Free daily newspapers have made Latin America one of the few areas in the world with rising newspaper circulation, although according to Bakker (2012), Latin America has a "low penetration of daily newspapers" compared to Western Europe and North America, but, spurred by free daily newspapers, circulation in Latin America grew by "15 percent between 2005 and 2010" (pp. 129–130). This free daily newspaper phenomenon was sparked worldwide by the introduction of *Metro* in Stockholm in 1995 (Wadbring, 2003). Though *Metro* launched in 16 other European markets in 1997, Latin America had been a selected growth area. This move touched off the expansion of many other free dailies. The question still remains whether or not advertising and other sources of revenues will be able to support the free dailies.

So technologies, changing readership patterns, shifting modes of behavior, and the emergence of different pricing and delivery structures are all factors being faced currently by daily newspapers, and in particular by their print versions. The question then becomes, what of the future? Finding a sustainable model is not easy.

Miller (2016), synthesizing data primarily from the World Association of Newspapers and News Publishing, identifies countries with the highest and lowest readership of newspapers. Variables include paid daily circulation, free daily circulation, number of paid dailies, number of free dailies, and total number of online editions, all based on per capita analysis. The average time spent reading a newspaper is also indexed. Countries with newspapers with higher ratings include Austria, Iceland, Japan, Luxembourg, Norway, and Sweden, while Argentina, Chile, Romania, and South Africa are the lowest rated.

Newspapers of the Future

Predicting the future of newspapers seems every bit as risky as forecasting the fate of libraries. Indeed, a consulting firm in the U.K. found out just how dicey an undertaking it can be, as Preston observes:

> Have newspapers a future? ... *The Guardian* asked one huge multi-national consultancy to tell us about that some nine years ago ... Hundreds of thousands of pounds later they declared *Fleet Street* dead for lack of advertising and circulation within five years, but it didn't quite happen. Indeed, it's absolutely not happened so far.

(2008, p. 318)

In that same year, the satirical paper, *The Onion* (2008), piled on. "It's nice to see," the writer quipped, "that the printed word, at least for now, is the most powerful medium for reporting on the death of the printed word." So while the trend lines clearly portrayed in this chapter indicate that there has been a long-term decline in newspaper circulation and revenue, and that the road ahead will be rocky, it seems highly unlikely that newspapers will become totally obsolete anytime soon. Ultimately, their fate will depend on their ability to adapt in the face of new challenges.

Nevertheless, if the past is any indication, newspapers are headed in the wrong direction fast. Granted, there appear to be opportunities in underserved markets and emerging economies, which still have low Internet penetration. There may also be a future for redesigned papers in other parts of the world, including developed countries. Yet, without substantive change, survival of newspapers in the future is a parlous prospect.

One of the major issues in the future of newspapers is discovering how to deal with dramatically changing demographics in the marketplaces of some of the countries with the largest newspaper circulations in the world. For example, in the United States, Katerina Matsa of the Pew Research Center reports:

> At 54 million in 2013, Hispanics account for 17% of the U.S. population and are responsible for half the nation's growth between 2000 and 2012. Much of this growth since 2000 has come from the births of Hispanics in the U.S. rather than the arrival of new immigrants. As a result, English use among Hispanic adults is on the rise. Today, about six-in-ten U.S. adult Hispanics (62%) speak English or are bilingual. One question this raises for the news media is to what degree this population turns to outlets dedicated to coverage – in both Spanish and English – presented through a Hispanic lens.
> (2015, p. 78)

Franklin (2008) offers a South African example of how newspapers have changed, and must continue to change, to reflect the changing demographics of the marketplace. He credits Wasserman (2007) as noting "the remarkable popularity of the new South African tabloids, like the *Daily Sun*, which have 'taken the market by storm,' creating a 'tabloid revolution.' They are highly popular with readers achieving unprecedented readership of 3.8 million. Their editorial content offers highly personalized, and often sensationalized, accounts of issues like poverty, HIV, and crime, but significantly offers its black working-class readership a voice in these and other issues" (p. 638).

An interesting alternative to the doom-and-gloom scenarios for newspapers was recently presented by Tom Engelhardt (2014). He addresses the question of whether or not we are in a new golden age of journalism. He recollects a time in his childhood when New York City was "papered with newspapers ... There were perhaps nine or ten significant ones on newsstands every day." He goes on to note that "it took the arrival of the 21st Century to turn the journalistic world of the 1950's upside down and point it towards the trash heap of history." He observes that "in so many ways it has been, and continues to be, a sad, even horrific tale of loss." He then suddenly shifts gears, portraying a new world of exhilaration and discovery:

> ...most of the major dailies and magazines of the globe, trade publications, propaganda outfits, Pentagon handouts, The Voice of Blogs, specialist websites ... are there ... You can read your way through the American Press and the World Press. You can read whole papers as they are edited and put together...You can become the editor of your own Op-Ed page every day, or three times, or six times a day ... You can essentially curate your own newspaper or magazine once a day, twice a day, six times a day ... For a reader it's also an experimental world, something thrillingly, unexpectedly new under the sun. For that reader, a strangely democratic and egalitarian era of the word has emerged.

As this quote suggests, digital sources present readers with a universe of possibilities because of their abundance and multiform nature. They also lead to high tension between the production of information and its dissemination. "Information yearns to be free," Stewart Brand famously remarked in the late 1960s. He was referring to the tendency of humans to share information and advocated for unrestricted access to it. The difficulty, of course, is that journalism is not a voluntary enterprise and the unchecked flow of information from producers to consumers can threaten a viable business model. Indeed, the word *free* in Brand's phrase can be interpreted in two ways. When it has meant without charge, the tab has so far been picked up by advertisers. This mechanism appears to be effective in most cases, and it has led to a variety of clever ad placements designed to catch the reader's eye. Certainly, there are many expanding advertising models with either optional or required "commercials" to be seen before the reading of an article.

The question of whether the reader attends to these ads or instead brushes them away like flies is vital to the future of newspapers. Increasing the chances that an ad will connect with a reader is already leading to changes in formatting and marketing. One of the most salient developments is *hyperdifferentiation*, a term introduced by Eric Clemons and his colleagues (2003) at the Wharton School to denote the process of tailoring a product's appeal to the consumer in order to increase the chances of its being purchased. Just as cable television enabled transmission of hundreds of channels, thereby allowing audiences to discover their niches, the same can be certainly said of online news. The news aggregators often include only a few sentences and a link to the total story. More differentiation is also being attempted in print, with multiple editions tailored to different locations, to different linguistic and cultural groups, and to various special interests.

The paper of the future will undoubtedly be smaller in size. It will contain far more local emphases. It will have more feature stories and less news as the news cycle becomes shorter and shorter. It may well be published fewer than seven days per week, and the personal relevance of stories will attempt to mirror the hyperdifferentiation of the online versions. In essence, the nature of a newspaper of the future is changing, along with its journalists, but neither seems likely to disappear.

Bookstores

The same factors that have influenced the past, present, and future of libraries and newspapers have strongly impacted bookstores as well. Digitally delivered print, content specialization, new distribution networks, and emerging economies with new buying power have all caused pervasive changes in bookstores. Clearly, the number of bookstores has declined in many, but not all, parts of the world. *Borders*, a major chain, as well as numerous smaller independent bookstores, have closed, and at this writing the fate of Barnes and Noble is unclear. But are bookstores altogether an extinct breed? We think not.

Murphy (1999) refers to a position articulated in *Scribner*'s magazine. She offers the following quote from Octave Uzanne, a writer of the late nineteenth and early twentieth century:

> If by books you are to be understood as referring to our innumerable collections of paper, printed, sewed, and bound in a cover announcing the title of the work, I own to you frankly that I do not believe (and the progress of electricity and modern mechanism forbids me to believe) that Gutenberg's invention can do otherwise than sooner or later fall into desuetude as a means of current interpretation of our mental products . . . our grandchildren will no longer trust their works to this somewhat antiquated process, now become very easy to replace . . .

Uzanne went on to speak of replacing print with what he referred to as phonography. In other words, in his version of the future, the technology that would unseat print was aural recording. His projection was offered in 1894 and is more significant for the fact that it was made at all rather than its accuracy. Granted, audio books presently enjoy immense popularity, but they have displaced neither their print versions nor the brick-and-mortar retailers who sell them. Nonetheless, change is coming and its pace is accelerating.

In addition to all the factors influencing reading in general, and libraries and newspapers specifically, there are additional factors that influence bookstores. Some of those factors operate quite differently in the case of bookstores than they do with respect to newspapers. Newspapers are a primary product of the companies that produce them, and those companies usually create their own distribution systems. In contrast, bookstores are more similar to libraries in that they are typically not the producers of the books they sell, just as libraries are no longer publishers of their holdings. There are notable exceptions. Some bookstore chains, such as Barnes and Noble, print their own lines, to be sure, especially reprints of classic titles. And in some countries nationalized bookstores are also publishers. Typically, however, publishers and bookstores are distinct entities, and the former seek other outlets for their products as well. For example, for a very long time, books have been sold by book clubs, through which the publisher, or an intermediate source, appeals directly to the customer without going through a retail outlet. Another example is that of book fairs, which existed long before the emergence of stores.

Another factor that influences the publisher and the bookstore's ability to sell materials is piracy. This is hardly a recent phenomenon, as copyright law dates back to 1709 during the reign of Britain's Queen Anne (Mumby, 1930). But digital formats make piracy easier whether texts are appropriated for personal use or sold for a fraction of their retail cost (see Idriss, 2013, on the emerging problem of piracy in the Arab world). Individuals who would be mortified at the idea of shoplifting a print copy of a bestseller often think nothing of reading an online version that may have been pirated. As with any retail business, book publishers will continue to fend off piracy with evolving digital safeguards and to estimate and write off losses where these fail.

Another important influence on bookstores is the language, culture, and traditions of varying countries. Naturally, the role of written language in cultural traditions varies widely across countries, and the importance of the oral versus the written tradition varies inversely. Tan (2009) in *Publisher's Weekly*, describes the minimal place occupied by written language in the tradition of many Arab countries. This is not to say that there is no culture of written language, but in describing the reading of children she observes, "In a region so rich in oral traditions, bedtime reading is not a common activity and early reading is only a newly introduced concept." Just as the advent of print in Europe eventually ended an oral tradition dating back thousands of years, a similar though belated phenomenon appears to be occurring in the Arab world. From a commercial perspective, an evolving role for books in countries with a minimal print tradition can only be viewed as a positive market force.

In contrast, another prevalent constraint on book sales and the popularity of bookstores is state censorship. Like piracy, this is far from new, as British examples make clear. During the Tudor era, for example, state censors were alert to any writing that threatened the existing power structure. They were likewise sensitive to perceived threats to the moral health of the populace, and a court official ironically called the "Master of the Revels" kept a close watch on publicly performed dramas. Thus began the genealogy of an official moral scrutiny traceable to the legal challenges to pornography in the twentieth century. Though state censorship is now rare in the West, it continues in some societies. Knezevic (2013) relates the following incident:

> A top selling Saudi Arabian science fiction novel has been removed from book shops across the country . . . An official handwritten letter was delivered . . . from the government body. It stated, among other things, that: "We purchased one copy of the book to review and we have counted 73 copies of *HWJN*, by Ibarheem Abbas, at your shop. You are requested not to dispose of, sell, or return these books until further notice."

In China, state censorship has been applied to entire bookstores. In one case, the government forbade the media from reporting on the forthcoming opening of a bookstore chain in a high-profile Shanghai high-rise. *The Christian Science Monitor* reported the following:

> "The matter about Taiwan Eslite Bookstore [intending] to open a branch in Shanghai should not be reported any more," read a terse message sent by SMS by the Shanghai office of the propaganda department to senior editors in charge of the city's major media outlets.
>
> (Haq, 2013)

Censorship is not only of the state variety. Pressure from cultural and religious groups has at times effectively censored the availability of books. Many will recall the furor over Salman Rushdie's *Satanic Verses* (1988), which was removed from many store shelves when a fatwa was issued against its author. Bookstores have been vandalized for selling it.

A far greater influence on the sale of books in bookstores is the competition from major multi-national e-bookstores such as Amazon, Google, and the Toronto-based Kobo. Carrenho (2012) describes the scramble for market share in Brazil:

> The beautiful Livraria Cultura bookstore at Paulista Avenue in São Paolo hosted a launch party on Wednesday to celebrate their partnership with Kobo. Actors were invited to read from Kobo devices and every digital enthusiast from the Brazilian publishing market was there. After all, Kobo was the first international company to set foot in Brazil with a national store and to sell devices locally. But Kobo's monopoly in Brazil lasted hours, as the serious competition looked to steal their thunder. And no, it was not Amazon, as had long been rumored, but Google, which actually started selling books at their local Google Play store at 11:45 p.m., Brasília time. Amazon would take another 35 minutes before its store went live. Yes, in a single day, they all arrived.

The effort of traditional brick-and-mortar companies like Barnes and Noble to operate parallel online stores may increase the bottom line overall, but it will ultimately be the profit margin of the physical stores that determines their fate.

Competition from online book sales is causing other changes in brick-and-mortar stores as well. Bookstores themselves are experimenting with many different models in order to compete. For example, the round-the-clock model used at the Taiwanese bookstore, Eslite, has been credited with sales "expanding at a time when bookstores around the world are folding. Nine months ago, Eslite opened the first overseas outlet in Hong Kong and another in mainland China" (Whitehead, 2013). This first Chinese location in Suzhou, outside of Shanghai, possibly emulated the 24-hour model already used in the store at Hong Kong's Causeway Bay shopping area, which itself was imported from Taipei.

Additional factors that exert varying impact in different parts of the world are price control, value-added tax, and price subsidies. These are imposed in a variety of ways. An article in *The Authors Guild* (2013) recounts the examples of Argentina and Korea:

> In Argentina, state-mandated price controls help brick-and-mortar bookstores thrive, while in Korea, which has no such restrictions, the success of a discount book chain is sparking calls for fixed pricing. In both countries there's debate over whether the need to preserve literary diversity should trump the free market.

The same phenomenon can be observed in European countries, in particular France, with varying amounts of price control.

Still another influence is the method of distribution. Some countries, such as China, have only localized distribution, and bookstores consequently tend to be limited to major cities. The need for a greater marketplace is evident. The Brazilian book market is another very large one with 100 million readers among a total population of 200 million. Yet, in a country this big, with a huge potential market, there is a striking lack of bookstores. Also growing are door-to-door sales, which have increased substantially.

Despite the assorted vagaries of the bookstore industry, it is important to realize that there are still bright spots and that not all bookstores have closed. Tagholm (2014) identifies India as a case in point:

> India would seem to be the place to be if you are a publisher ... when it comes to physical books the overall market was up 11% by volume and 23% by value in 2013 over 2012. In other parts of the world, many publishers would be happy just to take 1% up, thanks. Or even flat – yep, flat would be good.

Bookstores of the Past

As noted earlier, the terms *bookseller* and *bookstore* are not synonymous, but the histories of the two are closely intertwined. In fact, in periods of the past, the publisher, printer, distributor, seller, store, and in some cases, author, have all been one. Even as these functions began to separate, the concept of a "bookstore" was not common. Itinerant peddlers, selling books at fairs and outdoor locations in city streets and markets were the norm, even through the 1800s. Where there were "shops" around the squares, they often served as warehouses from which to supply the tables on the square. The emergence of modern stores came first to urban areas, where there was a significant population of potential customers; yet even in these areas, peddlers were common. Salman (2007) comments on the dual role of bookstore keeper and peddler in urban areas of the Netherlands:

> By the end of the eighteenth century, for instance, only 10% of the inhabitants of the cities of Middelburg and Zwolle patronized the bookshops there. Considering the high level of book production, the relatively high standard of living and the high literacy rates, it is more than likely that a large proportion of the urban population bought their printed matter in the streets. In cities like Utrecht and Amsterdam, research has revealed that there certainly was an extensive network of peddlers selling printed matter both inside and outside the towns. So, even in the Dutch Republic, where the economic position of the official book trade was relatively strong, itinerant bookselling played a crucial role in the distribution of print.
>
> (pp. 137–138)

Mumby (1930) describes the bookselling skills of Frederick Evans and his store. He tells the story of Bernard Shaw's tribute to Mr. Evans:

> While in Queen Street he was Mr. Shaw's "ideal bookseller." The author became interested in the shop, he explained, "because there was a book of mine [*The Quintessence of Ibsenism*] which apparently no Englishman wanted, or could ever possibly come to want, without being hypnotized; and yet it used to keep selling in an unaccountable way." The explanation was that Evans liked it. And he stood no nonsense from his customers. He told them what was good for them, not what they asked for.
>
> (pp. 290–291)

As we have stated, the early history of bookstores is difficult to separate from publishing. In many ways, the bookstores of the past were similar to today's "factory outlet" stores, in which the producer of goods, such as apparel, is also the retailer through a subsidiary store. The publisher of books has always marketed them in numerous ways, one being the ownership, entirely or in part, of the stores in which they were sold.

As the history of bookstores evolved in the late nineteenth and early twentieth centuries, independent bookstores remained on the scene, but an important new trend was the development of large bookstores, which eventually became familiar chains. The rise of the large chains began in the United States with Barnes and Noble. The original store was located in New York City, opening in 1917. Nearly a century later, the chain has expanded to over 600 retail stores and has also become the major operator of university bookstores at over 700 colleges and universities.

During roughly the same timeframe in Britain, the Foyles brothers began a bookstore empire centered in London. Their first (and still their largest) store opened in 1904 at Charing Cross. They quickly developed an international presence, particularly within the British Commonwealth, with stores in South Africa and Ireland.

Large-scale bookstores have historically experienced highs and lows in the evolution of their chains. For example, the period of the 1970s and 80s was one of major expansion for bookstore chains in the United States. Barnes and Noble purchased a number of smaller chains that were more specialized, such as B. Dalton, consisting of smaller bookstores found largely in malls. As is true of most international businesses, multi-national chains developed through mergers and acquisitions. But growth has hardly been steady. We have mentioned the fate of Borders, and Barnes and Noble has experienced perilous times as well. The company nearly went out of business in the early 1970s and in recent years the number of stores has declined.

Bookstores of the Present

The operation of bookstores has changed dramatically over the past decades. It is also apparent that this transformation has been due in part to an important interactive effect between the nature of the medium and the point of sale.

Consider the analogy of bookstores to record shops. When we were boys, a wonderful afternoon could be spent reviewing the most recent lists of the top 20, 40, and 100 bestselling records. The songs themselves were recorded on vinyl, and each individual item for sale was itself a piece of vinyl. Sometimes they were singles, called "45s" because of their revolutions per minute on a turntable. These generally contained a lead song on the "A" side and a second song on the "B" side. One could play only one side at a time on a turntable, listening with or without a headset. Longer playing (LP) records were larger in diameter and rotated more slowly. They contained a number of songs, many of which may have also been released as singles. These vinyl discs were delivered to the record store, where they were organized by artist and genre. Storeowners routinely permitted customers to play them prior to purchase.

Today, despite a recent but limited hipster comeback, record stores are found infrequently. Most of those in business today offer a piece of history, an anachronism, because the medium has changed and the world has moved on. Digital recordings can be heard through a variety of devices and they often do not take physical form, as CDs decline in popularity. Instead, music is frequently streamed from cloud-based sources or enjoyed through websites like Spotify and Pandora, some of which require subscriptions.

The situation is clearly analogous to bookstores today. Although the demise of bookstores has not been as prevalent as that of record shops, the change in the medium has caused a change in the point of delivery. Although the presence of print books is hardly the anachronism that vinyl records have become, two important trends that have characterized the transformation of the music industry are also apparent in the book business. One is the availability of print books through online ordering, making brick-and-mortar stores less relevant. The other is the increasing availability of digital versions. We will have more to say about the digital evolution of text in Chapter 8.

For now, there are three important trends to examine in current bookstores. The first is that the continuing existence of bookstores varies greatly from one country and culture to another. The second is that the intervention of government in the cost of books has had both positive and negative effects on sales in countries around the globe. Finally, the bookstores that survive, and in some instances thrive, are ones that have found new and different ways to compete.

One of the main reasons why the success of bookstores varies from country to country is that the culture of reading varies as well. Changes have gone on internationally, but they are far more prevalent in some cultures than in others. "There are two things you don't throw out in France," a famous saying goes, "bread and books" (Sciolino, 2012). And indeed, France continues to have a "bookstore culture."

In contrast, much has been made of the lack of reading culture in the Arab world, at least as far as it is possible to observe the behaviors that reflect such a culture. From all accounts, the Arab world is a difficult marketplace. Curley (2015) provides some specifics:

> Arabic book production and consumption is limited. The Arab World publishes one title per year for every 12,000 people who live in the region (about 25,000 books total), compared to one book for every 500 people in Britain, according to a 2008 UN study.

But even within the Arab world, there are large differences. As Curley goes on to note, "For online book retailers to become profitable, they must inevitably enter the Saudi market, where customers consistently buy between five and fifteen books per order."

In Korea, an Asian country with a strong "book tradition," the culture has turned away from reading in favor of other pastimes. Movies have become exceedingly popular. Korean boys are spending more time playing online games and less time reading books. This is not as true of girls, but it is a cultural phenomenon that cannot be ignored. In a summary of several American surveys, Common Sense Media (2014) concluded that "since 1984, the percent of 13-year-olds who are weekly readers went down from 70% to 53%, and the percent of 17-year-olds who are weekly readers went from 64% to 40%. The percent of 17-year-olds who never or hardly ever read tripled during this period, from 9% to 27%." In the next chapter we will examine some of the motivational forces that may be responsible for this shift, but from a commercial perspective, the change is associated with a downward trend in book sales, both in brick-and-mortar stores and in online sales. This phenomenon is not limited to Asian or Arab countries. Between 2000 and 2012 the number of physical bookshops in Denmark dropped from 423 to 338, with 18 shops closing in 2012 alone. Here, much of the competition comes from discounted books in grocery stores, and though Denmark does have a form of fixed-price agreement, which helps, it has not alleviated the downward pressure on bookstores.

Fixed pricing is a form of government subsidization that in some cases has kept book sales up, or at least the profitability of selling books. Subsidization is a costly policy, however, and there is a general trend to remove subsidies, after which declines in profits typically ensue.

In 1971, fixed pricing was eliminated in Finland. At that time there were approximately 750 booksellers. In 2012, there were only 450. In the same year about 31 percent of books were sold in bookstores; 18 percent in department stores, kiosks, and supermarkets; and about 16 percent over the Internet. Book clubs accounted for another 10 percent.

Norway retains a very regulated book industry based upon fixed pricing for new books, greatly increasing the price of a book compared to the same book in another country, such as the United States. It may also have led to the surprisingly large number of Norwegian bookstores:

> Norway has more bookstores per capita than any other land in Europe – a grand 618 in total. Oslo alone has 81 bookstores, compared to just 26 in Stockholm.... It's not unusual for a book to cost around NOK 400 or more (nearly USD 70).
>
> (Lindsay, 2013)

France has also enacted a number of laws to protect small retailers. One of the most interesting is the so-called "anti-Amazon" law. Independent and smaller booksellers complained they were being forced to compete with online companies like Amazon, who were selling at a 5 percent discount *and* providing free shipping. The result was a law preventing free shipping. Although France undeniably has a culture of literacy, this law is surely one of the reasons France has one of the highest numbers of traditional bookshops in the world – some 3,500 – of which about 800 are independent businesses. France compares favorably with the United Kingdom, which has fewer than 2,000 bookshops, and whose numbers are steadily being eroded by web competition. France compares even more positively with the United States. Writing in *The New Yorker* (2013), Alexandra Schwartz offers some stark comparisons between the two:

> To a New Yorker who spent her formative years witnessing the gutting of independent bookstores by Barnes & Noble, and then the gutting of Barnes & Noble by Amazon, the situation in Paris is luxurious beyond belief. In 1981, France passed the Lang Law ... The idea was to keep bookselling local; if they couldn't slash prices, megastores ... would hardly have an advantage over a tiny corner shop.

The French also provide bookstores with special subsidies, including interest-free loans for improvements and money to support reading events. Abrams (2013) quoted French Culture Minister, Aurélie Filippetti, who said that the government "wants to make certain that France never suffers the same fate as the United States with the collapse of several bookshop chains and ensuing difficulties for publishers." Hammad (2014) summarizes the result: "In France, in spite of rent, corporate competition and the economic crisis, large numbers of independent bookstores continue to exist – roughly ... double the amount in countries like the U.S., Spain, the U.K. and Germany."

Germany, however, while sharing a belief in the desirability of bookstores, reflects a different mindset about how to support them. Morris (2011) provides the German perspective:

> ... the German solution (is) saving books by keeping them expensive ... it makes perfect sense to prosperous, book-loving Germans to pay a fair, strictly regulated price for new books because they believe that the health of the book industry – that is, of publishers, booksellers, and writers, from famous to unknown – is vital to the health of the whole society.

Book readings in Germany are extremely common. Readings of an hour or more occur often in German literature houses.

The cultural dimension of gathering in the name of books may also underlie another challenge to the conventional store, one with a long history – the book fair. In many countries, book fairs have become a major source of competition for stores. Germany offers a striking example:

> Between 19 and 23 October 2005, 284,838 people descended on the exhibition grounds at Frankfurt am Main to visit the annual Frankfurt Book Fair, the most important regular event in the publishing world's calendar.
>
> (Flood, 2007, p. 1)

132 Supporting Literate Cultures

Likewise the Festival of the Book remains a vibrant part of American literary life, mingling lecture, discussion, and, of course, sales. And in the Arab world, fairs are all the rage. Curley (2015) quotes one bookstore owner:

> "It is difficult to move books in the Arab World," confessed Ala'a Al Sallal, founder of Jordanian bookseller, Jamalon. "Readers usually wait for book fairs to buy books."

The pressure on bookstores is clearly intense, and it has far more to do with economics than proficiency. Even in countries where the average reading ability is quite high – Korea, for example – support for bookstores is in decline. Over the past ten years 1,258 Korean bookstores have gone out of business.

Government intervention, in its many forms, has helped to curtail such closures and has in some cases had a positive effect on making bookselling profitable. In other cases, either by the elimination of subsidies or by the introduction of other competition, the price has come down so that books may be available to more people, but through a less profitable business model.

Finally, there is the entire issue of the types of bookstores that have continued to be able to compete successfully by changing their model. Germany has a somewhat successful bookstore industry, partly because of segmentation of the market. For example, there are stores that sell only crime novels. In others, owners sell only books that they have read themselves and can personally describe and recommend.

In Iceland, bookshop employees are all experts. They have bachelor's degrees in literature or Icelandic language, and a broad knowledge of Icelandic language books. They are generally far more conversant in literature than typical bookstore staff in either the U.K. or the U.S. In contrast to a worldwide trend, Icelandic bookstores carry fewer and fewer titles written in English. Thus, the marketplace, even though the population is extremely book-oriented, is limited to speakers of Icelandic. One consequence is that a profitable marketplace for the large-scale chains has not arisen.

Writing in *The New York Times*, Johnson (2014) discusses an interesting marketing anomaly concerning a bookstore in Seattle whose sales expanded greatly because the store marketed to people working at the Amazon headquarters nearby. Those employees enjoyed coming to a real store, where they could browse and sample the available books.

Among a myriad of trends and trajectories that are currently reshaping present-day bookstores, it is reasonable to arrive at several conclusions. To begin with, there is a trend away from brick-and-mortar bookstores, partly because they are no longer needed as warehouses for print books. Second, the decline of bookstores differs greatly from country to country. In some, stores still continue to be fairly successful, while in others the downtrend has been precipitous. Finally, the governmental policies of various countries can have a substantial impact on the success of the bookstores themselves. Any nation contemplating policy development would be well advised to examine the cases we have profiled here.

Bookstores of the Future

Several projections seem reasonable based on current trends. First, the overall model of bookselling will change if bookstores are to remain a viable participant in the distribution of texts. The competition among authors, publishers, libraries, and bookstores needs to be reduced and more ways found to help these groups collaborate for their mutual benefit. Eder (2013) discusses how the Swedish model has evolved, at least between libraries and e-book publishers. He describes the many differences between buying a single print copy of a book, after which a library lends it to clientele, and buying licenses to e-books. The point of Eder's article is captured in the title, "The Swedish Model: Or How We Learned to Stop Worrying and Love Ebook Lending." He discusses how e-books were treated as services, noting:

> Just over a decade ago publishers and librarians formed a joint task force that came up with a model for ebook lending which still to this day seems unique in the world: transaction fees for every loan; no cap on the number of concurrent loans; and access to full catalogues without entry fees.

This service-for-fee concept of library dissemination is made all the more likely by the demise of brick-and-mortar bookstores.

Norway provides an interesting model in which the leading bookstore chains are all owned by publishing companies. Hughes (2014) suggests this as a model that should be emulated in the U.S., even though it has been tried somewhat unsuccessfully before. Differences in national contexts appear to make such a plan viable in some places but not in others.

An intriguing variation on this model is the Finnish sample stock system. It entails shared risk between publishers and bookshops, and provides a wide range of books for the customers of those stores. Bengtsson (2013) describes the model as follows:

> Publishers send, free of charge, one copy of each of the trade titles they publish to each bookshop that participates in the sample stock system. The bookshop is obligated to put the books on display and to order a replacement copy when the sample stock copy has been sold. At the end of the sample stock period, which averages one year, the bookshop can either return any unsold books to the publisher or keep them in stock, in which case they must pay the publisher for the books. It is a requirement of the

sample stock system that booksellers must stock at least 80% of the titles in the sample stock system.

This consignment approach may have its advantages, and it is somewhat similar to the way that large discount wholesalers in the United States, such as Home Depot, interact with their suppliers. Regardless of the type, creative business models are a must for bookstores to survive in the future.

In order for bookstores to remain an important point of purchase, they will have to create stores that provide an interesting experience and that encourage face-to-face interaction. In the U.S., Barnes and Noble has also already reexamined its business model. Beyond its parallel industry of filling online orders for print books and developing its own line of eReaders (à la Amazon), its brick-and-mortar stores have diversified considerably. The Starbucks connection is an obvious move to draw in customers, but there are others. Authors frequently visit the stores to sign books and chat with their readers. Book readings are a regular occurrence in the children's section, where the youngest are welcome to play. Book clubs are invited to meet in the café. And sharing shelf space with print books one finds a wide assortment of kits and games geared mostly to the thoughtful and curious young. If many of these innovations sound similar to those we described earlier in reference to libraries, they are. Both libraries and bookstores are reinventing themselves to remain viable.

In the U.K., Foyles has embarked on a transition of its own, extending to the very architecture of its stores. Writing in *The Economist*, Alex Lifschutz (2013), an architect whose London-based practice is designing the new Foyles, suggests that for a bookstore to remain successful, it must improve "the experience of buying books." He suggests an array of approaches: "small, quiet spaces cocooned with books; larger spaces where one can dwell and read; other larger but still intimate spaces where one can hear talks from authors about books, literature, science, travel and cookery." The atmosphere, he adds, is vital. "Exteriors must buzz with activity, entrances must be full of eye-catching presentations and a bar and café is essential."

Somewhere between 2016 and 2017, it is predicted that digital books will for the first time outsell print titles, at least in major industrialized countries, and particularly in the West. So, in addition to a new business model and a new look, bookstores of the future must gain increasing footholds in e-commerce. Though the giants may appear to have outmaneuvered their smaller rivals in this endeavor, collective efforts utilizing common approaches and media can allow smaller independents to be successful e-marketers as well. Baker and Taylor Book Wholesalers announced the formation of TheRetailerPlace.com. This is an e-commerce turnkey solution similar in some ways to BookSense.com and BookSite.com. This collective effort gives participating retailers a chance to level the playing field and continue to grow their businesses. Internationally, there are similar efforts.

Saraiva has experienced success over the last several years competing in Brazil with such major industrial giants as Amazon. Part of the reason is that Saraiva "has more titles in Portuguese for e-books, accessible on Apple Inc.'s iPhones and iPads, as well as other tablet computers," than do the international giants (Sciaudone, 2013). Other countries and bookstores have not been as quick to adopt their own Internet models. For example, it has only been in the last few years that Waterstones, the largest single chain in the U.K., created its own web presence.

Another application of technology, which is beginning to have some impact on the bookselling industry, is publishing on demand. Technology has limited the need for large book inventories. Publishers and bookstores can partner to create both lower inventory for the publishers and lower inventory in the stores by using the expanded technologies enabling publishing on demand, in ways similar to lean manufacturing and "just in time" inventory supplies.

What then will bookstores be like in the future? First, they will continue to exist, although, there will be fewer of them. Undoubtedly, the major effects of consolidation will continue, but those effects will not only impact independent bookstores, but will also work against larger chains, as it did in the case of Borders. There will be physical restructuring and changed financial models. Finally, we anticipate more – and more creative – arrangements between the principal parties as they are compelled to collaborate out of self-interest.

Summary

In 1964, Marshall McLuhan, the Canadian philosopher and author sometimes credited with being the "High Priest of Pop Culture," published his seminal book, *Understanding Media: the Extensions of Man*. He further expanded his ideas in a sequel, *The Medium is the Message*.[1] An oversimplified distillation of his principal theme is that the content of any message interacts, in critical ways, with the medium by which it is transmitted. McLuhan observed that the actual study of communications might be better facilitated by studying the medium through which the content was communicated, rather than by analyzing the content itself. In short, he posited that the characteristics of the medium play an absolutely essential role in how information is perceived.

Extending this philosophy into our review of libraries, newspapers, and bookstores, we can conclude that the content they collect, organize, and transmit is undoubtedly affected, to a substantial degree, by the historical changes in the media of transmission. We have noted how changes in media, from wall paintings, to cuneiform clay tablets, to hand-transcribed volumes, to books printed with movable type, to digital media have created massive differences in how libraries store and retrieve information and make it accessible to broadly based populations. Similarly, newspapers have changed dramatically as well. They are transmitted and delivered in very new ways, and their delivery of content shapes how the information is read, perceived, stored, and utilized. Similarly, bookstores have changed dramatically, not necessarily because of the content, but because of the media by which the content is delivered and, in turn, sold.

Reasonable people might well debate the changes underway. From technology's impact on reading behaviors, a subject we take up in Chapter 8, to our growing accessibility to a superabundance of information, to the wisdom of subsidizing the print tradition, there is ample grist for spirited give-and-take. What cannot be debated, however, are the factual specifics of these changes and the need for policy to keep pace with them. Our modest aim is not to recommend policy but for policymakers to ground their decisions in the observable trajectories of change in order to meet the needs of those they serve.

In this chapter we have endeavored to describe the arc of these trajectories together with various reactions to them. We distil them here along with a few questions:

- Information has become accessible to far wider populations. But true access implies the proficiency needed to read with comprehension. How can a nation's educational system ensure that its citizens acquire such proficiency?
- The burgeoning amount of information is leading to far more segmentation. That is, technologically based delivery does not require the same scale of audience in order to be financially feasible. The blossoming of blogs aimed at specialized readerships is an example of how publishing can be profitable when the support previously required for the major delivery systems of print newspapers is not a factor. How can individuals navigate among a myriad of sources and be assured of their credibility?
- Just in time, or as needed, publishing of books means that there are more financially viable outlets for publications with a smaller number of potential readers. People who might not have been allowed to frequent libraries have much more "private" means of access. Should government incentives be provided to foster this kind of proliferation?
- Time sensitivity has become a much greater element in the delivery of information, and it has changed the habits and expectations of readers. Scarcely anyone reads the newspaper to find the price of a stock, for example. They can access its value by the minute with real time quotes. Consequently, the rapidity with which transmission occurs means that the content of print news sources has become far more focused on feature stories that are not as time-sensitive as "hard news." How can young readers be taught to navigate purposefully among print and digital sources?
- Finally, business models for media outlets, including libraries, newspapers, and bookstores, have changed dramatically. Not only have the roles of these enterprises been altered by the changing nature of the media that they collect, organize, and distribute, but the means by which they collect revenue

and remain financially viable, has changed as well. How can policy facilitate this transformation?

Technology, more egalitarian access, quicker turnaround of information, and lack of location-bound constraints all promise to shape the future of libraries, newspapers, and bookstores. As Internet access expands, so will the collecting, organizing, and dispersing of written language. Ironically, however, we believe that the value of the written word remains what it has always been, irrespective of technology. What the *Hartford Courant*, the oldest continuously published newspaper in the United States, stated about print in the lead article of its first edition on October 29, 1764, might just as well be applied to the digital formats of the present day:

> Of all the Arts which have been introduced amongst mankind, for civilizing Human-Nature, and rendering Life agreeable and happy, none appears of greater Advantage than that of Printing; for hereby the greatest Genius's of all Ages, and Nations, live and speak for the Benefit of future Generations.

Note

1 Curiously, this book first appeared as *The Medium is the Massage*, the apparent result of an error in typesetting.

References

Abrams, D. (2013, March 28). Can government intervention save bookstores? Maybe in France. *Publishing Perspectives*. Retrieved from http://publishingperspectives.com/2013/03/can-government-intervention-save-bookstores-maybe-in-france/

American Library Association (2008). *Internet connectivity in U.S. public libraries*. Chicago, IL: Author. Available: http://www.ala.org/research/sites/ala.org.research/files/content/initiatives/plftas/issuesbriefs/connectivitybrief.pdf

Auletta, K. (2012, October 8). Citizens Jain. *The New Yorker*. Retrieved from http://www.newyorker.com/magazine/2012/10/08/citizens-jain

Authors Guild. (2013, November 21). Not just the French: Argentina and South Korea debate limiting book discount. New York, NY: The Authors Guild. Retrieved from: https://www.authorsguild.org/industry-advocacy/reports-from-argentina-and-korea-do-fixed-book-prices-save-bookstores/

Bakker, P. (2012). The rise of free daily newspapers in Latin America. *Revista De Comunicación, 11*, 129–149. Retrieved from Academic Search Premier.

Barnard, H. (1849). *School architecture, or contributions to the improvement of school-houses in the United States* (2nd ed.). New York, NY: A.S. Barnes.

Bengtsson, N. (2013, September). The Finnish publishing industry. Retrieved from http://medienarchiv.buchmesse.de/keyword.html

Butler, P. (1945). *Books and libraries in wartime*. Chicago, IL: University of Chicago Press.

Carrenho, C. (2012, December 6). Google and Amazon launch Brazilian e-bookstores, minutes apart. *Publishing Perspectives*. Retrieved from http://publishingperspectives.com/2012/12/google-and-amazon-launch-brazilian-e-bookstores-minutes-apart/

Clemons, E.K., Spitler, R., Gu, B., & Markopoulos, P. (2003, May 7). Information, hyperdifferentiation, and delight: The value of being different. Information: *Strategy, Systems, and Economics*, Version 2.3. Available: http://opim.wharton.upenn.edu/~clemons/files/delight_info_paper_v2_1.pdf

Common Sense Media. (2014). New report from Common Sense Media reveals dramatic drop in reading among teens. San Francisco, CA: Common Sense Media. Retrieved from: https://www.commonsensemedia.org/about-us/news/press-releases/new-report-from-common-sense-media-reveals-dramatic-drop-in-reading

Curley, N. (2015, May 7–13). Challenges of selling books online in the Arab world. *Adbookfair.com*. Retrieved from http://www.adbookfair.com/the-challenges-of-selling-books-online-in-the-arab-world-by-nina-curley/

Douglas, G.H. (1999). *The golden age of the newspaper*. Westport, CT: Greenwood Press. Retrieved from EBook Collection (EBSCOhost).

The Economist. (2009, October 29). America's struggling newspapers: Big is best. London, U.K.: The Economist Newspaper, Limited. Retrieved from: http://www.economist.com/node/14770135?zid=292&ah=165a5788fdb0726c01b1374d8e1ea285

The Economist. (2013, June 4). Fold the front page. London, U.K.: The Economist Newspaper, Limited. Retrieved from http://www.economist.com/blogs/graphicdetail/2013/06/daily-chart-1?Fsrc=scn/fb/wl/bl/dc/foldthefrontpage

Eder, H. (2013, April 19). The Swedish model: Or how we learned to stop worrying and love ebook lending. *The Literary Platform*. Retrieved from http://www.theliteraryplatform.com/2013/08/the-swedish-model-or-how-we-learned-to-stop-worrying-and-love-ebook-lending/

Engelhardt, T. (2014, January 21). Tomgram: Engelhardt, the rise of the reader. Retrieved from http://www.tomdispatch.com/blog/175796/tomgram%253A_engelhardt%2C_the_rise_of_the_reader/

Esdaile, A.J.K. (1934). *National libraries of the world: Their history, administration, and public services*. London, U.K.: Grafton.

Ewing, J. (2008, August 13). Where newspapers are thriving. *Business Week*. Retrieved from http://www.businessweek.com/stories/2008-08-13/where-newspapers-are-thriving

Flood, J.L. (2007). "Omnium totius orbis emporiorum compendium": The Frankfurt Fair in the early modern period. In R. Myers, M. Harris, & G. Mandelbrote (Eds.), *Fairs, market and the itinerant book trade* (pp. 1–42). New Castle: Oak Knoll.

Franklin, B. (2008). The future of newspapers. *Journalism Studies, 9*(5), 630–641. doi:10.1080/14616700802280307

Future Library described. (1961). *The Science News-Letter, 79*(14), 215. Retrieved from http://www.jstor.org/stable/10.2307/3943289?ref=no-x-route:7f93f6fb760e6e9918ac9f032150e9a7

Galbi, D.A. (2008). Book circulation per U.S. public library user since 1856. *Public Library Quarterly, 27*(4), 351–371.

Galluzzi, A. (2009). New public libraries in Italy: Trends and issues. *The International Information & Library Review, 41*(1), 52–59. doi:10.1016/j.iilr.2008.12.002

Hammad, S. (2014, May 29). Indie bookstores alive and well in Paris. Retrieved from http://america.aljazeera.com/features/2014/5/bookstores-aliveandwellinparis.html

Haq, H. (2013, June 21). In China: An entire bookstore gets censored? *The Christian Science Monitor*. Retrieved from http://www.csmonitor.com/Books/chapter-and-verse/2013/0621/In-China-an-entire-bookstore-gets-censored

Hargrove, T., Miller, J., & Stempel, G., III. (2011). Study compares print, online use of metro, community newspapers. *Newspaper Research Journal, 32*(1), 84–89.

Harris, M.H. (1995). *History of libraries in the western world* (4th ed.). Metuchen, NJ: Scarecrow Press.

Hopper, L. (2013). Planning to thrive. *Public Libraries, 52*(3), 26–28.

Hughes, E. (2014, April 11). Norway is the best place in the world to be a writer. *The New Republic*. Retrieved from http://www.newrepublic.com/article/117337/norway-best-place-world-be-writer

Idriss, R. (2013, June 30). Debate: The Arab world is facing a publishing crisis. Retrieved from http://www.aawsat.net/2013/06/article55307810/debate-the-arab-world-is-facing-a-publishing-crisis

Jackson, J. (2013, February 11). Datawatch: Global newspaper circulation in decline as disruption reaches emerging economies. London, U.K.: TheMediaBriefing's Experts' Blog. Retrieved from: http://www.themediabriefing.com/article/datawatch-circulation-decline-developing-economies

Johnson, K. (2014, April 11). Bookstores in Seattle soar, and embrace an old nemesis: Amazon.com. *The New York Times*. Retrieved from http://www.nytimes.com/2014/04/12/us/bookstores-in-seattle-soar-and-embrace-an-old-nemesis-amazoncom.html

Jurkowitz, M. (2014, March 26). The growth in digital reporting. Retrieved from http://www.journalism.org/2014/03/26/the-growth-in-digital-reporting/

Knezevic, M. (2013, December 2). Saudi Arabia: Popular sci-fi novel banned. Retrieved from http://www.indexoncensorship.org/2013/12/popular-saudi-sci-fi-novel-banned-book-stores/

Lerner, F. (2009). *The story of libraries: From the invention of writing to the computer age* (2nd ed.). New York: Continuum.

Lewis, D.L. (2013, July 2). The New York Public Library must be saved from itself. *The Chronicle of Higher Education*. Retrieved from http://chronicle.com/blogs/conversation/2013/07/02/the-new-york-public-library-must-be-saved-from-itself/

Lifschutz, A. (2013, February 27). [Quoted in] The future of the bookstore: A real cliffhanger. *The Economist*. Retrieved from http://www.economist.com/blogs/prospero/2013/02/future-bookstore

Lindsay, E. (2013, December 26). Short shelf life for new book law. *Newsinenglish.no*. Retrieved from http://www.newsinenglish.no/2013/12/26/short-shelf-life-for-new-book-law/

Mallet, V. (2013, August 13). India's newspapers shrug off industry woes. *Financial Times*. Available: http://www.ft.com/cms/s/0/436ce7f4-027d-11e3-880d-00144feab7de.html#axzz3sJE37mxK

MarketingCharts. (2013, June 4). Global newspaper circulation and advertising trends in 2012. Thetford Center, VT: MarketingCharts.com. Retrieved from: http://www.marketingcharts.com/traditional/global-newspaper-circulation-and-advertising-trends-in-2012-30062/

Matsa, K.E. (2015, April). Hispanic media fact sheet. In A. Mitchell & D. Page (Eds.), *State of the news media 2015* (pp. 78–86). Washington, DC: Pew Institute Center. Available: http://www.journalism.org/files/2015/04/FINAL-STATE-OF-THE-NEWS-MEDIA1.pdf

Miller, J.W. (2016). *World's most literate countries*. http://www.ccsu.edu/globalliteracy

Morris, B. (2011, September 13). The German solution: Saving books by keeping them expensive. *The Millions*. Retrieved from http://www.themillions.com/2011/09/the-german-solution-saving-books-by-keeping-them-expensive.html

Mott, F.L. (1941). *American journalism; a history of newspapers in the United States through 250 years, 1690–1940*. New York: Macmillan.

Mueller, M.U. (2013, May 15). Crisis or strategy shift: Cuts planned at German tabloid Bild. *Spiegel Online*. Retrieved from http://www.spiegel.de/international/germany/axel-springer-said-to-be-planning-major-cuts-at-largest-german-newspaper-a-899742.html

Mumby, F.A. (1930). *Publishing and bookselling; A history from the earliest times to the present day*. London, U.K.: J. Cape.

Murphy, P.C. (1999, December 19). Books are dead, long live books. Retrieved from http://web.mit.edu/comm-forum/papers/murphy.html

Myers, S. (2011, July 8). India is now the world's fastest-growing newspaper market. Poynter. Available: http://www.poynter.org/news/mediawire/138502/india-is-now-the-worlds-fastest-growing-newspaper-market/

Nippon.com. (2014, December 5). Newspaper circulation in Japan: Still high but steadily falling. Tokyo, Japan: Nippon Communications Foundation. Retrieved from http://www.nippon.com/en/features/h00084/

Norman, M. (2012). Frail, fatal, fundamental: The future of public libraries. *Public Library Quarterly, 31*(4), 339–351.

Onion. (2008, May 1). Dying newspaper trend buys nation's newspapers three more weeks. Chicago, IL: The Onion. Retrieved from http://www.theonion.com/article/dying-newspaper-trend-buys-nations-newspapers-thre-6129

Piper, P.S. (2013, March/April). HathiTrust and Digital Public Library of America as the future. Retrieved from http://www.infotoday.com/OnlineSearcher/Articles/Features/HathiTrust-and-Digital-Public-Library-of-America-as-the-future-88089.shtml

Preston, P. (2008). The curse of introversion. *Journalism Practice, 2*(3), 318–325. doi:10.1080/17512780802280992

Preston, P. (2009). The curse of introversion. In B. Franklin (Ed.), *The future of newspapers* (pp. 13–20). New York, NY: Routledge.

Rogers, M. (1996). Internet shaping libraries' future. *Library Journal, 121*(20), 27–28.

Salman, J. (2007). Watching the pedlar's movements: Itinerant distribution in the urban Netherlands. In R. Myers, M. Harris, & G. Mandelbrote (Eds.), *Fairs, markets and the itinerant book trade* (pp. 137–158). New Castle, DE: Oak Knoll Press.

Schnibben, C. (2013, August 13). Extra, extra! Newspaper crisis hits Germany. *Der Spiegel International – Spiegel Online*. Retrieved from http://www.spiegel.de/international/germany/circulation-declines-hit-german-papers-a-decade-after-america-a-915574.html

Schwartz, A. (2013, October 9). Vive la bookstore! *The New Yorker*. Retrieved from http://www.newyorker.com/books/page-turner/vive-la-bookstore

Sciaudone, C. (2013, April 19). Amazon threat fails to damp Saraiva leading retail rally. *Bloomberg Business*. Retrieved from http://www.bloomberg.com/news/articles/2013-04-19/amazon-threat-fails-to-damp-saraiva-leading-retail-rally

Sciolino, E. (2012, June 20). The French still flock to bookstores. *The New York Times*. Retrieved from http://www.nytimes.com/2012/06/21/books/french-bookstores-are-still-prospering.html?_r=0

Swan, D.W., Grimes, J., Owens, T., Vese, Jr., R.D., Miller, K., Arroyo, J., Craig, T., Dorinski, S., Freeman, M., Isaac, N., O'Shea, P., Schilling, P. & Scotto, J. (2013). *Public Libraries Survey: Fiscal Year 2010* (IMLS-2013–PLS-01). Washington, DC: Institute of Museum and Library Services.

Tagholm, R. (2014, April 15). In the global book market, India and Brazil remain hot. *Publishing Perspectives*. Retrieved from http://publishingperspectives.com/

Tan, T. (2009, September 21). Publishing in the UAE. *Publishers Weekly*. Retrieved from http://www.publishersweekly.com/pw/print/20090921/7458-publishing-in-the-uae.html

Ten best libraries in the world. (2011). http://binscorner.com/pages/t/top-10-best-libraries-in-the-world.html

Tolzmann, D.H., Hessel, A., & Peiss, R. (2001). *The memory of mankind: The story of libraries since the dawn of history*. New Castle, DE: Oak Knoll Press.

Vallet, N. (2013). Becoming partners in urban development: A case-study research on the strategic roles of Flemish and Dutch public libraries in the future development of cities. *Library Management, 34*, 650–63.

van der Werf, H.H. (2010). The architecture of knowledge [Introduction]. In H.H. van der Werf (Ed.), *The architecture of knowledge: The library of the future – De architektuur van kennis: De bibliotheek van de toekomst* (pp. 10–19). Rotterdam, The Netherlands: NAi.

VanderKlippe, Nathan. (2014, February 10). Japan's thriving newspaper industry slow to learn from Western collapse. *The Globe and Mail*. Retrieved from http://www.theglobeandmail.com/report-on-business/international-business/asian-pacific-business/japans-thriving-newspaper-industry-slow-to-learn-from-western-collapse/article16792633/

Verschaffel, B. (2010). Guessing the future of the library. In H.H. van der Werf (Ed.), *The architecture of knowledge: The library of the future* (pp. 84–95). Rotterdam: NAi.

Wadbring, I. (2003). *En tidning i tiden? Metro och den svenska dagstidningsmarknaden*. Unpublished doctoral dissertation, University of Gothenburg.

Warsh, D. (2013, August 12). The golden age of newspapers: A short history. Somerville, MA: EconomicPrincipals.com. Retrieved from http://www.economicprincipals.com/issues/2013.08.12/1528.html

Wasserman, H. (2007, September). *Attack of the killer newspapers: The "tabloid revolution" and the future of newspapers in South Africa*. Paper presented at the Future of Newspapers Conference, Cardiff University.

Whitehead, K. (2013, April 30). Taiwanese bookstore chain Eslite expands aggressively into China. *Publishing Perspectives*. Frankfurt Book Fair. Retrieved from http://publishingperspectives.com/2013/04/taiwanese-bookstore-chain-eslite-expands-aggressively-into-china/

Zickuhr, K., & Rainie, L. (2014, September 10). *Younger Americans and public libraries: How those under 30 engage with libraries and think about libraries' role in their lives and communities*. Washington, DC: Pew Research Center. Retrieved from http://www.pewinternet.org/2014/09/10/younger-americans-and-public-libraries/

7

SKILL VERSUS WILL: IMPORTANT LESSONS FOR POLICY

The status of reading among Americans aged 18 and older is open to interpretation but the facts are rather clear. A recent Pew study (Zickuhr & Rainie, 2014), conducted with a random sample of just over 1,000 adults, reported the following:

- The average number of books read in the past year was 12, the median 5.
- These numbers have not changed from previous years.
- 76 percent reported reading at least one book in some format.
- There were no significant differences in reading frequency by age group.

These facts, though somewhat encouraging, may be viewed from a glass-half-empty perspective. What about the quarter of American adults who did not read a book of any kind in the past year? Why has the frequency of reading not increased in recent years?

All of this begs a more basic question – the wisdom of attempting to extend the percentage of the population for whom reading has become habitual. The answer to this question is not as self-evident as it might appear. Noted sci-fi author Ursula K. LeGuin (2008), for example, expressed a contrarian view of the alleged decline of reading. "I . . . want to question the assumption" she wrote, ". . . that books are on the way out. I think they're here to stay. It's just that not that many people ever did read them. Why should we think everybody ought to now?" Although LeGuin may well be right about a small but stable population of readers, we respectfully take issue with her conclusion that nothing needs to be done to increase their number. We argue that adding to the number of readers in any nation contributes to the mental and emotional health of its citizens, as surely as hospitals contribute to their physical well-being. Moreover, modes of behavior are subject to change, so that prudent policy initiatives can help make it happen.

We've made clear that our primary interest is in the practice of literacy rather than relative levels of achievement – in *how* and *how much* people read rather than *how well*. These two questions, however, are not easily dissociable. The simple fact is, achievement facilitates behavior. Reasonable proficiency is necessary to participate fully in literate activities, though it does not guarantee participation. We might extend this principle to nearly any endeavor in which one has a choice. Being reasonably skillful makes participation potentially more enjoyable, or at least less frustrating, and it therefore increases the likelihood that it will become habitual. The better an individual plays golf, the more likely it is that he or she will play regularly (a principle that explains why the first author has continued to play while the second author gave up the game). As in all endeavors, success breeds success. Those deficient in literacy skills are less likely to buy a newspaper, frequent a bookstore, or download a book to a device than those with higher-level skills.

The real possibility that students may acquire the ability to read but not the desire – skill without will – has prompted those who have designed large-scale studies such as NAEP, PISA, and PIRLS to include items intended to gauge the will to read as well as the skill required. For example, every administration of PIRLS has asked fourth graders how well they like to read. Their responses make it possible to observe a clear relationship between attitude and achievement. In the 2011 results, the average scale score of students who indicated they liked reading was 542; for those who responded they liked to read "somewhat," it was 506; and for those who reported they did not like reading, it was 488. These results are consistent over time and across national borders. The PIRLS assessments of 2000, 2006, and 2011 all show strong positive relationships within countries between attitude toward reading and achievement.

The chicken-and-egg question of whether positive attitudes lead to more reading and hence greater proficiency, or whether proficiency promotes positive attitudes is essentially a false choice. Both are true. This is because a reciprocal relationship exists between the attainment of reading proficiency and the acquisition of positive attitudes, at least up to a point (see Schaffner, Schiefele, & Ulferts, 2013). We have represented this relationship in Figure 7.1.

The first link in this cycle suggests that as a reader becomes more proficient, a greater variety of comprehensible materials opens up. Imagine a hypothetical student entering a large university library containing, say, 5 million print volumes, a library about the size of the University of Virginia's. To that student, all 5 million volumes would be available. However, it is safe to say that many of these volumes could not be read with adequate comprehension. This would be true regardless of the student's background and proficiency. That is, many would be available but not accessible. To put this idea in slightly different terms, the better a reader becomes, the more books become accessible. And so, even though many books could never

144 Skill versus Will

FIGURE 7.1 The reciprocal effects of skill and will.

be read, thousands would nevertheless be accessible to a student of moderate proficiency, enough volumes to propel a lifelong habit of reading. Now imagine a second student entering the library with a broader background and a higher level of reading proficiency. Clearly, this student has also surpassed the threshold necessary for extensive engaged reading. Even more of the volumes would be accessible and a different and arguably richer life of literacy engagement would be possible. This is well and good, of course. But it does not change the fact that the first student, by virtue of reaching the threshold of proficiency needed for a high level of engagement, is positioned to read frequently. Our point is that once a certain threshold of proficiency is attained, an individual will have more than enough to sustain a literate life. For this reason, we argue that policy should aim to make a wide range of materials available, materials written at varying levels of complexity.

The second link in the cycle, from more materials to greater motivation, is true only if certain conditions are met. The materials must be available to a given reader, they must contain titles the reader finds appealing enough to read, and the reader must have the time to read them. Then and only then can we expect more reading to occur and proficiency to rise as a long-term result (the last link). Under the right circumstances, this cycle recurs over time in an upward spiral, at least during the elementary years. Understanding how to ensure that these circumstances are created is clearly a challenge for educators and policymakers. As early as fourth grade the process has begun to unravel for many students. Despite the positive relationship between achievement and attitude, only about 28 percent of the students assessed in the 2011 PIRLS (Mullis et al., 2012) indicated that they liked to read.

Deconstructing Motivation

How do we go about ensuring that circumstances favorable to the upward cycle of motivation are realized? Let's start with a basic understanding of the affective factors at work. Psychologists investigating reading motivation have long operated amid a tangle of abstract terms representing concepts with multiple and sometimes overlapping definitions. We recently conducted a concept analysis of an entire decade of studies and proposed some consensus definitions (Conradi, Jang, & McKenna, 2014). Without getting too technical, we invite you to introspect as we walk you through the most important of these concepts.

Let's begin with the end in mind – with reading motivation. Derived from the Latin *movere* ("to move"), motivation simply means the drive or intent to act. This intent is typically described as originating either from within or from without. We suspect you view yourself as intrinsically motivated to read. You know that reading can help fulfill certain perceived needs – the need for pleasure, edification, or knowledge, for instance. These are precisely the qualities we want to foster more broadly. Just as Plato dreamt of a country populated by philosophers, we dream of one populated by readers, by individuals intrinsically motivated to read. We suspect this is a dream you share with us. But motivation can also arise from factors outside the individual. The need to read a book for a test or to interpret an email from your boss are examples of motivation that is extrinsic in nature.

The origins of motivation, whether from within and from without, can coexist at the same time for the same individual. (You might actually enjoy reading that book you'll be tested over.) However, extrinsic motivation (to earn rewards or outperform others, for example) has often been observed to have a negative impact on intrinsic motivation (Schaffner, Schiefele, & Ulferts, 2013). These examples begin to illustrate just how complex the construct of motivation actually is. Many factors have a hand in influencing it at any particular time and in shaping it over an extended period.

Let's think about these factors as they relate to the criminal mind, an odd but instructive analogy. If you enjoy a good mystery, you undoubtedly understand that three conditions must be met in order for the police to regard a person as a suspect: means, motive, and opportunity. If your motive is to read, your decision to act will depend upon the other two. In the case of reading, we can equate means with proficiency. What we sometimes lose sight of in the equation is opportunity. You may be both willing and able to read, but unless a suitable text is available, reading will not occur. This is the reason that various initiatives to make books available in the developing world are so crucially important. It is also an idea that operates at the family level. Dan Willingham (2015) recommends, for instance, that parents place a tub of books next to their child's car seat. Doing so provides opportunity.

And now a morbid question. Imagine you could eavesdrop at your own funeral as a close friend delivers a eulogy. Would you be surprised to hear yourself described as a "reader"? This question gets at the very heart of your self-concept. If you are in fact intrinsically motivated to read and if you regularly choose to read, then that label would be fitting indeed. The key is the place that reading occupies in your life, and regularity has a great deal to do with it. As Aristotle remarked, we are what we repeatedly do. True readers belong to a category that is best defined by the frequency of elective reading. Membership in that category depends on proficiency and availability as prerequisites. To say that students who struggle to read do not view themselves as readers is painfully obvious, and teachers have long sought to supply the two prerequisites, by building proficiency and supplying good things to read.

Next, imagine that an interviewer asks how well you enjoy reading. The question suggests a spectrum from negative to positive. If you answer "very much," your response would indicate a favorable orientation toward reading in general. This predisposition to act in a consistently negative or positive way is called attitude. Its relationship to motivation is fairly obvious, but it is primarily an emotional response to the idea of reading. An individual can be motivated to read despite a negative attitude, for example. If you value reading, even though you don't especially like doing it, you may still be motivated to read. Going to the gym or swallowing a foul-tasting medicine are everyday examples of the same phenomenon.

Attitudes turn out to be complex in themselves. They exist in hierarchies, from general to specific. You probably have a very positive attitude toward reading in general. But when we narrow the target, you might find that your attitude is not so positive after all. Figure 7.2 represents a tiny part of the vast hierarchy of reading attitudes. At the top of the hierarchy is one's attitude toward reading in general. The notion of reading becomes more specific as we move down the branches of the hierarchy. The complexity of attitudes and the importance of using that term in the plural are evident at once. Two people with the same general attitude toward reading may have quite different attitudes toward reading

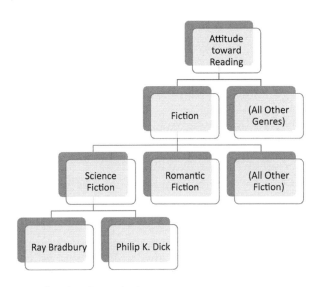

FIGURE 7.2 Hierarchy of reading attitudes.

romantic versus science fiction. And science fiction buffs, ostensibly cut from the same cloth, might have very different views of Ray Bradbury and Philip K. Dick.

The lesson for policy at the level of the family, school, and community is a simple one: It is not enough that one likes to read. One must like to read something that's available. You've surely had the experience of sitting in the waiting room of a doctor's office with time on our hands. You look through a stack of magazines, all of which are at least six months old. Some of them are about topics that do not interest you in the least. Remember that you have already described yourself as intrinsically motivated to read, someone who would be comfortable if characterized as a reader in a eulogy. But now you're faced with the prospect of reading something you find at worst distasteful and at best, dull.

This is why developing questionnaires that tap into a person's attitude can be tricky. In a recent study, we asked a group of adolescents how they would feel if they received a book as a present (one of the PISA questions). "That would depend," one girl responded. "Can you tell me which book? And would it be the only present I got?" This particular student claimed to enjoy reading, but her attitude clearly depended on a number of contingencies. We are not arguing that surveys are not valid, only that they must be developed with care. Researchers have learned a great deal about their construction in recent years. Our point is that attitudes are but one factor in the decision to read.

Abundant evidence suggests that attitudes are acquired, not inherited. We all know siblings with remarkably different perspectives on reading despite originating from the same gene pool. This is both good news and bad. The good news for educators and policymakers is that attitudes can be shaped over time. By taking steps to build proficiency and make plenty of good books available, they can do much to ensure the development of positive attitudes. The bad news is that these steps are often countered by other factors in a student's environment. In Chapter 2, we spoke of the social norms that influence how students perceive reading and how they view academics in general. Students who are inclined to fit in by adhering to those norms are unlikely to become readers if reading is not valued by their peers.

Contributing to the gradual development of reading attitudes is the competition from other forms of activity. As students grow older, an increasing number of leisure options are open to them, options that eventually include driving and dating. Consequently, reading must fight for shelf space in a student's expanding cabinet of leisure options. Such choices follow us into adulthood. Imagine yourself seated at home in your living room. On the end table next to you is the novel you've been reading. In front of you is the television. Do you reach for the book or the remote?

Mind you, choices like this are not necessarily a negative outcome. There is a case to be made for well-roundedness, and a nation of readers is not the same as a nation of bookworms. We simply intended this exercise in introspection as a means of making you aware of how complex the problem of motivation can be. Perhaps this is one reason it is typically ignored by policymakers, who prefer to focus on

148 Skill versus Will

achievement. In our view, however, we ignore motivation at our peril when we take a tunnel view of literacy and assume that nothing matters but achievement.

Lessons from Other Countries

Rather than profiling individual countries, we consider here some overall trends. In Chapter 3, we listed the highest-achieving countries on PISA 2009. Achievement is, quite understandably, the most important way to rank the participating countries. But it isn't the only way. What if we ranked them on the basis of motivation instead? In Table 7.1, we have done just that. The left-hand column shows the achievement ranking of the top 20 countries, but on the right we list the top 20 based on the Enjoyment of Reading Index, a standardized composite of 11 affective items to which 15-year-olds are asked to respond.

TABLE 7.1 Top 20 PISA Countries Ranked by Achievement versus Enjoyment

	Combined Literacy Scaled Score	*Reading Enjoyment Mean Index Score (SD)**
1	Shanghai-China	**Albania** 0.67 (.02)
2	Korea	**Turkey** 0.64 (.02)
3	Finland	Shanghai-China 0.57 (.01)
4	Hong Kong-China	**Kazakhstan** 0.54 (.02)
5	Singapore	**Thailand** 0.54 (.01)
6	Canada	**Indonesia** 0.43 (.01)
7	New Zealand	**Azerbaijan** 0.39 (.01)
8	Japan	**Kyrgyzstan** 0.39 (.01)
9	Australia	**Chinese Taipei** 0.39 (.02)
10	The Netherlands	**Jordan** 0.37 (.02)
11	Belgium	**Tunisia** 0.37 (.02)
12	Norway	**Peru** 0.35 (.01)
13	Estonia	Hong Kong-China 0.32 (.01)
14	Switzerland	Singapore 0.29 (.01)
15	Poland	**Dubai (UAE)** 0.28 (.01)
16	Iceland	**Brazil** 0.27 (.01)
17	United States	**Portugal** 0.21 (.02)
18	Liechtenstein	**Montenegro** 0.21 (.01)
19	Sweden	**Trinidad and Tobago** 0.21 (.01)
20	Germany	Japan 0.20 (.02)

*OECD mean = 0.

Skill versus Will **149**

It is plain to see that a very different list emerges. Sixteen of the 20 (in bold) are not among the top 20 achieving countries. The fact that only four countries are on both lists runs counter to the assumption that motivation and proficiency are strongly related. What can explain the fact that 15-year-olds in many of the highest-achieving countries report substantially lower levels of enjoyment? Loveless (2015) describes this as "a curious pattern" (p. 28) and traces it back to the first international assessments in the 1960s. It is a pattern observed in other school subjects as well, not just reading, and it prompted Loveless to caution against the conventional wisdom that if we take steps to increase motivation, achievement is sure to follow. This conclusion calls into question the cycle depicted in Figure 7.1, at least as it pertains to older individuals. And although we agree with Loveless up to a point, we believe the situation is more complex. We argue that the explanation lies in the fact that the cycle does not continue indefinitely. Once a certain threshold is reached, the law of diminishing returns takes effect and the relationship plateaus. That is, the highest achievement levels are not always associated with the greatest enjoyment of reading.

There is good evidence for this claim in the results of PIAAC. Figure 7.3 displays the relationship between the reading proficiency of adults and the extent to which they reported engaging in reading outside of work, reading they did for

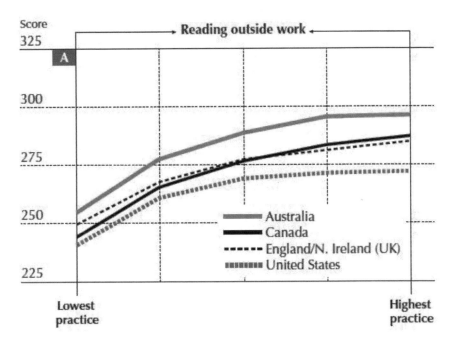

FIGURE 7.3 Relationship of reading outside work to reading proficiency in four countries.

personal rather than professional purposes (OECD, 2013, p. 217). The left-hand portion of the graph portrays the predictable connection between ability and practice, but only for low-to-moderate levels of proficiency. Beyond that point, the difference in reading ability does not rise appreciably between the moderate and highest levels of reading outside the workplace. Instead, the connection stalls. What this means is that the threshold required for extensive engagement in reading is not particularly high. In fact, the difference in ability between those moderately and highly engaged in reading is actually quite modest. At first blush, this finding seems counterintuitive, but a likely explanation lies in job-related reading. The most proficient readers are typically employed in positions that require extensive reading of technical material. When they are off the job, leisure options that require little or no reading may have greater appeal. (Think of our scenario involving the choice between a book and a remote.)

Consequently, we need not wait to encourage extensive reading until high levels of proficiency are widely achieved. Quite the contrary. It is just that such efforts can be expected to have greater impact on readers of lower proficiency. The pattern displayed in Figure 7.3, though correlational, suggests that efforts to motivate adults who are already moderately good readers may not result in appreciable gains in proficiency, and, conversely, that efforts to increase their proficiency may not result in increased engagement.

Recommendations for Policy

What does all of this mean for national policy? That countries make no effort to encourage wide reading? Certainly not. We suggest that there are at least three compelling reasons for launching concerted initiatives designed to promote reading at all age levels. The first is that the relationship between motivation and achievement does appear to hold for weak-to-average readers. Motivating them to read more is therefore likely to improve their proficiency. A second reason is to foster a citizenry that is connected in part by an engagement in reading. Although reading is an individual activity, it is inherently social in nature. Reading completes the act of communication initiated by the writer, and it positions the reader to interact with others in ways that center about a common text. It seems hardly necessary to add that a habit of doing so can lead to a life of greater fulfillment through literacy. The third reason is less obvious but quintessentially important. A society in which reading is central to life – meaning that its members not only can read but regularly do – is better informed and far more likely to safeguard a democratic culture. This sentiment is hardly new. Writers from Jefferson to Dewey have stressed the importance of an electorate informed through reading.

Each of these three reasons is compelling in its own right. Together they make a strong case for altering national policy in ways that encourage motivation and broaden the lens through which educators view reading itself. The following recommendations are intended to provide such encouragement.

1. Think outside the achievement box

If we had to distill a single recommendation for policymakers it would be to think beyond the narrow confines of achievement. Motivating a citizenry to become readers must be seen not merely as an optional add-on to the real work of building proficiency. When motivational programs share the limelight with achievement, both aspects of reading development reinforce one another. And it is reasonable to speculate that a country populated by readers may be an eventual outcome.

2. Make broadened policy goals explicit

Some 15 years ago, we argued that national and international assessments include measures of motivation and that reports generated after each administration highlight both achievement *and* motivation and that they track trends in both over time (McKenna, 2001). As we have noted, items that target student feelings and habits are included in PISA, PIRLS, and NAEP, but they are not given anything resembling equal play when results are announced or when they are subsequently analyzed. Only when policymakers demand that the reports be broadened in this way will they have the data necessary to make informed decisions concerning the direction of their countries.

3. Strive to make reading a cultural given at multiple levels

Schools and their broader communities should be encouraged to develop literate cultures. Specific guidance should be provided about how to achieve this goal, and it should be championed by national and local leaders alike. Here is a modest idea for a mantra: *In this country, we read*. Parents should be targeted as key players in the transmission of cultural values. When these values include literacy, good things can be expected to happen. To suggest that this is an easy goal to achieve would be naïve. And yet we believe that specific measures can be reasonably effective. Legislative support for parent education, book distribution, grant competitions, and volunteer programs are among the promising possibilities.

References

Conradi, K., Jang, B.G., & McKenna, M.C. (2014). Motivation terminology in reading research: A conceptual review. *Educational Psychology Review, 26,* 127–164.
LeGuin, U.K. (2008). Staying awake: Notes on the alleged decline of reading. *Harpers Magazine.* Available: http://harpers.org/archive/2008/02/staying-awake/.

Loveless, T. (2015). *2015 Brown Center report on American education: How well are American students learning?* Washington, DC: Brookings Institution, Brown Center on Education Policy. Available: http://www.ewa.org/sites/main/files/file-attachments/brown_ctr_2015_v2.pdf

McKenna, M.C. (2001). Development of reading attitudes. In L. Verhoeven & C. Snow (Eds.), *Literacy and motivation: Reading engagement in individuals and groups* (pp. 135–158). Mahwah, NJ: Lawrence Erlbaum.

Mullis, I.V.S., Martin, M.O., Foy, P., & Drucker, K.T. (2012). PIRLS 2011 international results in reading. Chestnut Hill, MA: TIMSS & PIRLS International Study Center, Boston College. Available: http://timssandpirls.bc.edu/pirls2011/international-results-pirls.html

OECD. (2013). *OECD skills outlook 2013: First results from the survey of adult skills* (Revised version). Paris, France: OECD. Available: http://www.keepeek.com/Digital-Asset-Management/oecd/education/oecd-skills-outlook-2013_9789264204256-en#page1

Schaffner, E., Schiefele, U., & Ulferts, H. (2013). Reading amount as a mediator of the effects of intrinsic and extrinsic reading motivation on reading comprehension. *Reading Research Quarterly, 48,* 369–385.

Willingham, D.T. (2015). *Raising kids who read: What parents and teachers can do.* San Francisco, CA: Jossey-Bass.

Zickuhr, K., & Rainie, L. (2014). *E-reading rises as device ownership jumps.* Washington, DC: Pew Research Center. Available: http://pewinternet.org/Reports/2014/E-Reading-Update.aspx

8
ARE BOOKS OBSOLETE? EXAMINING TRENDS IN MEDIA USE

For readers, the transition from print to pixels is the new future shock. Despite a few constants in a changing universe (the need to recognize words, and so forth), how we read is undeniably changing, and changing fast. Developments in digital texts are occurring so rapidly in fact that staying current is a full-time job.

It may also be a fool's errand. We say this because appreciating the overarching course of these trends is far more important than keeping up with day-to-day developments.

From Tablet to Tablet

To do so, it's useful to place recent developments in historical context, noting that the rise of digital texts is only the most recent transition in how reading happens, an evolution that has taken us from tablet to tablet, as we illustrate in Figure 8.1. The first was the replacement of scrolls with the codex book, beginning some two thousand years ago. Navigation and rereading were suddenly far easier. Imagine the inconvenience of unrolling a scroll to a point you'd passed much earlier. First-century Roman poet Martial quipped that his readers could stroll down the street holding his writings in one hand, without the bother of a scroll:[1]

> You who long for my little books to be with you everywhere and want to have companions for a long journey, buy these, which parchment confines within small pages. Give your scroll-cases to the great authors – one hand can hold me!
> (Epigram I.2)

The second transition came with the advent of the printing press in the fifteenth century, ensuring that books would forever be widely available. The arrival of electronic texts during the 1980s and 90s further increased the availability of texts, this time to an exponential degree. Their arrival was heralded by many and lamented by others. In a series of essays, Sven Birkerts (1994) waxed elegiac about the unavoidable demise of the printed word. Parallels can be found in the recording industry (vinyl enthusiasts) and even in money (cash diehards). Christopher Harris (2014) has little patience with such sentiments:

> There can be no question: Digital is the future of information. For those bemoaning the shift, often evoking arguments centered around the smell and feel of paper tomes, be assured that your protestations are all for naught. In the end, digital content will win because it is faster, easier, more connected, and more flexible. E-books, like digital music in the early 2000s, are a disruptive technology steadily gaining in the public mindset. Disruptive technologies, initially rejected by experts as being inferior to the status quo, are embraced by the masses. The widespread adoption drives rapid development, leading to improvements that quickly overshadow the technology being replaced.
>
> (pp. 20–21)

Since the late 1940s, when the binary math of digital communication was laid out by Claude Shannon and others (Shannon, 1948; Shannon & Weaver, 1949), the trajectory of advancements has been clear. We note a few of the important developments in Table 8.1.

To sum them up, hardware has become cheaper, quicker, easier, and smaller. At the same time, software has grown smarter, more adaptive, and breathtakingly simpler to use. Conjecture about the next development has become a cottage industry, and the interval between science fiction and fact has narrowed. Twenty years ago, Neal Stephenson, in his 1994 novel, *The Diamond Age*, described the use of paper-like sheets embedded with electronic "ink" consisting of nanoprocessors that could be activated in varying ways to display particular patterns, including text. Each morning the embedded pixels were activated in different configurations to represent the *London Times*. Today, electronic ink is yesterday's news, a commonplace of engineering.

The sense of inevitability in this tide of events is inescapable. And yet we suspect that rumors concerning the death of print, to borrow from Mark Twain, appear to have been greatly exaggerated. The millennials grew up as digital natives, having never known a world without the Internet. Their predecessors, Generation X and the boomers, have entered the digital world, of course, but as immigrants, carrying with them the baggage of print reading habits that are hard to break. We might expect the elderly, reared in an era of print, to keep books alive through their purchasing power. But it is surprising to learn that many millennials likewise prefer print to digital texts, despite their higher cost (Rosenwald, 2015). Given the price of print textbooks, along with the other imposing costs of college, it is

FIGURE 8.1 Cuneiform tablet from the 24th century BCE (Library of Congress) and the iPad Mini 3 (registered trademark of Apple, Inc.).

TABLE 8.1 Key Firsts in Digital Reading[1]

1941	Konrad Zuse introduces Z3 computer in Berlin
1941	Bombe computer completed in the U.K.
1947	First keyboard introduced
1950	First digital computer developed in Japan
1963	First mouse is developed
1971	Michael Hart launches Project Gutenberg to house public domain e-books
1972	First video game is marketed
1975	First portable computers are introduced by Altair
1991	World Wide Web is launched on August 6
1993	Peter James publishes *Host*, a thriller, on two floppy disks
1994	First use of HTML to publish e-books
1998	Google is launched
1998	First handheld e-book reader is introduced by NuroMedia
1999	Simon & Schuster is first publisher to offer digital and print versions
2001	Five other publishers follow suit, launching e-book divisions
2004	Facebook is launched
2007	Amazon introduces the Kindle
2009	E-books first become available for checkout at libraries
2010	Apple introduces the iPad
2013	More than a quarter of adult trade books are sold as e-books

[1] For a detailed history of early landmarks in computing, visit http://www.computerhistory.org/timeline/

little short of astonishing that these apparent dinosaurs have maintained a viable market niche.

Rosenwald (2015) reports that the typical reasons given by millennials are that storylines are easier to follow and that print versions of nonfiction invite slower and more careful reading. Linguist Naomi Baron (2015) speculates that print books make it easier to form a mental "map" of where information is located, a process that helps us comprehend complex material. Though the popularity of reading on digital devices is undeniable, she points out that most of the texts that we read in that format are lightweight in nature. For the kind of careful reading required for academic learning, digital texts have disadvantages:

> Despite the thousands of hours logged reading and writing digitally, I cannot perform a careful analysis this way. I need to see the work as a whole, cross-reference back and forth, keeping multiple passages in view.
>
> (p. xii)

We can relate. At the same time, however, we believe it is important to note that developments in technology are driven by market forces. The limitations Baron notes, if voiced by sufficient numbers of consumers, may very well lead to changes deliberately brought about to address them. For example, the need to see multiple documents open at once can already be met through large and/or multiple screens, on which a number and variety of texts can be displayed simultaneously. Similarly, there are digital equivalents available for any number of practices with a print origin. They include dog-earing, glossing, highlighting, note-taking, and many others. We suspect that as these become more commonplace the idea of going back to their print ancestors will seem more and more anachronistic, just as the idea of drafting a manuscript with pencil and pad is already an archaic notion.

For whatever reasons, the rise of digital reading is occurring at different rates for different kinds of reading. It has been meteoric in social media and more gradual where books are concerned. A recent Pew report presented the following findings:

> Though e-books are rising in popularity, print remains the foundation of Americans' reading habits: Among adults who read at least one book in the past year, just 5% said they read an e-book in the last year without also reading a print book. In general, the vast majority of those who read e-books and audiobooks also read print books. Of the three (overlapping) groups, audiobook listeners have the most diverse reading habits, while relatively fewer print readers consume books in other formats:
>
> - 87% of e-book readers also read a print book in the past 12 months, and 29% listened to an audiobook.
> - 84% of audiobook listeners also read a print book in the past year, and 56% also read an e-book.
> - A majority of print readers read only in that format, although 35% of print book readers also read an e-book and 17% listened to an audiobook.
>
> Overall, about half (52%) of readers only read a print book, 4% only read an e-book, and just 2% only listened to an audiobook. Nine percent of readers said they read books in all three formats.
>
> (Zickuhr & Rainie, 2014)

It's important to keep evolving technologies in mind when interpreting factoids such as these. Print books are a constant that we all know and understand. The nature of e-books changes with each advance, and improvements are likely to make them more appealing. In the music industry (our analogy in Chapter 6), the transition from vinyl records to compact discs was incremental, but the larger trend – from records to CDs to downloads to the cloud – lends perspective to the direction digital literacy appears to be taking. It's true that we can't predict the next stage in their development, but we can safely anticipate that it will make them more attractive to readers.

The Unique Affordances of Digital Texts

More than 40 years ago, Isaac Asimov (1974) related his thoughts during a presentation on the topic of videocassettes. As the speaker celebrated their many advantages, Asimov inwardly speculated about where this development was headed. Specifically, he wondered what the "ultimate" cassette might offer. He began with the limitations inherent in all cassettes – that they require machinery to play them, that they provide information at the same pace for every user, and that they create an identical visual and auditory experience for all. Could the ultimate cassette overcome these limitations? To do so, it would require no player, it would proceed at different rates for different users, and, most importantly, it would provide unique visual and auditory impressions. As you may have guessed, Asimov's point was that the ultimate cassette already existed in the form of a book. Although as the author of more than 500 books Asimov might be accused of reaching a self-serving conclusion, we find the basic logic compelling. The limitations he listed will continue to apply to each new technological advance. This is because every experience with text, regardless of format, results in unique interpretations, in personal takeaways that depend on prior knowledge and experience. As critic Edmund Wilson once put it, no two persons ever read the same book.

Of course, Asimov was describing a distinction that is now blurred. No one disputes that reading a descriptive passage will elicit mental images unique to each reader. But reading in digital environments often involves blended media, particularly in online contexts. Present-day news sites offer the traditional form of news stories, as prose texts, but they typically appear side-by-side with video background and commentary. Even proficient readers are faced with unparalleled choices – which path to follow first, which ones to steer clear of, and how to assemble the pieces to make sense of it all. When viewed in the context of the Internet as a whole, these choices can become overwhelming in their impact. By a series of clicks, we can follow the slightest inclination to satisfy a moment's whim. It is perhaps the dream of those with attention deficits and time on their hands – and a nightmare for others.

In a way, many of these choices have always been possible. Imagine sitting in a public library, pouring over a single print volume. The author makes a reference that interests you. You get up, find the second book, and locate the relevant text. But doing so takes time and requires effort and focus. Before you act, you must weigh the wisdom of pursuing the thread, and you make your decision on a cost-benefit basis. Is what you stand to gain worth the time and effort required? In an online setting, though, following an interesting lead is only a click away.

Although we certainly acknowledge that frivolous choices might occasionally distract us from constructive actions, we argue that the network of branching options available in digital settings (hypermedia) offers advantages that far outweigh the risks. In classroom settings, for example, the range of pathways can be constrained by teachers so that they can keep their students focused without eliminating the motivating power of choice. Internet projects are in fact well documented as conducive to learning and motivation to read (e.g., Miller, 2003).

Another affordance of digital texts is their potential to provide support for those who struggle. The notion of supported text has been the subject of research and speculation since the early days of desktop computing. Improved technology now brings the long-awaited potential of text supports closer to realization. Researchers such as Bridget Dalton (e.g., Dalton, 2014; Dalton & Proctor, 2008) have led pioneering efforts to test various supports, alone and in combination. The overarching idea is to embed within text digital scaffolds that give struggling readers the support they need to function independently. The architectural metaphor of "universal design" (Rose & Meyer, 2002) conveys the rationale perfectly:

> Every child has the right to access the general education curriculum. For students reading below grade level, this can be quite frustrating. Providing struggling readers with e-texts that offer Text to Speech (TTS) or human voice narration allows them to read, listen, and learn from the text without worrying about decoding or fluency issues. Their e-book reading might also contribute to vocabulary and comprehension development.
>
> (Dalton, 2014)

Table 8.2 lists the kinds of supports that can now be incorporated into texts that individuals might encounter in digital settings. You will easily discern that many could be helpful to proficient readers as well.

We've found two other metaphors helpful as well in framing the role of supported text. We can classify a support designed specifically to help struggling readers either as a scaffold or a prosthesis (McKenna & Walpole, 2007). A digital scaffold, such as pronunciations on demand, can eventually be removed when the reader's word recognition sufficiently improves. A digital prosthesis, in contrast, must continually be available for adequate comprehension. An extreme example is TTS for the visually impaired. Both prosthetic and scaffolded supports fall within the broad category of assistive technology.

Equipping a text with digital supports is a labor-intensive process. In our experience there are no shortcuts to first carefully analyzing a text and then customizing the supports included. Not long ago, one textbook publisher touted the electronic version of one of its titles. Among the features it contained were on-demand definitions of selected words. However, the company simply tied the definitions to the existing dictionary function without taking the time to suppress

TABLE 8.2 Digital Supports Useful to Struggling Readers and Writers (and Everyone Else)

Text to speech	Entire segments read aloud
	Single words pronounced on demand
Definitions	Meanings of unfamiliar words provided on demand
Language modifications	Simplified text, paraphrasing the original
	Translations into a second language
	American Sign Language pop-ups
Animated graphics	Diagrams that change
	Screencasts and podcasts that provide additional explanation
Background knowledge	Annotations and links that supply what an author incorrectly assumes that a reader knows
Writing	Voice recognition for dictation (speech-to-text)
	Spellcheckers/predictors
	Grammar checkers
Strategic aids	Highlighting
	Note-taking
	Bookmarking
	Searching
Metacognition aids	Comprehension checks

irrelevant definitions. Taking this shortcut presented already-struggling students with the task of choosing among competing meanings couched in academic language.

At their best, however, supported texts live up to the claim of universal access, and they can facilitate advanced readers as well. We created two mock-ups of supported texts that we invite you to explore. Each is based on a short canonical piece of English literature: "The Eagle," a poem by Tennyson, and "The Open Window," a short story by Saki. These examples contain a range of supports, though by no means all of those listed in Table 8.2! They appear in two of the many professional learning modules created with our colleague, Sharon Walpole, and are available free, on an open-access basis, at ComprehensiveReadingSolutions.com. To view the two texts, follow these steps.

For "The Open Window":

1. Go here: http://www.comprehensivereadingsolutions.com/reading-guides/
2. Click on Page 10.

For "The Eagle":

1. Go here: http://www.comprehensivereadingsolutions.com/technology/
2. Click on Page 9.

To sum up, the support afforded by digital scaffolds has the potential to be applied broadly, assisting individuals of all ages as needed. It is a proper focus of funded research and dissemination efforts.

The Economics of Digitization

When we compare the cost of an e-book with its print equivalent, the e-book is the hands-down winner. This simple economic argument is undeniably compelling. The e-book clearly passes the Cheerios Test, an approach proposed by Tom and David Gardner of the Motley Fool investment site to gauge the cost effectiveness of entertainment media, but we can easily extend it to the print-digital question. Basically, this hypothetical test presents the consumer with a choice between two ways of packaging the same product. Assuming that you were inclined to buy Cheerios, would you be more likely to purchase a 21-ounce family-size box at 19 cents an ounce or an 8.9-ounce individual-serving box at 52 cents an ounce? The point of the test is that when the product we want is held constant (Cheerios in this case), the packaging is likely to influence our choice of how to buy it.

Let's apply the test to books. If you wish to read a particular bestseller, the choice between the print and digital versions may well propel you toward a download. Your reasoning would be sound, as far as it goes, but the reality is that a number of contingencies may ultimately influence your choice. As Asimov would have noted, for example, e-books require hardware and print books do not. And bestsellers are often read on a one-off basis – once we finish we tend not to return. The digital choice is attractive in this case. But consider a student purchasing a textbook. The digital version is not as easy to navigate, let alone dog-ear and mark up. Considerations like these complicate the transition from print to pixels, as Rosenwald discovered to his surprise. Where books are concerned, the Cheerios Test is far from clear-cut. It turns out to be an essay exam, not true-false quiz.

This does not mean, however, that print versions offer enduring advantages that can never be surmounted. And it certainly doesn't mean that anything like a reversal is in the works. Anna Baddeley (2015) has charted trends in e-book sales that put to rest claims that print books are making a comeback. One of her points seems especially salient, the fact that Apple reports that its iBooks platform is adding a million new users a week.

Is Digital Reading Hazardous to Your Health?

Critics of digital literacy offer a number of arguments, ranging from persuasive to compelling to alarmist. It makes sense to consider them seriously. Mark Bauerlein (2008), as we noted in Chapter 4, contends that digitization has led to adolescents and young adults who lack the stamina and depth to engage long stretches of text. He collectively calls these individuals "the dumbest generation" and points to the lack of evidence that their involvement in digital literacy has resulted in the improvements some proponents have claimed:

> [H]owever much the apologists proclaim the digital revolution and hail teens and 20-year-olds for forging ahead, they haven't explained a critical paradox. If the young have acquired so much digital proficiency, and if digital technology exercises their intellectual faculties so well, then why haven't knowledge and skill levels increased accordingly? ... If the Information Age solicits quicker and savvier literacies, why do so many new entrants into college and work end up in remediation? Why do one-third of students who go straight to college out of high school drop out after one year?
>
> (p. 68)

Bauerlein points out that although engagement with text may be up overall, much of it involves social networking. Like Baron, he challenges the lack of depth associated with what passes for reading through social media, but he also raises the specter of its effects on emotional and intellectual development. He points to "peer absorption" (p. 133) as a particular threat where adolescents are concerned, and one that social media exploit.

This objection may seem at odds with another criticism of social media – that they tend to isolate individuals, removing them from the here and now. Sherry Turkle's (2011) turn of phrase, "alone together," sounds the alarm by recounting scenes that are all too commonplace: individuals glued to their devices in the presence of friends and family. It is one thing to be online in the presence of strangers – traveling by train or waiting in line – and quite another to use a device in situations where others expect one's attention. But the idea of being alone together conjures images of monastic solitude, when in fact nothing could be further from the truth. The person who reads emails or answers texts at a luncheon is socially connected, just not with those present in physical space. Given the rapidity of change, we believe that such apparent breaches of etiquette are examples of social conventions lagging behind technology. What matters more is the claim that engaging in social media may lead to maladjusted adults, and we can find no convincing evidence for it.

Yet another charge leveled at social media is that their frequent use may result in a shortened attention span. By facilitating, if not encouraging, fleeting engagement with text and other media, is it possible that our brains might be conditioned to function only in this manner? Dan Willingham, our colleague and a cognitive scientist at the University of Virginia, was asked in a recent NPR interview whether digital devices are in fact leading to shorter attention spans:

> There's no evidence they're keeping us from being able to focus. If you look at the way psychologists typically measure span of attention, there's no evidence that it's really declined in the last 50 years or so. The brain is plastic, but I think attention is so central to so much of what we do that it seems pretty improbable to me that attention span could shrink significantly. If it did, either we would all get really stupid or lots of other cognitive processes would have to adjust in some way.
> (*Raising Kids Who Want to Read*, NPR Interview, March 17, 2015)

Until convincing evidence emerges that reading in digital spaces entails real risks – whether emotional, social, or neurological – it seems pointless to militate against the tide of technological change. In any event, the matter appears to be moot given the direction in which the world is clearly moving. A far more prudent policy is to embrace the reality of change and champion the best outcomes. Doing so is especially important in schools.

The Message of the Standards

When we consider the workplace for which a society must endeavor to prepare its children, an environment now dominated by digital applications, it would seem ludicrous for educators to function exclusively in a traditional mode, privileging print above technology. Certainly the Common Core is explicit about appropriate expectations. At first blush, however, it may appear that the Standards ignore technology, for there is no strand bearing this label. This is because technology use is infused throughout the English language arts (ELA) standards (see McKenna, Conradi, Young, & Jang, 2013) – beginning in kindergarten! Of the 10 CCSS Anchor Standards for Writing in grades K–5, two require students to function in digital environments:

6. Use technology, including the Internet, to produce and publish writing and to interact and collaborate with others.
8. Gather relevant information from multiple print and digital sources, assess the credibility and accuracy of each source, and integrate the information while avoiding plagiarism.

As early as first grade, children are expected to begin acquiring navigational skills that are specific to Internet use:

> 5. Know and use various text features (e.g., headings, tables of contents, glossaries, electronic menus, icons) to locate key facts or information in a text.

By grade five, they are expected to integrate information across sources, and to use both print and digital sources to research the answers to questions:

> 7. Draw on information from multiple print or digital sources, demonstrating the ability to locate an answer to a question quickly or to solve a problem efficiently.

Implicit in these standards is the assumption that comprehension of text in print settings does not map perfectly onto digital environments. If comprehending were the same in each, the standards would not need to specify that students be proficient in both. The reality, however, is that online comprehension requires additional strategies that need to be taught and monitored in schools. These range from interpreting icons to navigating purposefully through a maze of links. Through the ORCA Project (Online Reading Comprehension Assessment), Donald Leu and his colleagues (Leu et al., 2015) have identified a well-thought-out taxonomy of these skills and they have developed practical ways of assessing them (http://www.orca.uconn.edu/). Their home page message puts the matter simply: "Online reading comprehension requires additional skills, beyond those required during offline reading comprehension." They credit French researcher Jean-François Rouet as being among the first to acknowledge the national importance of targeting such proficiencies: "Developing online reading comprehension skills is increasingly important for any nation determined to lead a global information economy."

We find this observation spot-on in defining a national policy that affords digital literacy the attention it merits. Our hope is that the impetus of the Common Core in the U.S. will foreground technology use so that schools fulfill their mission to prepare students for the world in which they will live and work. That some impetus was needed lies in the fact that language arts teachers have been among the most resistant to technology. (See Turbill and Murray, 2006, for an account of Australian primary teachers that is typical elsewhere.)

Adherence to such standards is a necessary but insufficient precondition for literacy to thrive in digital settings. Access is clearly vital, together with workforce opportunities for extending and refining skills. These factors are among the most important contributors to an adult population capable of applying digital literacy skills to solve problems. Table 8.3 presents PIACC rankings of countries in which the assessment of this proficiency was conducted in 2013.

TABLE 8.3[1] Percentage of 16–65 Year-olds in OECD Countries with Strong[2] Problem-Solving Skills in Technology-Rich Environments

Country	Percentage	Significance	Digital Literacy Reflected in National Secondary LA Standards
Sweden	44	Significantly Above Average	Yes
Finland	42		Yes
Netherlands	42		Yes
Norway	41		Yes
Denmark	39		Yes
Australia	38		Yes
Canada	37		NA[3]
Germany	36	Average	Yes
England/Northern Ireland	35		No
Flanders (Belgium)	35		No
Japan	35		No
Average	34		
Czech Republic	33		No
Austria	32		Yes
United States	31	Significantly Below Average	No[4]
Korea	30		No
Estonia	28		Yes
Slovak Republic	26		No[5]
Ireland	25		No
Poland	19		No

[1] We are indebted to Sarah Lupo for her assistance in researching these standards.
[2] Defined as Level 2 or 3 (see OECD, 2013).
[3] No national standards (provincial only).
[4] The Common Core was implemented in 2010, after these respondents were in school.
[5] The Digipedia 2020 initiative was launched in 2013.

As with all OECD assessments, national rankings are best viewed in light of whether they differ significantly from the OECD average – and in what direction. One surprise is that the two Asian countries did not perform as well as their PISA scores might lead us to predict. In any case, those with below-average means have much to consider.

Surely one consideration is the prominence given to digital literacy in schools. We undertook an analysis of the secondary language arts standards of the

17 countries other than the U.S. that participated in PIAAC 2013. Our findings are represented in the last column of Table 8.3. Although we cannot draw causal conclusions, the relationship between public school standards and later digital proficiency is plain to see.

Recommendations

1. Look to the overarching trends

A prudent policy is to avoid reading too much into the latest trends because of the likelihood that still newer developments will put society on a different course. (Remember MySpace? Atari? The Apple 2e?) The important goal is to note the overarching trends that subsume many of the developments we read about in news outlets. MySpace gave way to Facebook and Instagram, but the megatrend was social media, and this is what remains a driving force in tech applications.

2. Support the infrastructure needed to drive digital reading

Reading in digital environments requires ongoing commitment to a support system, from power grids to Internet access and bandwidth. It's true that the print publishing industry has an infrastructure of its own, but once a book is published its portability permits it to be read offline and off the grid, from children attending school in the developing world to hikers pausing along the Appalachian Trail. Unless care is exercised to maintain the infrastructure needed for digital reading, problems soon arise. A striking example is the Los Angeles Unified School District's project to provide iPads to every student. As the *Los Angeles Times* reported, failure to estimate the cost of upgrading the bandwidth needed to drive the project together with failure to account for advances that would render the devices obsolete have led to a boondoggle of mammoth proportions. "Doing innovative things involves risks," Karen Klein observed (2014), "but those risks should have been better calculated." We can to some extent sympathize with the LA planners. It isn't possible, after all, to foresee the many vagaries of technological advancement. But that is all the more reason to plan as carefully as possible for the "known unknowns," as a former defense secretary might have put it.

3. Support supported text

The potential of digital text supports is well worth the effort to further their development, particularly through low-cost apps that will make challenging texts accessible to some readers and a deeper appreciation available to all.

4. Target technology through educational standards

Demands of the twenty-first-century workplace require a corresponding demand for early preparation reflected in public school standards of learning. It is not enough that this focus involve STEM subjects; it must include the language arts. Teachers at every level must receive the professional development they need to implement such standards, and outcome measures must include digital competencies.

5. Let policy reflect the reality that reading in digital environments is here to stay

We must exercise caution with regard to minor reversals in the movement toward digital literacy. A quality separating the digital transition from the two before it is the speed of change. New developments occur so rapidly that it is hard to keep pace, and the fact that some of them falter has already defined a movement that is anything but smooth, advancing by fits and starts that keep us guessing. The fact that college students may be willing at present to pay more for print textbooks doesn't necessarily mark a reversal that will take us back to a collegiate world where print was dominant. Odds are, a market-driven economy will soon lead to new products designed to address the shortcomings voiced by consumers. Again, the larger picture is becoming clear, and occasional bumps in the road do not change its direction. As the novelist Macaulay once put it, "A single breaker may recede, but the tide is . . . coming in."

Note

1 An amusing video of the transition from scrolls to books portrays a Norwegian IT specialist attempting to explain the new format to a clueless monk. Similarities to the modern-day help desk are all too apparent. View it at https://www.youtube.com/watch?v=pQHX-SjgQvQ

References

Asimov, I. (1974). The ancient and the ultimate. *Journal of Reading, 17*, 264–271.
Baddeley, A. (2015, February 1). The ebook is dead. Long live the ebook. *The Guardian*. Available: http://www.theguardian.com/books/2015/feb/01/the-ebook-is-dead-long-live-print-digital-sales
Baron, N.S. (2015). *Words onscreen: The fate of reading in a digital world.* New York, NY: Oxford University Press.
Bauerlein, M. (2008). *The dumbest generation: How the digital age stupefies young Americans and jeopardizes our future.* New York, NY: Tarcher.
Birkerts, S. (1994). *The Gutenburg elegies.* New York, NY: Faber & Faber.
Dalton, B. (2014). E-text and e-books are changing the literacy landscape. *Phi Delta Kappan, 96*(3), 38–43.

Dalton, B., & Proctor, C.P. (2008). The changing landscape of text and comprehension in the age of new literacies. In J. Coiro, M. Knobel, C. Lankshear, & D. Leu (Eds.), *Handbook of research on new literacies* (pp. 297–324). Mahwah, NJ: Lawrence Erlbaum.

Harris, C. (2014). Fact or fiction? Libraries can thrive in the digital age. *Phi Delta Kappan, 96*(3), 20–25.

Klein, K. (2014, February 12). As the tab for L.A. Unified's iPads grows, so does the confusion. *Los Angeles Times*. Available: http://www.latimes.com/opinion/opinion-la/la-ol-lausd-ipad-20140211-story.html

Leu, D.J., Forzani, E., Rhoads, C., Maykel, C., Kennedy, C., & Timbrell, N. (2015). The new literacies of online research and comprehension: Rethinking the reading achievement gap. *Reading Research Quarterly, 50*, 37–59.

McKenna, M.C., Conradi, K., Young, C.A., & Jang, B.G. (2013). Technology and the Common Core Standards. In L.M. Morrow, T. Shanahan, & K.K. Wixson (Eds.), *Teaching with the Common Core Standards for English language arts, PreK-2* (pp. 152–169). New York, NY: Guilford Press.

McKenna, M.C., & Walpole, S. (2007). Assistive technology in the reading clinic: Its emerging potential. *Reading Research Quarterly, 42*, 140–145.

Miller, S.D. (2003). How high- and low-challenge tasks affect motivation and learning: Implications for struggling learners. *Reading and Writing Quarterly, 19*, 39–57.

OECD. (2013). *OECD skills outlook 2013: First results from the survey of adult skills* (Revised version). Paris, France: OECD. Available: http://www.keepeek.com/Digital-Asset-Management/oecd/education/oecd-skills-outlook-2013_9789264204256-en#page1

Rose, D., & Meyer, A. (2002). *Teaching every student in the digital age: Universal design for learning*. Alexandria, VA: ASCD. Available: http://www.cast.org/teachingeverystudent/

Rosenwald, M.S. (2015, February 22). Why digital natives prefer reading in print: Yes, you read that right. Washington Post. Available: http://www.washingtonpost.com/local/why-digital-natives-prefer-reading-in-print-yes-you-read-that-right/2015/02/22/8596ca86-b871-11e4-9423-f3d0a1ec335c_story.html

Shannon, C.E. (1948). A mathematical theory of communication. *Bell System Technical Journal, 27*, 379–423, 623–656.

Shannon, C.E., & Weaver, W. (1949). *The mathematical theory of communication*. Urbana, IL: University of Illinois Press.

Turbill, J., & Murray, J. (2006). Early literacy and new technologies in Australian schools: Policy, research, and practice. In M.C. McKenna, L.D. Labbo, R. Kieffer, & D. Reinking (Eds.), *International handbook of literacy and technology* (Vol. 2, pp. 93–108). Mahwah, NJ: Lawrence Erlbaum.

Turkle, S. (2011). *Alone together: Why we expect more from technology and less from each other*. New York, NY: Basic Books.

Willingham, D.T. (2015, March 17). *Raising kids who want to read*, NPR Interview. Text available: http://www.npr.org/blogs/ed/2015/03/17/387774026/q-a-raising-kids-who-want-to-read

Zickuhr, K., & Rainie, L. (2014). *E-reading rises as device ownership jumps*. Washington, DC: Pew Research Center. Available: http://pewinternet.org/Reports/2014/E-Reading-Update.aspx

9

OVERCOMING THE SES/LITERACY RELATIONSHIP – MAKING EXCEPTIONS THE RULE

It has long been known that economic advantage is associated with academic success. The question of whether it *causes* success has long been debated. Many contend that although the relationship is sometimes causal, as when affluent parents buy their children books, take them on background-building trips, or hire tutors, the relationship is more often tied to other factors, such as level of parental education and the cultural views parents harbor toward education in general, and literacy in particular. In this chapter, we challenge the assumption that poverty and literacy are inevitably bound. Examples of individuals, schools, and countries that are exceptions to the relationship do exist and they have important lessons to teach. We will examine them here.

A brief refresher on the distinction between a correlational and a causal relationship is warranted first, however. A correlation is simply an indicator of the degree to which two variables change together. They may be positively correlated, meaning that as one variable increases, the other does as well. Conversely, they may be negatively related, meaning that when one variable increases, the other decreases. For example, when the temperature goes up, the amount of electricity used to cool homes and businesses goes up. There is a positive correlation. On the other hand, when the outside temperature goes down, the amount of fuel to run heaters and furnaces goes up. In this case, there is a negative correlation. The important point is that when one variable changes, so does the other.

Cause and effect is a particular kind of correlational relationship. Not only does one variable change as the other does, it *causes* the change to occur. In a cause-and-effect relationship one variable has a direct impact of on another. Use of a vaccine is one example. When it is administered, incidence of the disease declines. Vaccination and cases are negatively correlated, but they are also causally connected as experimental studies have revealed.

Difficulties occur when we attribute causation to a relationship that is merely correlational. Consider this example: A city's crime rate is positively correlated with the number of churches it contains. A novice statistics student might be tempted to conclude that the presence of churches somehow contributes to a higher crime rate. This conclusion is counterintuitive, to say the least. A much more likely explanation is the city's size. Large cities tend to have higher crime rates and they also contain more churches simply because of their size. A valuable rule of thumb is this: Correlation is necessary for causation but it is not sufficient in itself.

The importance of understanding the difference between correlational and causal relationships is clear as we look at examples of the relationship between socioeconomic status and literacy level. The connection is not necessarily a causal one, but rather one in which both variables are associated with a multitude of other factors that may cause both of them to change, just as population density affects *both* the number of crimes and the number of churches. Because human nature does not manifest itself in a confined laboratory environment, but in the real world, it is not easy to experimentally control for all of the correlated variables to determine which of them are causally related to one another.

It is also important to note that the SES-literacy relationship is anything but absolute. That is, a change in one is not associated with an "identical" change in the other. Whether socioeconomic status and literacy are simply correlated or exist in a cause-and-effect relationship, the correlation is far from perfect. In fact, there are many examples of non-conforming data points in the relationship between the two. In some of the poorest of homes with the least emphasis on school achievement and the least concern for books and learning, there are individuals who grow academically, eventually becoming highly literate and reaching elevated levels of achievement. Similarly, even in cities where the schools, in general, are beset by high crime and poverty, and in which achievement levels lag well below the national average, there are schools that excel. Finally, at the macro level, there are countries whose citizens achieve proficiency well beyond the level we might expect on the basis of their economic vitality. Such countries demonstrate the takeaway we suggested in Chapter 3, that socioeconomic status isn't a deal breaker. Later in this chapter, we will consider examples of outliers at each of these levels.

Evidence of an SES-achievement connection is so widespread that it is difficult to select among the many studies documenting it. Perhaps the most frequently cited example in the early U.S. research literature is the Coleman Report (Coleman et al., 1967). This report has been interpreted in various ways, but the essential finding was that socioeconomic status, variously defined as home and family background, economic vitality of the family, etc., was a greater determinant of student achievement than the school a student attended. This is not to say that there was no correlation between schooling and achievement, but instead that other factors accounted for a greater part of the variability. As we noted, this phenomenon has been borne out in hundreds, perhaps thousands, of studies, conducted in different societies over the years. Kahlenberg (2001) noted the following:

> [A]fter conducting what was then the second largest social science research project in history – involving 600,000 children in 4,000 schools nationally – Coleman and his colleagues issued Equality of Educational Opportunity ... it contained a number of surprising findings. First, the disparities in funding between schools attended by blacks and whites were far smaller than anticipated. Second, funding was not closely related to achievement; family economic status was far more predictive. Third, a different kind of resource – peers – mattered a great deal. Going to school with middle-class peers was an advantage, while going to school with lower-class peers was a disadvantage, above and beyond an individual's family circumstances ... Today, in public memory, Coleman's report has been largely reduced to the second proposition: that "family matters more than schooling."
>
> (pp. 55–56)

Coleman and his colleagues went further in noting the following:

> Schools are successful only insofar as they reduce the dependence of a child's opportunities upon his social origins (1966, p. 72) ... This is a task far more ambitious than has ever been attempted by any society; not just to offer, in a passive way, equal access to educational resources, but to provide an educational environment that will free a child's potentialities for learning from the inequalities imposed upon him by the accident of birth into one or another home and social environment.
>
> (1967, p. 21)

This "accident of birth" involves a two-edged sword: slower development of academic skills, such as delayed letter recognition and phonological awareness, in comparison with more affluent children (Morgan, Farkas, Hillemeier, & Maczuga, 2009) and attendance in schools that are often under-resourced (Aikens & Barbarin, 2008). The cumulative effects of these disadvantages are well documented and predictable. In 2007, the high school dropout rate among persons 16–24 years old was highest in low-income families (16.7 percent) and lowest for high-income families (3.2 percent) (National Center for Education Statistics, 2008).

The prevalence of the SES-literacy relationship aside, there are exceptions. Among them are children now described as *resilient*. Debra Viadero (1995), writing in *Education Week* two decades ago, noted that a "growing body of research suggests that a fair number of children touched by adversity fare reasonably well.... These patterns of resiliency don't look the same in all children," she went on to observe, however. "But experts say a handful of common factors do tend to build on one another in multiple and complex ways throughout the course of a lifetime." For example, they often discover conducive environments like organizations and clubs.

But generalizing across cases is difficult, particularly if our interest lies in shaping policy to facilitate resilience. Nevertheless, we believe the key to understanding exceptions to the relationship between socioeconomic status and achievement level lies in real-life examples. There are lessons to be learned at three levels: the individual, the school, and the nation.

Individuals

Coleman's observations and Kahlenberg's comments on them illustrate how strong the perception of the SES-literacy relationship is, and also the inadvertent tendency to regard it as an ineluctable fact of education. One consequence, in the words of Michael Gerson, can be the "soft bigotry of low expectations," an acceptance by educators of the futility of fighting against the rule that demography is destiny. The key lies in closely considering exceptions to this rule – the examples of resilient individuals.

Khadijah Williams

Millicent Pierre-Louis, in a 2014 blog post entitled, "Ten Students Who Overcame Massive Obstacles to Achieve Their Dream of an Education," profiles the example of Khadijah Williams:

> By the time she turned 18, Khadijah Williams had attended twelve schools in as many years. She had lived in shelters, in parks and in motels, never in a permanent residence for more than a few months. She had endured the leering of pimps and drug dealers, and the tauntings of students at a dozen schools who pegged her as "different."... at age 18, Khadijah had also been accepted at Harvard University. Homeless since early childhood, Khadijah struggled all her life to hide her circumstances from teachers and fellow students. At age 9 she placed in the 99th percentile on a state exam, and her teacher told her she was "gifted." From that moment forward, Khadijah decided to do whatever it took to keep herself in that category. "I was so proud of being smart I never wanted people to say, "You got the easy way out because you're homeless," she told the LA Times. "I never saw it as an excuse."
>
> By her sophomore year of high school, she realized that she could not succeed in getting the education she dreamed of without getting help to go beyond what her current school could offer. She talked to teachers and

counselors who helped her apply to summer community college classes, scholarships, and enrichment programs. And in 11th grade, when she enrolled at Jefferson High School, she decided to complete the rest of her career there – a decision that meant taking a bus each morning at 4 a.m. and not getting home until 11 p.m.

When it came time to apply for college, Khadijah finally told the whole story of her life, including how difficult it had been to keep up at school, in her application essay. By focusing not on the hardships she endured, but rather on the lessons and skills she learned from them, she was accepted into Harvard.

Once Khadijah felt ready to tell her story, it won her notice not only from college admissions boards, but also from the news media, including Oprah, who profiled Khadijah on her show.

(Para. 1–4)

Inspiring though it is, Khadijah's story is not just an exception to the rule, but one likely to evoke a dismissive response due to its rarity. To those who would discount it, we caution that the real lesson lies in the conclusions we can reach across cases.

Oprah Winfrey

Oprah Winfrey, born in rural Mississippi to teenage parents, one a maid and the other a barber, led anything but an advantaged life as a child. After her mother left to go north, she was raised by her grandmother and they lived under the poorest conditions. While her grandmother could not give her material things, however, she did impart a strong set of religious values and a belief in God, and she taught her to read and write before she entered school.

During her upbringing and education, she moved from her grandmother's home and went north to rejoin her mother in Milwaukee. She then caromed back and forth between her mother's and her father's home in Tennessee. This period was marred by far more than a lack of permanence. It included multiple instances of sexual abuse, a teenage pregnancy at the age of 14 with a child that died soon after birth, and various economic hardships. Through it all, she was an excellent student. She was elected school president and won a scholarship to Tennessee State University. She chose to go to work for a television station instead of graduating and eventually became a talk-show host, first in Baltimore and then in Chicago. *Bam Chicago* later became the *Oprah Winfrey Show*. In the process, Oprah has become one of the most successful media personalities in history, an Academy Award nominee, and one of the wealthiest African Americans.

Oprah's story is a portrait of resilience not only in the face of economic hardship, but in response to grievous injustice suffered in her youth. The latter challenge might well have proved insurmountable to even an affluent child. If we can distil a single important lesson from her success, it is that there is hope even when the effects of poverty are compounded by additional factors. Any examination of outliers from the poverty-achievement norm must account for the ironic possibility that other obstacles were overcome as well.

Malala Yousafzai

Next we return to the case of Malala Yousafzai, whom we first mentioned in Chapter 1 as an exemplar of the sacrifice an individual might make to achieve literacy. The youngest winner of the Nobel Peace Prize, she is a courageous young woman who defied the efforts of the Taliban in Pakistan to deprive her of educational opportunities. Her resistance occasioned a live address at the U.N., a blog entitled, *Diary of a Pakistani School Girl*, sponsored by the BBC, and a lengthy explanation of her circumstances in a 2015 book, *I am Malala: The Girl Who Stood up for Education and Was Shot by the Taliban*. Malala's younger years were not spent in poverty. Though not wealthy, her family was intact and included her mother, father, and brothers. The family valued education, and Malala's father, who had studied at Jahanzeb College, founded in the early 1950s, was running his own school even when Malala was born. He had established an educational enterprise that had grown to serve over a thousand girls and boys. Politically, the area of Pakistan where her family lived had grown relatively tranquil after the offensive to push back the Taliban. The Swat Region had a proud history of trying to educate all of its children. It was in this environment, one relatively conducive to learning, that Malala grew up.

She attended school and spoke up for her rights. She stated openly that she did not want her life to be imprisoned by the four walls of a house, the fate of many a Pakistani woman. She noted that it was rather easy for low-skilled boys to find work outside the home but that females were largely confined to work that they could do inside. She was not content to settle for this traditional role. She wanted an education and a career. These high aspirations were shared by many of the females at Malala's school.

All of this changed dramatically on October 9, 2012. Two Taliban stopped the bus on which Malala was traveling home from school. They asked the students to point her out. The fame she had acquired through speaking out on behalf of education, especially for females, was her undoing. Though no one answered the Taliban, several looked towards Malala, and at that point she was shot in the head. The bullet traveled down her neck and lodged in her back.

Her eventual recovery has been well documented. It involved stays at three different medical facilities in Pakistan, and eventually a move to Birmingham, England. The outrage caused by the incident brought her international acclaim and furthered her role as a spokesperson for the education of females.

Malala provides an interesting contrast with Oprah. In Oprah's case, a combination of poverty and social factors within the family posed formidable obstacles. Malala faced neither of these. The obstacle that confronted her was social in nature but it resided in the larger context of her culture rather than in her family.

Deval Patrick

A fourth high-profile outlier is Deval Patrick, whose autobiography, *A Reason to Believe* (2011), recounts the inspiring events of what he calls his "improbable life," an apt phrase to say the least. Deval and his sister, Rhonda, were raised by their mother and grandparents. Their mother had dropped out of high school to be with their father, Pat, a musician. They married, but soon after the children were born Pat left to follow his career. The family moved from place to place on Chicago's South Side.

Deval attended Mary C. Terrell Elementary School, named for one of the first African American women to earn a college degree, and later a founding member of the NAACP. By his own recollection, he did well at Terrell. "School came easy to me," he writes (2011, p. 26). Deval's challenge, however, lay outside of school. The family was living in Robert Taylor Homes at that point, one of the most notorious housing projects in the United States. The complex extended some 15 blocks and housed over 27,000 residents though it was built to accommodate 11,000. Drug deals were prevalent and gunfire not uncommon. In the early 2000s the Homes were demolished.

It was in this environment that Deval Patrick succeeded in school, first at Terrell then at DuSable Middle School. But the trek between school and home was a daily gauntlet. He was harassed, jumped, and robbed on numerous occasions. In the end, it was worth the trouble. In his autobiography, he discusses a particular teacher "who would radically broaden my vision of what was possible." She was something of an anomaly herself – a white woman coming to the South Side to teach. He observed that many of the students were discovering that they could intimidate whites on a regular basis, and they attempted to do so with this teacher. She continued undeterred, however, serving in Deval's case not only as a teacher but as a broker matching him with options. She connected him with the Better Chance Foundation, an organization that ultimately enabled him to move on with a scholarship to the largely white, and very wealthy, Milton Academy in Massachusetts. From there the path led to Harvard College and then Harvard Law School.

Deval Patrick has since led a storied career as an activist, serving, among other things, as an attorney with the NAACP Legal Defense in Education Fund. President Clinton appointed him as U.S. Assistant Attorney General for the Civil Rights Division of the Department of Justice. He was later elected governor of Massachusetts, serving two terms, from 2007 to 2015. Deval L. Patrick has led an improbable life indeed, far eclipsing the level of achievement we might have predicted based on his socioeconomic status. His story has elements of the others', but the combination is unique. Like Oprah, he lacked the stability of a two-parent family. Like Malala, he faced adverse circumstances between home and school. Like Khadijah, he was aided by a teacher who saw within him something exceptional.

Conclusions from Individuals

Two relevant dimensions contribute to the departure of these individuals from the expected relationship between academic achievement and socioeconomic status. The first is a determination to succeed, a quality that must ultimately arise from within. The second is facilitation by others, who serve as a source of motivation and support after recognizing a child's potential. With Khadijah Williams, this occurred when a teacher took her aside, told her that she was gifted, and encouraged her to work hard. In Oprah Winfrey's case it was a father who instilled a sense of self-discipline and a grandmother who helped her acquire a set of positive values. Malala Yousafzai enjoyed the support of an educated family, who transmitted to her an appreciation for the value of learning and who encouraged her to persevere in an adverse cultural context. Finally, Deval Patrick, grew up in difficult circumstances, but school was a safe haven where he could develop his abilities. It was also a place where he received the support of a remarkable teacher, herself a resilient individual.

Schools

Schools that succeed despite the lack of social and economic advantage have long been the holy grail of educational researchers. If their success can be traced to qualities replicable elsewhere, then scaling up might be feasible. That, at least, has been the rationale. And such schools do exist, in fact, though prying loose their secrets is a complex task. If any conclusion can be safely reached, it is that there is a connection between these schools and the creation of resilient students like those we've profiled.

In their book, *Turning High-Poverty Schools into High-Performance Schools,* Parrett and Budge (2012) clarify the situation:

> As a nation, are we content that 70 percent of our entering 9th graders read below grade level? Is it acceptable that one out of every three minority students attends a high school where 40 percent of the students drop out? Are we willing to continue spending $2.6 billion a year replacing teachers, half of whom choose to leave the profession before they begin their sixth year in a classroom? . . . While our crisis is one that is being successfully countered

in hundreds of public schools across the United States. These schools enroll high proportions of underachieving children and adolescents who live in poverty but have reversed long-standing traditions of low achievement and high dropout rates. They are models of the possible, where the mind-set of it's impossible has been proven wrong.

(p. 1)

In Chapters 4 and 5, we summarized recent results of the National Assessment of Educational Progress in grades 4 and 8. Although the headline-grabbing findings are at the state and national levels, the connection between poverty and achievement is clear through a more fine-grained analysis. Indeed, irrespective of the achievement measure used, the relationship is a dependable finding. For example, children who do not qualify for lunch subsidies regularly outperform those who qualify for reduced-price lunches, who in turn score higher than those who qualify for free lunches (National Center for Education Statistics, 2013).

Approaches to reform have been implemented with varying degrees of success. Borman and Overman (2004) explored several models of promoting academic success in elementary mathematics. Not surprisingly, the most effective actively fostered resilience. Specifically, they noted that "the most powerful school characteristics for promoting resiliency were represented by the supportive school community model, which unlike the other school models, included elements that actively shielded children from adversity" (p. 177).

In a Canadian study, D'Angiulli, Siegel and Hertzman (2004), observed that the relationship between socioeconomic status and achievement was substantial in kindergarten but that as students progressed through the years the relationship declined, and in some cases was not statistically significant by grade three. In short, they noted that the school literacy program might have attenuated that association.

Other studies of schools that defy the SES-achievement relationship indicate that principals are the most important factor. One report indicates that among New York City's poorest schools and neighborhoods, 14 of the highest achieving were marked by hard-charging principals willing to work long hours to improve teaching and learning (Archibold, 1999).

Such studies give an inkling of the complexity of the problem and some glimmers of replicable strategies with the potential to inform policy. Inspecting a few examples of against-the-odds schools can deepen our appreciation of the issues.

Hp Keluskar Marg Municipal School No. 2

It is hard to imagine a more challenging environment in which to attend school than the slums of Mumbai. The Municipal Schools serve children who are among the poorest in the country, and given the need for child labor, poverty itself is a disincentive to attend school. Sometimes parents send their children to school only to receive a midday meal or obtain free uniforms. To make school an attractive place for more acceptable reasons, a series of schools have been jointly sponsored by UNICEF and the Municipal Corporation of Greater Mumbai, with additional support from McKinsey & Company and the NAANDI Foundation.

School No. 2 is an instructive example. Children who study there work almost exclusively in cooperative groups. They do so partly out of a belief that learning occurs best in this manner and partly because the numbers of students are so high that they must be relied on to teach each other.

The first, and one of the most important, goals of the school is simply to get children to attend. On a given day, the attendance rate is about 70 percent. The goal is to raise this figure to 90 percent, and to reduce the dropout rate to less than 5 percent.

The school follows a standard curriculum, but also allows for substantive variation under the School Excellence Programme. The syllabus is the same as that of all other government schools, but extra materials for practice are provided. Teachers receive professional development ("forum" training) twice a year plus on-the-job assistance from instructional coaches.

Parents also play a significant role. Numerous counseling and guidance services are provided on a variety of topics, including parenting. In addition, a parents' committee helps keep parents involved with teachers while encouraging attendance and school success.

Gauging achievement must be viewed in relative terms. While the academic success rate is still a work-in-progress, available data document a 19 percent improvement in reading skill development. Observers witness students sitting in groups, engaged in productive learning activities. The school seems poised to become the first to achieve a targeted 25 percent improvement rate.

School administrators recognize the challenges, of course, but are committed to ensuring that teachers receive the professional learning they require. Together with program coaches, they acknowledge their efforts on a continuing basis. Teachers receive annual awards and recognition, and also smaller acknowledgements on a monthly, and even daily, basis.[1]

In short, this is a school whose faculty and administration are working hard to overcome formidable obstacles in order to improve the achievement of students living in extreme poverty. Instructional growth is the result of a basic approach well suited to the context, an approach that involves professional development, parent involvement, curricular flexibility, side-by-side coaching, and collaborative learning.

Lane Technical High School

Lane Technical High School, in Chicago, is a large public school with an impressive history of student success. When it opened in 1908, Lane's mission was largely technical in nature, offering programs in areas that included foundry, welding, machining, electrical work, and similar fields. By the early 1930s, Lane had grown to over 7,000 students and a new building opened in 1934. At that time the school was all male, and on opening day 9,000 boys marched from Wrigley Field (then Cubs Park) to the new school.

Today, Lane Tech is co-educational and serves 4,000 students. It still maintains a technology-oriented curriculum, emphasizing STEM areas and offering advanced placement programs. The largest single ethnic group is Hispanic (40%), and approximately 60 percent of all students receive lunch subsidies. Lane operates as a magnet, attracting students from across the city. Consequently, it can be argued that the high performance of students is due in part to the volunteer nature of the student body. Given the history of American magnet programs, however, this factor seems unlikely to account for the exceptional achievement at Lane. In 2014, 93 percent of the students met the state's standard on the 11th-grade Prairie State Achievement Examination (PSAE) Reading Assessment, compared with only 38 percent in the district and 56 percent statewide. Scores for math and science are similar. In 2014, Lane Tech Middle School (the feeder for Lane Tech High) outranked 99.5 percent of the middle schools in Illinois, and Lane Tech High School exceeded 99.1 percent of the high schools in Illinois.

It hardly bears mentioning that parents, students, and teachers take justifiable pride in what they have accomplished. A history of high performance has contributed to a culture of success, and we suspect that this is key to explaining Lane's outlier status. In today's parlance, there is now a distinctive Lane "brand," a signature quality that all involved recognize and that guides the rapid acculturation of new-hires: "Welcome to Lane. This is how we teach here."

Leap

Next consider the example of the three-building set of schools known as "Leap." These are part of a new approach to what might be considered "bare-bones private schools" in South Africa. In a *New York Times* article, Dugger (2010) notes that "[i]n fact, researchers discovered far more of these low-fee private schools exist than official statistics suggest." Surprisingly, they noted that "public school teachers dissatisfied with their own workplaces were among the parents of students in these schools."

Leap schools have extended days during the week, with classes running from 8:15 a.m. to 5:15 p.m., and continuing on Saturday mornings. Extra time is spent on math, science, and English. Students also have orientation classes, where they talk freely about personal problems that might cause them to discontinue their education.

Dugger chronicles the experience of Gcobani Mndini, a 17-year-old male, who, prior to enrolling in the school, was a gang member. He spent his time stealing, fighting, drinking, and smoking marijuana. Needless to say, Gcobani had never felt that he truly fit into a school setting – until he found Leap. After that, his aberrant behavior vanished. His story is typical of the many students who have achieved success in these schools. At this writing, data are being compiled to formally document the impact of Leap on achievement and school finishing. Meanwhile, the schools continue to engage students in productive learning. If we were to speculate about an effective ingredient in the Leap recipe, it would be the fact that Leap has made the nurturing of adolescents a central priority. Students know that teachers care about them, and whenever that occurs engagement tends to follow.

Conclusions from Schools

Noreen Connell and her colleagues, in *Beating the Odds: High-Achieving Elementary Schools in High-Poverty Neighborhoods*, examined 14 schools that achieved academic success despite economic disadvantage. Their conclusion was succinct and hopeful: "Socioeconomic status is not a destiny" (quoted in Archibold, 1999). While there were many differences among the 14 schools, there were also common attributes. The schools were characterized by "a principal who managed instruction; mastery of curriculum by principal and teachers; a code of professional respect in caring for children; a no-nonsense communication style on the part of the principal; open-door classrooms in which teachers were freely observed; parent engagement; and attention and rewards for good academic performance" (Connell et al., 1999, pp. 5–6).

We can extend her list by distilling lessons from the schools we've profiled. Successful schools provide a safe haven for learning. The Leap schools help students escape the streets into a nurturing environment where they are given an education and a future. Development of the most important human resource, teachers, is essential for schools to overcome the long odds of trying to turn low-income students into high achievers. The schools in Mumbai emphasize the professional development teachers require to best serve their students. Lane Tech exemplifies the power of high expectations and the synergy of creating a true culture of learning and an enduring brand.

Countries

Just as individual students and schools tend to conform to the fateful relationship between literacy and socioeconomic status, such is the case with countries. This conclusion makes sense for the simple reason that countries comprise individuals and schools. As we will see, however, there are instructive outliers at the national level as well.

To identify them, we will return to the international assessments discussed in Chapter 3—specifically, the scores from PISA 2012 and PIRLS 2011, which we will compare with an expected literacy level, based on socioeconomic status. Here, SES is defined as the per capita gross national product as of 2013. This is a commonly used indicator of a country's economic standing, in essence a proxy for standard of living. We recognize that our approach is simplistic in that a complex of other factors impact standard of living, but it works for these purposes. Gross Domestic National Product (GDNP) is calculated by summing the value of all final goods and services produced during a given period. The per capita GDNP is then determined by dividing GDNP by the total population of the country. (We will also consider a few other definitions of socioeconomic status.)

While most of the assessments that link socioeconomic status to literate behavior, in particular PIRLS and PISA test scores, use a financial indicator as an index for socioeconomic status, there are some studies, such as Chiu and Chow (2010), in which researchers define SES as family cultural capital. Numerous other indicators have been used as well, but here PIRLS and PISA scores are compared based on the per capita GDNP of individual countries.

Table 9.1 presents results from PISA and PIRLS, together with per capita GDNP. (In our analysis we excluded countries that participated only in PIRLS.) Singapore is a country that adheres, fairly directly, to the socioeconomic status and literacy achievement correlation. Singapore's mean score of 542 on PISA made it the highest-ranked country, its PIRLS mean score of 567 made it the fourth-ranked country, and its per capita income made it the fourth-richest.

In Table 9.2, we have identified countries near the endpoints of wealth and literacy. The vertical axis relates to an informal analysis of achievement test scores. The scores either include both PISA and PIRLS scores, or only PISA scores if the country did not participate in PIRLS. Higher-scoring countries fall above the mid-line and lower-scoring ones below. Again, our analysis is simply an informal examination of the results from Table 9.1. Recognizing that "richer" and "poorer," and "higher" and "lower" are relative terms, we can nonetheless identify countries that either conform with or depart from, to a substantial degree, the anticipated strong relationship between literacy and socioeconomic status. Countries listed as poorer are not always the very poorest countries, but they are definitely lower in per capita GDNP than we would anticipate on the basis of their literacy scores. The same reasoning applies to wealthier nations.

Examining the four cells, we see that countries such as Singapore and the Netherlands have relatively high income and do well on the standardized tests. They conform to the anticipated relationship. Singapore we have already noted. The Netherlands is 11th on PISA, 13th on PIRLS scores, and 8th in terms of income level.

Some countries conform, but in the negative direction. They are poorer and do not score well on literacy assessments. They include Indonesia, ranking 55th (of 57) on PISA and 43rd (next to last) on PIRLS. This country was also 58th (again, next to last) on income level, ahead of only Vietnam.

TABLE 9.1 PISA and PIRLS Results Compared with Per Capita GDNP[1]

Country	PISA 2012 Score	PISA 2012 Ranking	PIRLS (2011) Score	PIRLS (2011) Ranking	GDNP (2013)[2] Score	GDNP (2013)[2] Ranking
Singapore	542	1	567	4	62,400	4
Japan	538	2			37,100	21
Korea	536	3			33,200	24
Finland	524	4	568	2	39,812	18
Canada	523	5	548	12	43,247	15
Ireland	523	6	552	11	46,140	9
Poland	518	7	526	28	23,649	36
Estonia	516	8			25,462	34
Australia	512	9	529	26	43,544	13
New Zealand	512	10	531	24	34,826	23
Netherlands	511	11	546	13	46,298	8
Switzerland	509	12			56,565	6
Belgium	509	13	506	32	41,663	17
Germany	508	14	541	17	44,469	12
Vietnam	508	15			5,294	59
France	505	16	520	29	37,872	20
Norway	504	17	507	31	65,461	3
United Kingdom	499	18			38,452	19
United States	498	19	556	6	53,042	7
Denmark	496	20	554	7	43,445	14
Czech Republic	493	21	545	14	28,770	28
Austria	490	22			45,493	10
Italy	490	23	541	19	35,597	22
Latvia	489	24			22,560	40
Luxembourg	488	25			90,410	2
Portugal	488	26	541	20	26,759	30
Spain	488	27	513	30	32,925	25
Hungary	488	28	539	21	23,482	37
Israel	486	29	541	18	32,760	26
Croatia	485	30	553	9	21,366	42
Iceland	483	31			41,939	16

Country	PISA 2012 Score	PISA 2012 Ranking	PIRLS (2011) Score	PIRLS (2011) Ranking	GDNP (2013)[2] Score	GDNP (2013)[2] Ranking
Sweden	483	32	542	16	45,148	11
Slovenia	481	33	530	25	28,996	27
Lithuania	477	34	528	27	25,467	33
Greece	477	35			25,705	32
Russian Federation	475	36	568	3	24,114	35
Turkey	475	37			19,020	44
Slovak Republic	463	38	535	22	26,643	31
Cyprus	449	39	494	34	28,224	29
Serbia	446	40			13,020	52
United Arab Emirates	442	41	439	41	59,845	5
Thailand	441	42			14,394	49
Chile	441	43			21,911	41
Costa Rica	441	44			13,876	51
Romania	438	45	502	33	18,991	45
Bulgaria	436	46	532	23	15,732	47
Mexico	424	47			16,463	46
Montenegro	422	48			14,132	50
Uruguay	411	49			19,594	43
Brazil	410	50			15,037	48
Tunisia	404	51			11,124	56
Colombia	403	52			12,424	53
Jordan	399	53			11,785	54
Malaysia	398	54			23,338	38
Indonesia	396	55	428	43	9,561	58
Albania	394	56			10,374	57
Kazakhstan	393	57			23,211	39
Qatar	388	58	425	44	136,727	1
Peru	384	59			11,774	55

[1]Missing data indicate that a country did not participate in a given assessment.
[2]In USD.

TABLE 9.2 A 2 × 2 Comparison of Wealth and Literacy

	GDNP Per Capita	
Literacy Scores	Richer	Poorer
Higher	*Netherlands* *Singapore*	*Finland* *Korea* *Poland* *Vietnam*
Lower	*Norway* *Sweden* *Qatar* *U.A.E.*	*Indonesia* *Peru*

Our principal interest, of course, was identifying countries that depart from the expected relationship. Norway, Sweden, Qatar, and United Arab Emirates are all countries where economic level is significantly greater than their PISA and PIRLS scores. Norway has the third highest socioeconomic status, yet ranked 17th on PISA and 31st on PIRLS. Similarly, Sweden is the 11th highest country in terms of socioeconomic status, yet ranked 32nd on PISA and 16th on PIRLS. Qatar was 58th (next to last) on PISA, and 44th (last) on PIRLS, yet it is the single richest country. Similarly, United Arab Emirates ranked 41st on PISA and 41st on PIRLS but was the fifth-richest participating country. The cases of Norway and Sweden are somewhat similar to one another in that in recent years they have admitted large numbers of immigrants who speak a second language. In contrast, Qatar and the United Arab Emirates are countries whose per capita GDNP scores are partly attributable to a relatively small population, enriched by extreme mineral wealth.

The quadrant of greatest interest is the upper right. Here we find those countries for which achievement test scores are higher than expected based on SES. This diverse group includes Korea, Finland, Poland, and Vietnam. Of the four, the country with the lowest economic ranking is Vietnam, and yet it ranked 15th, well above the median, on PISA. Vietnam is beginning to align itself with the Asian education culture, which, of course, also includes South Korea. South Korea ranked third on PISA (it did not participate in PIRLS) and was 24th in GDNP. Finland was 4th and 2nd in PISA and PIRLS, respectively, but 18th in GDNP, while Poland was 7th and 28th on these assessments, and yet 36th in GDNP.

These four countries are positive outliers in much the same way as the individuals and schools we described earlier in this chapter. Their educational attainment runs counter to their economic status, and for this reason they warrant closer scrutiny. Because we have profiled Korea and Finland in Chapter 3 and Korea again in Chapter 4, we will examine Poland and Vietnam in some detail here.

Vietnam

Vietnam is one of the more interesting countries in terms of the quality of its educational system. Javier Luque (2014) states the matter clearly:

> Vietnam's impressive results in the 2012 Program for International Student Assessment (PISA) became a big surprise following their publication last December. Vietnam ranked 17 among 61 participating countries and its mathematics score was 511, which is higher than the 494 Organisation for Economic Co-operation and Development (OECD) countries' average. This is particularly relevant because Vietnam is one of the worst off countries socioeconomically speaking.

In the 2013 OECD report *Ready to Learn: Students' Engagement, Drive and Self-Beliefs*, an analysis of PISA results, it is noted that one of the key elements of a successful country, educationally speaking, is "a culture that values effort, perseverance, and motivation" (p. 188). Vietnam is clearly such a country. Luque (2014) reported that: "[i]n 91 percent of all schools, questionnaire respondents admitted that parents exert pressure for students to improve their learning" and that "Vietnamese students themselves also highly value their math education." Such qualities, he concluded, "allow us to visualize an education system that upholds a great commitment from all actors involved to improve its education results, and whose experience could possibly be replicated in other countries."

Though still poor, the economy is being improved by developing substantial oil reserves and other natural resources. The food export industry is also strong, particularly in the areas of seafood and rice. This economic growth is particularly notable considering that Vietnam's economy had been severely damaged by years of war. From 1975 forward, the first period of relative tranquility since French colonization has involved the development of an economy that has expanded to include light manufacturing and government investment in a wide range of areas. Tourism has also grown steadily as Vietnam becomes a safer, more productive country. The nation seems poised to join the rest of the Pacific Rim as an economic force, propelled in part by an exemplary educational system.

Poland

Following World War II and the Yalta Conference, Poland was left under Russian control. The Russians and the Germans had, of course, fought a considerable part of the War in Poland, and over 20 percent of its pre-war population was killed. From the end of World War II through the 1990s, there was constant strife and unhappiness with Soviet rule. The rise and fall of Solidarity in the 1980s was marked by the declaration of martial law by the Soviet Union in 1981, during which Solidarity was disbanded. The first democratic elections took place in 1990, resulting in victory for Polish icon, Lech Walesa. Hopes were high, but there was little economic improvement. Skyrocketing prices were coupled with declining wages.

Poland's more recent economic growth can be traced back to a new constitution in 1997, together with the country's engagement with NATO and membership in the European Union. All were signs that the country was beginning to reawaken.

Poland has had a very long history of valuing education. In 1773, the first Ministry of Education in the world was formed in Poland. Many positive developments have been attributed to its formation, including some standardization of the curriculum, with emphases on language, the sciences, and mathematics. Textbooks were aligned with the established curriculum and were generally well written. Agricultural education was instituted with the aim of economic improvement. One possible ancillary benefit of Soviet rule was the expansion of education and literacy to the masses. While economic support remained meager, the idea of all individuals becoming increasingly well educated was consistent with the Soviet concept of developing the common person. On the other hand, there was substantial pushback from some of the particulars of the Soviet approach. The Polish population balked at learning the Russian language, for instance, and held fast to a desire to return to religious education and the subsidization of private schools.

More recently, educational progress has resulted from Poland's participation in such initiatives as the Bologna Process, which enables large-scale European credit transfer by institutions. Poland has also enacted compulsory education beginning at age five so that all students spend a year in what is essentially the equivalent of kindergarten. Pearson Publishing, using the resources of the Economist Intelligence Unit (EIU), examined a combination of PIRLS, PISA, and TIMSS results, together with college graduation rates, school participation rates, and other metrics, to rank Poland 10th among the world's countries in education, ahead of Germany, Russia, and the United States.

As part of the EU, in 2004, Poland became part of the Erasmus Project, which offered opportunities to improve school reform, emphasize vocational education, and have greater participation in higher education. Paralleling Poland's educational advancement has been a rise in its economy. Although it has not yet kept pace with the growth in literacy, it is steadily improving. Participation in numerous trade initiatives, such as those enhanced by the EU, and the advancement of the educational level of the citizenry, bode well for Poland's future. Hopefully, an extended (and unprecedented) period of tranquility will afford Poles the opportunity to further improve both their socioeconomic status and their literacy achievement.

Conclusions from Countries

There can be no question that these four countries are outliers, marked by characteristics that have enabled them to exceed, in a relatively short time, expectations based on economic status. As Barber and Mourshed (2007), have observed:

> South Korea and Singapore demonstrate that a school system can go from low performance to high performance within a few decades. This achievement is even more remarkable given that it typically takes a long time to see the impact of a reform effort.
>
> (p. 40)

The question is which qualities these countries share and whether other nations might emulate them to advantage. One quality, though not one to be voluntarily copied, is resilience under adversity. We note in these four nations a trend not unlike the one observed in resilient individuals and schools. Vietnam, Korea, and Poland have all suffered historically from recurring periods of war and occupation by foreign powers. Finland has experienced some of these misfortunes but has generally enjoyed a more tranquil history.

The Vietnamese have suffered devastating invasions by the Chinese, the French, and the Americans, and they have witnessed a withering partitioning of their country. Ongoing battles have made it difficult for schools to remain open and successful. The Vietnamese people's commitment to culture and education, however, is sustaining them as they work toward improving their economy. Koreans have suffered under occupations by the Chinese and the Japanese and, like the Vietnamese, from the effects of partitioning. The industrial and commercial emergence of the South has been partially led by improvements in their educational system. The Poles have likewise suffered many of the same tribulations. Occupation by neighboring powers Germany and Russia have caused numerous setbacks, but they have been steadfast in their commitment to rebuilding their educational system and have managed to achieve considerable continuity of practice.

Finland was born out of Sweden less than 250 years ago and was subsequently occupied by Russia. Today it differs considerably from both countries. The Finnish language is only remotely related to Swedish and their GDNP far smaller. Toward the Russians the Finns harbor a long-standing apprehensiveness that history no doubt justifies. The image of the composer Sibelius standing in his yard during World War II, firing a shotgun (more or less symbolically) at Russian planes reflects an animosity that endures. Only since World War II have the Finns been free from foreign domination, a fact that makes a strong case for their resilience.

What is now occurring in each of these countries is relative tranquility shaded by an enduring collective memory of adversity. This tranquility has afforded each the opportunity to develop its schools and economy. They have taken it upon themselves to reform and reorganize their educational systems. As is true of many countries with emergent educational systems, there is often a need in the beginning for rigorous standardization. While this prospect does not appeal to all educators in all countries, it is a place to start.

Although resilience in the face of diversity is (fortunately) not a replicable quality, another may be. These countries, as well as others that achieve well beyond expectations, also share a divergent perspective on the selection and preparation of teachers. Barber and Mourshed (2007) have noted two principal options:

> Option 1: The first model selects people before they start their teacher training and limits places in the training program to those who are selected.
>
> Option 2: The second model leaves the selection process until after the prospective teachers have graduated from teacher training and then selects the best graduates to become teachers.
>
> While almost every school system in the world uses the second option, most of the top-performers use variations on the first.... Failing to control entry into teacher training almost invariably leads to an oversupply of candidates, which, in turn, has a significant negative effect on teacher quality.
>
> (p. 20)

Not only are teachers selected wisely, they are held in greater esteem in ascending countries. In Finland, as we observed in Chapter 3, teachers are viewed on a professional level comparable to that of doctors and lawyers. In Korea, a similar attitude is prevalent. Darling-Hammond (2010) quotes a Korean proverb "reflective of the deep respect for knowledge and teaching that is part of its Confucian heritage" (p. 173): *Don't even step on the shadow of a teacher*. Ascribing so high a value to education reflects the commitment of parents to ensuring that the work of their schools succeeds in helping their children realize their potential. These examples suggest that policies designed to uplift the profession may be practical as well as idealistic.

Conclusions

There is little doubt that a strong relationship exists between socioeconomic status and literacy, regardless of how either is measured. Whether SES is operationally defined in terms of income, social/cultural capital, or some other metric, there is almost always a strong positive correlation with literacy, whether indexed by test scores or the presence of numerous other literate behaviors. Some portion of the relationship may be causal, but a portion can be attributed to variables that impact both.

The connection may elicit serious concern, and even a sense of helplessness, in those endeavoring to teach students how to read. Yet there is reason for optimism because there are instructive exceptions to the SES-literacy relationship. That the correlation is neither absolute nor causal is reflected in the Connell quote cited earlier in this chapter: "Socioeconomic status is not a destiny."

One idea we find helpful in understanding why some people succeed, even under the most difficult of circumstances, and others do not, is that of mindset (Dweck, 2007). In the simplest of terms, an individual can be said to possess either a fixed or a growth mindset. The individual with a growth mindset is receptive to new challenges and undertakings. The person with a fixed mindset avoids these out of an assumption that failure will follow.

Dweck illustrates growth mindsets through the amazing accomplishments of certain individuals, such as Darwin and Tolstoy. She also illustrates the power of mindset in educational contexts. She cites some amazing accomplishments such as those achieved by students at Garfield High School, in Los Angeles, under the direction of Jaime Escalante, the teacher portrayed by Edward James Olmos in the movie *Stand and Deliver*. We mentioned in Chapter 2 how his efforts overcame the cultural norms that operated to suppress achievement. Those efforts can be described in terms of altering the closed mindset of his students, who reached incredible heights in AP Calculus. In fact:

> only three other public schools in the country had more students taking the Advanced Placement Calculus Test. Those three included Stuyvesant High School and the Bronx High School of Science. Both elite math- and science-oriented schools in New York. . . . In the whole country that year, only a few hundred Mexican-American students passed the test at this level.
>
> (p. 64)

Escalante fostered in his students a growth mindset, a can-do perspective that propelled their learning.

As another example of the power of growth mindsets, Dweck cites the example of Marva Collins' work in Chicago, both in a regular public school and an academy she founded later. Dweck illustrates the power of changing students' perspectives about what they can accomplish when they abandon the fatalism of the fixed mindset.

In this chapter we have described outliers from the relationship between SES and literacy. We have offered multiple examples of individuals, schools, and countries deviating positively from expectations. We have also observed that the characteristics for defying the SES-literacy death grip are similar for individuals, schools, and countries. Such defiance first requires a certain innate willingness to persevere against long odds. Second, it takes a period of relative tranquility in the environment. Third, it demands leadership and positive direction from others, whether they be parents, mentors, coaches, teachers, principals, or ministers of education. Fourth, it requires adequate structure in a life, a school, or a national education system. Finally, it takes the hope, belief, and optimism associated with a growth mindset, not the defeatism, cynicism, and pessimism of the fixed mindset.

These five ingredients constitute a recipe for success against long odds. They are within reach of those who raise children, those who teach them, and those who make policy that affects them. And they have the potential to make the exceptions the rule.

Note

1 For a more detailed account of these schools, see UNICEF India (2013).

References

Aikens, N.L., & Barbarin, O. (2008). Socioeconomic differences in reading trajectories: The contribution of family, neighborhood, and school contexts. *Journal of Educational Psychology, 100,* 235–251.

Archibold, R.C. (1999, June 29). Success at poor schools, despite the odds. *The New York Times.* Available: http://www.nytimes.com/1999/06/29/nyregion/success-at-poor-schools-despite-the-odds.html

Barber, M., & Mourshed, M. (2007). *How the world's best-performing schools systems come out on top.* New York, NY: McKinsey & Company. Available: http://www.smhc-cpre.org/wp-content/uploads/2008/07/how-the-worlds-best-performing-school-systems-come-out-on-top-sept-072.pdf

Borman, G.D., & Overman, L.T. (2004). Academic resilience in mathematics among poor and minority students. *The Elementary School Journal, 104,* 177–195.

Chiu, M.M., & Chow, B.Y. (2010). Culture, motivation, and reading achievement: High school students in 41 countries. *Learning & Individual Differences, 20,* 579–592.

Coleman, J.S. (1966). Equal schools or equal students? *The Public Interest,* Summer, No. 4, 70–75.

Coleman, J.S. (1967). Toward open schools. *The Public Interest,* Fall, No. 9, 20–27.

Coleman, J.S., Campbell, E.Q., Hobson, C.J., McPartland, J., Mood, A.M., Weinfeld, F.D., & York, R.L. (1967). *Equality of educational opportunity.* Washington, DC: U.S. Department of Health, Education, and Welfare.

Connell, N., Mendelow, N., Tyson, D., & Educational Priorities Panel. (1999). *Beating the odds: High-achieving elementary schools in high-poverty neighborhoods.* New York, NY: Educational Priorities Panel.

D'Angiulli, A., Siegel, L.S., & Hertzman, C. (2004). Schooling, socioeconomic context and literacy development. *Educational Psychology, 24,* 867–883.

Darling-Hammond, L. (2010). *The flat world and education: How America's commitment to equity will determine our future.* New York, NY: Teachers College Press.

Dugger, C.W. (2010, September 8). New schools in South Africa serve the underserved. *The New York Times.* Available: http://www.nytimes.com/2010/09/09/world/africa/09safrica.html?pagewanted=all&_r=2

Dweck, C.S. (2007). *Mindset: The new psychology of success: How we can learn to fulfill our potential.* New York, NY: Ballantine Books.

Kahlenberg, R.D. (2001). Learning from James Coleman. *Public Interest, 144,* 54.

Luque, J. (2014, February 26). *Vietnam: The big surprise.* Inter-American Development Bank Blog. Available: http://blogs.iadb.org/education/2014/02/26/the-big-surprise-vietnam/

Morgan, P.L., Farkas, G., Hillemeier, M.M., & Maczuga, S. (2009). Risk factors for learning-related behavior problems at 24 months of age: Population-based estimates. *Journal of Abnormal Child Psychology, 37,* 401–413.

National Center for Education Statistics. (2008). *Percentage of high school dropouts among persons 16 through 24 years old (status dropout rate), by income level, and percentage distribution of status dropouts, by labor force status and educational attainment: 1970 through 2007.* Retrieved from http://nces.ed.gov/programs/digest/d08/tables/dt08_110.asp

National Center for Education Statistics. (2013). *The nation's report card: A first look: 2013 mathematics and reading. National Assessment of Educational Progress at grades 4 and 8.* Washington, DC: U.S. Department of Education. Available: http://nces.ed.gov/nations reportcard/subject/publications/main2013/pdf/2014451.pdf

OECD. (2013). PISA 2012 results: Ready to learn: Students' engagement, drive, and self-beliefs (Vol. 3). Paris, France: OECD. Available: http://www.oecd.org/pisa/keyfindings/PISA-2012-results-volume-III.pdf

Parrett, W.H., & Budge, K.M. (2012). *Turning high-poverty schools into high-performing schools.* Alexandria, VA: ASCD.

Patrick, D. (2011). *A reason to believe: Lessons from an improbable life.* New York, NY: Broadway Books.

Pierre-Louis, M. (2014). Ten students who overcame massive obstacles to achieve their dream of an education. Available: http://overcomingchallengeswithfaith.blogspot.com/

UNICEF India. (2013, March 14). Children in Mumbai slums learning better with the school excellence programme. Available: https://www.facebook.com/notes/unicef-india/children-in-mumbai-slums-learning-better-with-the-school-excellence-programme/10152638815435284

Viadero, D. (1995, May 1). Against all odds. *Education Week.* Available: http://www.edweek.org/tm/articles/1995/05/01/8success.h06.html?tkn=PZMDFTEUwLy6y3sC4PjXl MduGOogW0x6gt9G

Yousafzai, M. (2015). *I am Malala: The girl who stood up for education and was shot by the Taliban.* New York, NY: Back Bay Books.

10
THE FUTURE OF THE KNOWLEDGE-BASED ECONOMY AND CHANGE IN THE WORLD ORDER

"The multitude of books," complained Voltaire, "is making us ignorant." Put differently, whenever a new book appears, our ignorance is increased, by definition, until we have read it. Fast-forward to the present, and the observation could come to mean that society is disadvantaged by the geometrically increasing appearance of new sources of information until they are found and digested. Our concern here is with sources of knowledge related to livelihood. That knowledge is power – at least certain forms of knowledge – is a fact few would dispute. We argue in this chapter that such access will increasingly determine whether individuals and nations will flourish or flounder. Trends linking literacy growth with economic success were explored, to some extent, in the previous chapter. How economic and political power, on a national scale, are inextricably tied to knowledge growth is considered here. Most importantly, trends identified in previous chapters will be consolidated into reasoned trajectories of where the nations of the world have been and where they are headed.

Author and sought-after consultant in the 1980s and 90s, John Naisbitt, wrote three books during that period pertaining specifically to what he referred to as "megatrends." In his first book in 1982, *Megatrends: Ten New Directions Transforming Our Lives,* he discussed a transformation that was already well underway as society shifted from an industry-based to an information-based economy. In *Megatrends 2000: Ten New Directions for the 1990's,* he described how the economic locus of control had shifted from European countries and the United States, Canada, and Mexico, to the Pacific Rim. Naisbitt and Aburdene quote John Hay, U.S. Secretary of State at the beginning of the twentieth century: "The Mediterranean is the ocean of the past, the Atlantic the ocean of the present, the Pacific the ocean of the future" (1990, p. 179). They observe that his prophecy had already become a reality, and they cite five specific points to remember about the Pacific Rim:

1. The Pacific Rim shift is economically driven – and at a *pace* that is without precedent.
2. The shift is not only economic but cultural as well. The countries of the Pacific Rim speak more than 1,000 languages and have the most varied religious and cultural traditions in the world.
3. Although Japan is the region's economic leader today [1990], the East Asia region (China and the Four Tigers – South Korea, Taiwan, Hong Kong, and Singapore) will eventually dominate.
4. The Pacific Rim's economic thrust is being reinforced with a commitment to education. As early as 1985, a higher percentage of young Koreans attended schools of higher education than young Britons.
5. In a global economy the rise of the Pacific Rim need not signify the decline of the West unless the West ignores the significance of this trend and fails to capitalize on it.

(Naisbitt & Aburdene, 1990, p. 179)

By 1996, when Naisbitt had written his next book on Megatrends, the title told it all: *Megatrends Asia: Eight Asian Megatrends That Are Reshaping Our World*. He made clear that one of the major influences that will continue to impact economies in the future is that "as the global economy continues to shift from its industrial past to the full potential of the information-based future, the key to productivity will not be inexpensive labor but the best use of high technology" (p. 175).

He further noted:

> The twin forces of global change – the decline of Western dominance and the rise of the East and the shift from industrial to information societies – are producing the need for painful adjustments. The shock waves are enormous in speed and magnitude.... The time has come to fully recognize and accept the East. And the East is not just Japan and China ... Thailand, Malaysia, Singapore, Indonesia, the Philippines, Brunei and Vietnam have a population of almost 450 million; the Indian subcontinent has 940 million people.
>
> (p. 231)[1]

To these nations, South Korea must surely be added. In fact, as we have noted in early chapters, their change in educational level in concert with their change in economic level has been nothing less than astounding.

Pre-Industrial, Industrial, and Post-Industrial Economies

Daniel Bell was a noted American sociologist and journalist. From his birth in 1919 to his death in 2011, his life stretched from the middle to the end phases of the industrial society and well into the post-industrial age. Two of his better-known books are *The End of Ideology* (1960) and *The Coming of Post-Industrial Society* (1973). His influential work is important in defining changes in societal values.

Bell offered instrumental definitions of the Pre-Industrial, Industrial, and Post-Industrial Eras. He characterized pre-industrial society as one dependent upon nature. The few collective economies in existence were largely agrarian. Individuals depended upon nature for collecting food and natural resources. Their work depended on simple, non-motorized tools, powered by people and domesticated animals.

As the industrial society emerged, the power of the individual gave way to mechanization. Manufacturing became a leading economic activity. Societies with extensive natural resources still were advantaged, but the ability to convert those resources into useful products was the hallmark of the Industrial Era. Society became much more urban, and work was done in collectives. While there were advantages in these developments, there were numerous drawbacks, such as poor living conditions, low wages, and exploitation of child labor.

Bell thought of the post-industrial societies as ones in which the raw materials became digitized information while production, or manufacturing, had largely been replaced by technology transfer. Large-scale masses of employees, one of the hallmarks of the transition from pre-industrial to industrial societies, again reversed itself as more employees in a knowledge economy work at individual locations. Opportunities for economic success became much more distributed, with knowledge made portable through technology.

In light of Bell's conceptualizations, a key question arises: Is the Post-Modern society the first economy in which knowledge is of critical importance? The answer is a resounding "no." Knowledge has always been associated with influence, power, and economic success. And literacy has always been the essential vehicle for the acquisition of knowledge. So, while referring to the Post-Industrial, or Post-Modern, Era as the period of the Knowledge-Based Economy (KBE) is not a misnomer, it would be a mistake to assume that the Pre-Industrial and Industrial economies were not knowledge-driven as well. In Chapter 1, we offered multiple examples of how knowledge and literacy created power in the world. Advantages, both financial and otherwise, were afforded to those who could read and thus acquire, organize, and use knowledge. In Chapter 6, we described the literate as those who held important positions, such as translators and scribes. By virtue of those positions, they often determined what others could read. In Chapter 9, we demonstrated that high literacy levels correspond strongly with the current, and potentially the future, economic success of countries. What then are the basic tenets of the new world KBEs? How has the post-industrial society varied from the past, and where are these changes occurring more often? These questions are central to understanding the role of literacy and shaping policy to advance it.

Technology is the Driver

After even a cursory reading of the nine previous chapters of this book, there can be little doubt about one overriding theme in today's world of literacy. Technology is the driving force. Its impact is seen in the approaches to educational systems and in the ways we produce, store, and disseminate the written word. We have noted how libraries, bookstores, and newspapers have all undergone transformative changes, which have occurred at an ever-increasing pace. Not only what we read, but how we read, has been radically changed by the forces of technology.

Access to information has become far more egalitarian, and though there is much to do before all individuals can equally access knowledge, the power divide created by differential access has diminished. David Audretsch and his colleagues offer the following observation:

> The emergence of new technologies is acting both as a driving force and an enabling factor to globalization. At the same time, these technologies are changing rapidly, shortening the life cycles of products and the underlying processes, and raising technology costs. Technology transfer from academic and scientific institutions has thus transformed into a strategic variable for companies and nations to cope with these challenges in a global economy.
> (2014, p. 301)

There is no doubt that technology is one of the driving forces in the new KBEs and changes in the world economic order. Those who are literate have access to knowledge and, as a result, are the more likely benefactors of KBEs.

Knowledge is Product

Perhaps the most important characteristic of the Post-Industrial period is that knowledge is not only the key that unlocks economic success, it is ever increasingly the product of that success. Knowledge driven by technology becomes not only the means but the end. This was not true of the pre-industrial and industrial economies. In a discussion of knowledge as a product in New Zealand, Bogunovich (2014) discusses the future of "smart manufacturing":

> New Thinking might be about lifting Exports by directing more Investment into the planning of Regional Development and design and construction of Housing, in a manner that not only does not damage the Environment, but in fact enhances it.
>
> Sounds like a bad idea if you wish to export – since new subdivisions cannot be shipped overseas – but it isn't. Knowledge is portable. And the knowledge of how to build and operate cities and suburbs which do not cost the earth is rapidly emerging as the most sought-after item in the global market.
> (p. 20)

Consider also a recent description of Singapore's postal service and how it has reinvented itself:

> When a German lingerie brand wanted to sell bras online in Malaysia, it turned to Singapore's nearly 200-year-old national postal service.
>
> Singapore Post built a website, developed a marketing strategy and now delivers packages for the company, Triumph International. As postage stamps give way to keyboard clicks, SingPost is redefining the role of the letter carrier, by creating a one-stop shop for retailers' e-commerce needs in Asia.
>
> In South Korea, SingPost is helping to sell Levi's jeans. In Singapore, it is stocking Toshiba laptops. In Malaysia, it is delivering Adidas sneakers.
>
> With traditional mail services in decline, post offices around the world are scrambling to reinvent themselves for the digital age.
>
> SingPost's makeover is among the most ambitious. Besides its regular postal duties, it offers a basket of services for companies, including website development, online marketing, customer service and, of course, package delivery.
>
> (Stevenson, 2015)

Vinnychuk et al. (2014) describe economic growth, in the context of KBEs, in the Ukraine, Poland, Germany, and Lithuania:

> Economic growth increasingly depends on the ability to acquire new knowledge and apply it in all areas of life. Relocation of scientific knowledge at the centre of the key factors for sustainable economic growth caused concentration-date research on the problem of becoming a knowledge economy.

The examples are almost endless, and the point is clear. Those who are literate can access knowledge. While this principle has been important throughout history, it becomes especially critical as the knowledge also becomes the product of human labor.

New Workforce, New Education

Throughout this book, changes in literacy and the commensurate changes in teaching and learning have been emphasized. As a new world order evolves, being part of ascending economies, rather than descending ones, in large part depends on the ability to transform educational systems. While this transformation means having a scientific/technological emphasis, it does not mean developing a system to mass produce technocrats. The ability to think critically, solve problems, and act ethically is still an integral part of comprehensive education for KBEs. This point notwithstanding, the ability of individuals to work in the emerging fields of biomedicine, engineering, and computer sciences will have a very large impact on a country's economic well-being.

Andreas Schleicher (2007), head of the Indicators and Analysis Division of OECD's Directorate for Education, wrote in the Foreword to a report on new world education and its top-performing school systems:

> The capacity of countries – both the world's most advanced economies as well those experiencing rapid development – to compete in the global knowledge economy increasingly depends on whether they can meet a fast-growing demand for high-level skills. This, in turn, hinges on significant improvements in the quality of schooling outcomes and a more equitable distribution in learning opportunities.

Chun-Yao Tseng (2014) refers to this new workforce as "knowledge workers":

> The evolution of a knowledge economy has created a new workforce of highly skilled professionals, called knowledge workers . . . Academia and industry agree on the importance of knowledge workers in a developed economy for economic growth.
>
> (pp. 1–2)

Concern abounds about the development of a competitive knowledge-based workforce. In 2002, the British journal *Business Europe* published a discussion of the evolution of a knowledge-based workforce, particularly as it relates to EU countries and eastern European countries poised to associate with the EU at the time. The EU Lisbon Summit in 2000, at the change of the millennium, looked closely at how "fit" countries were in the development of their workforce:

> The key ingredients of a knowledge-based economy are highly skilled, flexible knowledge workers. East Europeans score high on literacy, numeracy and other basic skills. Education spending as a percentage of GDP hovers around west European averages. Enrollment in higher education is very high, with more than 90% of workers enjoying some form of secondary education or training in countries such as Estonia and Hungary. However, east Europeans are still much less likely to get a university degree than their western counterparts.
>
> (Anonymous, 2002, p. 8)

The simple fact is that countries either already have an educational system producing students with the skills and abilities to work in a KBE, or they must transform what they do. They also need to produce students who possess not only the ability to work in technological fields but an interest in doing so. Some countries have very high numbers of students engaged in engineering, computer sciences, and other technological fields. Examples include many of the Asian nations, including India, and a number of eastern European countries. However, in the United States and many northern and western European countries, the level of participation in those fields is lower.

In other areas of the world, participation is lower still because the educational system has not yet been extended to the full range of the population. Even where there is some emphasis on educating workers for the KBE, the percentage of people accessing the system remains modest. This is true of many parts of Africa and the Middle East.

As noted, the purpose of educating KBE workers is not simply to create single-job functioning technocrats. Those who guide the education system must not focus on its research mission at the expense of its larger cultural charge. Ramesh (2013) examines the Chinese context:

> Higher education is not only the teaching centre, but also an important scientific research community, the center of technological innovation, and an opportunity to create in different kinds of culture. The most important function of higher education is to increase the quality of the Chinese national identity and to develop the Chinese personality.
>
> (p. 487)

The ability of countries to reinvent their educational systems will determine, in significant ways, their participation in the KBE. Knowledge is critical and literacy is the point of access.

All Countries See Themselves as "In"

In an earlier chapter, we cited the emergence of cellular telephones as a tremendous advancement in telecommunications, particularly for underdeveloped countries. In essence, countries that had not made significant infrastructure investments for landline telephones were now provided a "second chance" to create widely distributed telecommunications for their citizens. Countries with extensive investment in landlines were not at a disadvantage, but their advantage was greatly diminished.

The same can now be said about the emergence of KBEs in the Post-Industrial Era. Countries that ruled the economic world, largely through manufacturing and an abundance of natural resources, were not placed at a disadvantage when KBEs emerged, but their advantages were diminished. The second chance represents a new opportunity that cannot be ignored by less-developed countries. And virtually all of them are positioned to see themselves as active participants in the new KBE.

Bringing about this vision is challenging, to be sure, but it cannot occur without the optimism to make the attempt. Rasim Aliguliyev, Director of the Institute of Information Technologies of the Azerbaijani National Academy of Sciences expresses such optimism for Azerbaijan:

> In recent years, the ICT sector has played an increasingly important role in the socioeconomic development of Azerbaijan. In recognition of that important role, the government has identified ICT as one of the priority sectors of the national economy, and has taken significant steps toward the formation of an information society and knowledge economy in Azerbaijan.
>
> (Aliguliyev & Gurbanov, 2012, p. 150)

Clearly, this is a nation of individuals who see themselves as "in."

Rwanda has started from a different point of entry, but the end goal is the same and its leaders have taken pains to spell it out:

> In 2000, Rwanda adopted Vision 2020 which aimed at building a knowledge-based economy. This strategy was centered on investing in its main asset, the Rwandan population . . . Having inherited an education system where few were allowed to go to school from regimes prior to 1994, the main challenge was to ensure that Rwanda provide free basic education to all students in primary and secondary schools.
>
> (Bakuramutsa, 2013, para. 1, 5)

Rwanda sees the future as one where opportunity exists to overcome past injustices. Like the Azerbaijanis, they too see themselves as "in."

In Sri Lanka, policymakers view building a knowledge-based economy as a means to stem the tide of emigration of some of their most talented people. In 2011, the *Daily News* of Colombo ran this comment:

> It's the most important thing for a country like Sri Lanka. We have less than 21 million people. There is a brain drain within. Why? Other lucrative countries offer better ways to manage their knowledge and thrive. We have a capable HR base running on a discarded infrastructure. Only solution is leapfrogging the IT for development.

Sri Lankans likewise see themselves as "in."

Iran recognizes both the need to change and the difficulty of doing so when the economy has been able to rely heavily on natural resources in the past. In 2015, the FARS news agency reported a policy statement made by Iran's Vice-President for Science and Technology, Sorena Sattari:

Sattari underscored the necessity for paying special attention to the development of knowledge-based economy in Iran.

"Today we should move toward changing the old approach towards research, a kind of approach which has been created based on reliance on oil revenues and has influenced the research environment of the country," Sattari said.

Changing the old habits needs firm determination for moving toward innovation by Iranian enterprises because reliance on mere oil revenues in research and technology has led to creation of luxury but inefficient infrastructures in the country.

Iranians too see themselves as "in."

Other countries, such as India, see human capital, whether fully developed or not, as having great potential for a KBE. In 2014, the Asian National Bank (ANB) released a report that reached this conclusion:

India, with its youthful population and thriving information and communication technology (ICT) industry, can become a leading knowledge-driven economy as long as regulatory, education, and infrastructure barriers are overcome.

Indians see themselves as "in."

In short, a surprising array of developing nations now perceive themselves as poised to participate in the Post-Industrial KBE. While this perception may not be entirely realistic at present, each has reason for optimism. Knowledge, and access to it through literacy, is the critical component, and the right policies can place it within their grasp.

Who's Really In?

Despite the broad desire to be recognized as active participants in a KBE, common sense dictates that some nations are better positioned than others to realize this goal. Which ones? There have been attempts to benchmark countries in relationship to others based on their actual participation. One such attempt is the Knowledge Economy Index (KEI), created by the World Bank Institute. An overall metric combines measures of various aspects of a knowledge-based economy, including education and human resources, innovation, and communication technology. Results of the 2012 KEI appear in Table 10.1.

Although more countries are included in this analysis than those appearing in the achievement tables presented in Chapter 3, almost all of the countries that have been engaged in PIRLS, PISA, and PIAAC are included in the KEI rankings. In some ways, the results of this analysis confirm common impressions concerning various countries, but some of the findings run counter to these preconceptions.

TABLE 10.1 Knowledge Economy Index (KEI) 2012 Rankings

2012 Rank	Country	Change from 2000	2012 Rank	Country	Change from 2000
1	Sweden	0	32	Lithuania	2
2	Finland	6	38	Poland	−3
3	Denmark	0	48	Malaysia	−3
4	Netherlands	−2	55	Russian Federation	9
5	Norway	2	56	Ukraine	−2
6	New Zealand	3	60	Brazil	−1
7	Canada	3	66	Thailand	−6
8	Germany	7	72	Mexico	−11
9	Australia	−3	79	Azerbaijan	15
10	Switzerland	−5	84	China	7
11	Ireland	0	92	Philippines	−15
12	United States	−8	94	Iran, Islamic Rep.	1
13	Taiwan, China	3	101	Sri Lanka	−14
14	United Kingdom	−2	104	Vietnam	9
15	Belgium	−1	110	India	−6
16	Iceland	3	★★		
17	Austria	−4	117	Pakistan	5
18	Hong Kong, China	7	118	Uganda	2
19	Estonia	7	119	Nigeria	5
20	Luxembourg	2	120	Zimbabwe	−6
21	Spain	2	121	Lesotho	−12
22	Japan	−5	122	Yemen, Rep.	6
23	Singapore	−3	123	Malawi	−6
24	France	−3	124	Burkina Faso	9
25	Israel	−7	125	Benin	−10
26	Czech Republic	7	126	Mali	−7
27	Hungary	2	127	Rwanda	14
28	Slovenia	0	128	Tanzania	−2
29	South Korea	−5	129	Madagascar	−2
	★★		130	Mozambique	5

(Continued)

TABLE 10.1 Continued

2012 Rank	Country	Change from 2000	2012 Rank	Country	Change from 2000
131	Lao PDR	−2	139	Djibouti	−3
132	Cambodia	−16	140	Ethiopia	−2
133	Cameroon	−15	141	Guinea	−9
134	Mauritania	−11	142	Eritrea	−11
135	Nepal	−10	143	Angola	−1
136	Cote d'Ivoire	−15	144	Sierra Leone	−4
137	Bangladesh	−3	145	Myanmar	−8
138	Sudan	1			

**Table consists of the top 20%, bottom 20%, and other countries mentioned throughout.

First, it might be appropriate to observe that a Matthew Effect is clearly at work – that "the rich get richer and the poor get poorer." Although many countries wish to become a part of the knowledge-based economy, those that were economically developed in the past continue to be. Northern and Western European countries, Canada, and the United States all top the KBE rankings. The bottom of the list is largely made up African and Middle Eastern nations. None of this is surprising.

What is surprising is the lack of the preeminence of the Asian Rim nations. The highest ranked of those is Taiwan (13th), Hong Kong[2] (18th), Japan (22nd), Singapore (23rd), and South Korea (29th). Some of the rising Asian countries are working their way up the knowledge-based economy list. China, at 84th, moved up seven places and Vietnam, at 104th, moved up nine. The lack of correspondence between KBE rankings and those of PISA and PIRLS may lie in the inevitable lag time between education and economic payoff. In other words, successes in literacy and school reform may best be viewed as leading indicators of future success in the KBE – a future that has yet to be fully realized.

As to the overall KBE rankings, Finland, a perennial high finisher on international literacy assessments is the second highest ranked country in KEI. Other Scandinavian and Western European countries continue to occupy places near the top of the KEI list, even as their literacy test scores have declined. Examples include Sweden, Denmark, the Netherlands, and Norway, all of which have moved down the literacy rankings. If literacy is indeed a leading indicator of a knowledge-based economy, then a downward pattern should be cause for concern.

The low rankings of some countries on the KEI list can be explained through lack of educational access. UNESCO's 2014 report, *Teaching and Learning: Achieving Quality for All*, is the eleventh assessment of progress in providing such access.

Unfortunately, the report makes clear that many countries have not made substantial enough improvements, especially related to the goal of universal primary education:

> Sub-Saharan Africa is the region that is lagging most behind, with 22% of the region's primary school age population still not in school in 2011. By contrast, South and West Asia experienced the fastest decline [in those out of school], contributing more than half the total reduction in numbers out of school.
>
> Girls make up 54% of the global population of children out of school. In the Arab States, the share is 60%, unchanged since 2000.
>
> (p. 2)

Though hope may spring eternal – and there are surely opportunities created by the emerging KBE – those countries already successful during the industrialized period continue to experience success. The fastest rising economies are those of the Pacific Rim and those making the least progress are those in Africa and some areas of the Middle East. Thus these data do tend to support the contention that the rich get richer, but they also illustrate the opportunity for the "have-nots" to move up. The "second chance" offered by KBE has permitted those willing and able to change their educational approaches to increase literacy levels and experience success in the KBE.

Multi-national Agreements

What will unquestionably drive changes in the world order based on the KBE is the development of multi-national cooperative agreements – not just forming them, but actually making them work. Reaching these agreements, and abiding by them, is sometimes more difficult for countries used to having the superior economies of the past, and far easier for those who had less and are striving to emerge.

Such agreements often encounter opposition from forces within a nation, sometimes to the point of derailing movement toward an agreement. Much was made in 2015 of the United States' developing extensive cooperative agreements with Asian Rim countries. Trade unions, owners of certain manufacturing companies, and those skeptical of some foreign cultures all had serious concerns about that development.

A similar situation occurred in the early 1990s with regard to the North American Free Trade Agreement (NAFTA). William Daley worked with U.S. President Clinton on trying to arrange passage of that agreement, but apprehension abounded. Daley (2015) described the context as follows in the *New York Times*:

> During the NAFTA debate, America was on the precipice of great change. In plain view was the collapse of the Soviet empire, the further liberalization

of China's economy and the intensification of international efforts to integrate economies worldwide. On the horizon was a technological revolution to rival any we had known. In 1993, the Internet was made up of just 130 websites.

(Para. 2)

Countries perceiving themselves as having the most to lose are often concerned about entering into multi-national arrangements, while countries who feel they have little to lose are more willing to participate. Those that benefited during the Industrial Era now perceive jobs as having been lost in the manufacturing sector in the Post-Industrial Era.

This perception is not altogether wrong. While it is a not true that production is down, even in the U.S., it is true that jobs have been lost. As Samuelson (2013) points out:

> The truth is that output has continued to climb ... U.S. manufacturing production [in 2010] of nearly $1.8 trillion was the largest in the world; it was slightly ahead of China's [though now slightly behind], about two-thirds higher than Japan's and nearly triple Germany's. Manufacturing's "decline" refers mostly to job loss, which is stark and long-term. In 1970, the 17.8 million manufacturing jobs represented 25 percent of all 71 million U.S. jobs. By 2012, the 11.9 million manufacturing jobs were only 9 percent of the 133.7 million total. The declines reflect two forces: automation and imports, especially of labor-intensive products.

(Para. 4)

Despite these concerns, multi-national arrangements have been achieved. The European Union and its multi-national, highly interactive cooperative environment and its eurozone consisting of all EU countries that fully incorporate the euro as their national currency, provides one of the most highly developed cooperative arrangements. It can be argued that less-developed European nations have benefited more from their participation than others, but the more-developed countries have benefited from additional access to markets. Blackstone (2015) notes that the eurozone "is never going to be a locomotive for the global economy, but at the least you hope it's not going to act as a brake." It helps all participants, though some more than others.

Opportunities for new connections exist as well. The BRIC countries (Brazil, Russia, India, and China) hold tremendous potential economic (and therefore political) power. Over 40% of the younger people in the world live in these countries. All four have placed emphasis on developing a technology workforce, albeit with differing degrees of success (Carnoy et al., 2013). Most of the transformation in the educational systems in these countries has taken place since the 1980s. Consequently, the full impact of their transformation is hard to assess. If literacy test scores are truly leading indicators, there is real potential, especially for Russia and China.

The economic power of producers in a KBE is strong, but the economic power of consumers of the products of a KBE is equally powerful. In short, the future for all economies of the world that plan on taking a significant place in the world's KBE is dependent upon the ability to form meaningful and trustworthy multi-national agreements for both selling and buying. Consider the simplicity of this one fact, that 95% of the world's consumers live outside of the United States. The ability to prosper is not only dependent on the ability to produce, but also on having open access to international consumers.

This does not mean that any multi-national agreement will do. There are certainly rules of human decency, worker care, and ecological imperatives that must be considered in forming multi-national agreements. There is also the need to find common ground between countries on these issues. And it is equally important to insist on a level of mutual respect for the human dignity of workers and for the future of the planet.

Conclusion

As the post-industrial society and the KBE have unfolded over the last half century, much change has occurred and its pace is increasing. Discussing the rapidity of this evolution and its impact on India, Ray (2013) observes:

> Gone are the days when the abundance of cheap labour and natural resources was enough to propel economic growth. If GM crops are increasing acreages in agriculture, robots are scaling up factory output and software development is changing the face of a wide range of services from banking to telecom. In fact, it is a no-brainer that technology is the key factor now for any economy to accelerate its growth.
>
> But what is equally important is the level of skill that the future labour force must have, coupled with R&D efforts to improve productivity.
>
> (Para. 1–2)

Changes in the world order and the KBE are driven by technology. There can be no doubt of that. Knowledge has become both the mechanism by which products are created, and a product itself. This new KBE requires a different workforce, a demand that calls for transformation in how people are educated. This does not mean that all aspects of liberal education should be foregone in order to place an exclusive emphasis on the STEM fields. It means that both science and the humanities must be a part of education in a successful culture.

All countries see themselves either as active or potential participants in the KBE. However, the idea that all countries will participate equally and be successful in the new knowledge-based economy is clearly inaccurate. The struggle for those who were less advantaged during previous periods is not only to transform their education systems, but to improve at a rate equivalent to those of more advantaged countries, *just to stay even*. Then, they must grow and improve at a rate fast enough to overcome past inequalities. That is asking a lot, but there are role models, particularly in Asian countries.

Knowledge has always been the true coin of the realm and literacy "the key to the kingdom of knowledge." It will continue to be so, even as what is read, how it is stored, how it is retrieved, and even how it is read changes. The new world order is "defined more by Google than by General Motors" (Samuelson, 2013).

Of the ten largest publicly held companies in the world, defined by Forbes rankings, five are Chinese and five are American (Chen & Murphy, 2015). Investment and banking enterprises dominate the top ten, with two petroleum companies, ExxonMobil and PetroChina, the highest "production" companies at 7th and 8th. Technology-heavy industries include Apple, Verizon, Microsoft, Intel, Deutsche Telekom, Cisco Systems, and Google. All are ranked in the top 100 largest public companies in the world and all have been founded in the last 50 years (Chen & Murphy, 2015). It is indeed a new economy for a new world. And as ever, literacy will again provide the "keys to the kingdom."

Notes

1 These statistics were based on 1990 Census figures.
2 Evaluated as a unit distinct from China.

References

Aliguliyev, R., & Gurbanov, G. (2012). Big ambitions in a rapidly changing world: Azerbaijan. Chapter 2.1 in S. Dutta & B. Vilbao-Osorio (Eds.), *The global information technology report 2012: Living in a hyperconnected world* (pp. 149–159). Geneva, Switzerland: World Economic Forum. Retrieved from http://www3.weforum.org/docs/Global_IT_Report_2012.pdf

Anonymous. (2002). Towards a knowledge-based economy? *Business Europe, 42*(6), 8. Retrieved from http://0-search.proquest.com.www.consuls.org/docview/221284398?accountid=9970

Asian National Bank. (2014, September 12). India can be a leading knowledge-based economy with the right steps. Manila, Philippines: ANB. Retrieved from http://www.adb.org/news/india-can-be-leading-knowledge-based-economy-right-steps-report

Audretsch, D.B., Lehmann, E.E., & Wright, M. (2014). Technology transfer in a global economy. *The Journal of Technology Transfer, 39*(3), 301–312. Retrieved from http://0-dx.doi.org.www.consuls.org/10.1007/s10961–012–9283–6

Bakuramutsa, N. (2013, June 18). Towards a knowledge-based economy. *The New Times*. Retrieved from http://www.newtimes.co.rw/section/article/2013–06–18/66794/

Bell, D. (1960). *The end of ideology: On the exhaustion of political ideas in the fifties*. New York, NY: Free Press.

Bell, D. (1973). *The coming of the post-industrial society: A venture in social forecasting.* London, U.K.: Penguin Books.

Blackstone, B. (2015, March 6). Central bank boosts outlook for Eurozone. *The Wall Street Journal,* p. A14.

Bogunovich, D. (2014, January 26). Adding value. *The Sunday Star-Times,* p. 20.

Carnoy, M., Loyalka, P., Dobryakova, M.S., Dossani, R., Froumin, I.D., Kuhns, K., Tilak, J.B.G., & Wang, R. (2013). What do BRIC higher education strategies imply for the future? In *University expansion in a changing global economy: Triumph of the BRICs?* Stanford, CA: Stanford University Press.

Chen, L., & Murphy, A. (2015, June 5). The world's biggest public companies. *Forbes.* Retrieved June 10, 2015, from http://www.forbes.com/global2000/

Daley, W.M. (2015, May 19). Free trade is not the enemy. *The New York Times.* Retrieved from http://www.nytimes.com/2015/05/19/opinion/free-trade-is-not-the-enemy.html

Naisbitt, J. (1982). *Megatrends: Ten new directions transforming our lives.* New York, NY: Warner Books, Inc.

Naisbitt, J. (1996). *Megatrends Asia: Eight Asian megatrends that are reshaping our world.* New York: Simon & Schuster.

Naisbitt, J., & Aburdene, P. (1990). *Megatrends 2000: Ten new directions for the 1990's.* New York: Morrow.

Ramesh, S. (2013). China's transition to a knowledge economy. *Journal of the Knowledge Economy, 4,* 473–491.

Ray, R.K. (2013, November 18). Shaping up a knowledge economy. *The Financial Express.* Retrieved from http://archive.financialexpress.com/news/shaping-up-a-knowledge-economy/1196123

Samuelson, R.J. (2013, April 7). Myths of post-industrial America. *The Washington Post.* Retrieved from http://www.washingtonpost.com/opinions/robert-jsamuelson-myths-of-post-industrial-america/2013/04/07/775d1062–9fb2–11e2–82bc-511538ae90a4_story.html

Schleicher, A. (2007). Foreword. In M. Barber & M. Mourshed (Authors), *How the world's best-performing school systems come out on top.* Retrieved from http://mckinseyonsociety.com/how-the-worlds-best-performing-schools-come-out-on-top/

Stevenson, A. (2015, May 18). Singapore's postal service reinvents itself for the Digital Age. *The New York Times.* Retrieved from http://www.nytimes.com/2015/05/19/business/international/singpost-reinvents-for-digital-age-of-ecommerce.html?_r=0

UNESCO. (2014). *Teaching and learning: Achieving quality for all.* New York, NY: Author. Retrieved from http://unesco.nl/sites/default/files/dossier/gmr_2013–4.pdf?download=1

Vinnychuk, O., Skrashchuk, L., & Vinnychuk, I. (2014). Research of economic growth in the context of knowledge economy. *Intelektine Ekonomika, 8*(1), 116–127. Retrieved from http://0-search.proquest.com.www.consuls.org/docview/1551172833?accountid=9970

INDEX

Abrams, D. 131
Aburdene, P. 192
access to texts 18–20, 59, 103, 104, 106, 143–7, 164, 195
achievement: achievement gap 88–9; gender gap 59; international comparisons 25; skill versus will 143, 148–51; socioeconomic status 41, 170, 177, 184
Adams, John 4
Adams, Marilyn 75, 76
adolescents 162
adult literacy: Finland 52–3; IALS 42–6; long view 25; Morocco 55; PIAAC 47–52
Adult Literacy and Lifeskills Survey (ALL) 25, 57, 61
advertising 114–20, 122
Afghanistan 8, 12
Africa 5, 29, 198, 202, 203
Aftonbladet Dagens 115
A Gazetta 113
Age of Kits 97
Albania 38
Alexandria 12, 102
Aliguliyev, Rasim 199
aliteracy 2, 19, 20
Amazon 119, 125, 130–2, 134, 135, 156
American Library Association 107
American Sign Language 160
America's Most Literate Cities (AMLC) report vii

Anchor Standards for Writing 163
Angola 60
Apple 135, 156, 161, 206
Arab world 8, 12, 59, 124, 129, 132, 203
Argentina 120, 126
Aristotle 145
Asia: knowledge-based economy 198, 202, 203, 206; measured reading ability 59; newspapers 115, 116; wealth and literacy 184
Asian National Bank (ANB) 200
Asian Rim 202, 203
Asimov, Isaac 158, 161
assistive technology 79, 159
Assurbanipal, King 101
Assyrian libraries 101
Atmir, Mohammad Haneef 8
attention span 162–3
attitude to reading 143, 146–7
audio books 17, 18, 110, 123, 157
Audretsch, David 195
Auld, Hugh 6
Auletta, K. 118–9
Australia 38, 51, 69–70, 72, 81, 110, 116, 149, 164
Austria 120
availability *see* access to texts
Avedon, J. 10
Axel Springer 116
Azerbaijan 38, 199

Baddeley, Anna 161
Baker and Taylor Book Wholesalers 134
Bakker, P. 120
Barber, M. 186–7, 188
Barnard, Henry 103
Barnes and Noble 123, 124, 126, 128, 131, 134
Baron, Naomi 156, 157
Battles, M. 11
Bauerlein, Mark 80, 162
B. Dalton Bookseller 128
Belgium 30, 107, 108
Belize 33, 54
Bell, Daniel 193–4
Benavot, A. 53
Bengtsson, N. 133
Benin 60
bestsellers 161
Better Chance Foundation 175
Bibliothèque Nationale 102
Biemiller, Andrew 67
Bild 115, 116
Birkerts, Sven 154
Black Robe 1
Blackstone, B. 204
Blesk 115
Bloomberg Business Week 116
Bodleian Library, Oxford 109
Bogunovich, D. 195
Bologna 108
Bologna Process 186
book burning 2, 9–13
book clubs 124, 130, 134
book fairs 124, 131–2
book floods 19
book readings 131, 134
books: economics of digitization 161; is digital reading hazardous to your health? 162–3; message of the standards 163–6; policy recommendations 166–7; sales 130, 134; from tablet to tablet 153–8; trends in media use 153–68; unique affordances of digital texts 158–61
bookstores 123–35; access to texts 19; bookstores of the future 133–5; bookstores of the past 127–8; bookstores of the present 128–33; skill versus will 143; supporting literate cultures 100, 105, 135–7
Borders 123, 128, 135
Borman, G.D. 177
Boston 4, 112, 113

Boston Public Library 101, 103, 109
Botswana 29, 31
Brand, Stewart 122
Brazil 38, 125, 126, 135, 204
British Museum 109
Brodsky, Joseph 2
Buddhism 10
Budge, K.M. 176
Bulgaria 33
burning books 2, 9–13
Business Europe 197
Butler, P. 112
Buzz Feed 113

cable television 113, 122
Canada: elementary schooling 82; IALS 43, 45; IEA Study 31; Knowledge Economy Index 202; measured reading ability 52, 58; PIRLS 32, 33; PISA 38; skill versus will 149
Canadian Parliamentary Library 110
"Can Ivan read better than Johnny?" 75
Carnegie report 86
Carrenho, C. 125
Carr, Nicholas 80
Catherine the Great 103
CCSS *see* Common Core State Standards
censorship 12, 124–5
Center for the Improvement of Early Reading Achievement (CIERA) 58
Center for the Study of Reading 66, 73, 75, 77
Center on Instruction 77
Central African Republic 60
Chall, Jeanne 73, 75
Chang, J. 10
Cheerios Test 161
Chicago 112, 178–9, 189
Chile 45, 120
China: book burning 9–10; bookstores 125, 126; elementary schooling 71–2, 83; knowledge-based economy 193, 198, 202, 204–6; language 29; libraries 110; newspapers 115, 116; regional shifts in proficiency 59; secondary schooling 94–5, 96
Chiu, M.M. 181
Chow, B.Y. 181
Christianity 5, 7, 12
Christian Science Monitor 125
Cisco Systems 206
City Library of Stockholm 109

Clemons, Eric 122
Clinton, Bill 175, 203
closed-captioning 53
coaching movement 78
codex 153
Cold War 74, 75, 80
Coleman Report 170, 171, 172
Collins, Marva 189
The Coming of Post-Industrial Society 193
Common Core State Standards (CCSS): elementary schooling 69, 74, 77, 84; measured reading ability 44, 47, 61; message of the standards 163, 164; secondary schooling 86, 87, 88
Common Objectives 70
Common Sense Media 130
compact discs (CDs) 110, 129, 157
Composite Development Index (CDI) 27
comprehension 61, 66–8, 75, 143, 164
computers 91, 106–8, 156, 197, 198
Condon, Mark 19
Connell, Noreen 180, 188
content literacy 97, 98
copyright 124
Cornelius, Janet Duitsman 14
Council of Chief State School Officers 69
country profiling: Finland 52–4; Korea 55–6; Morocco 54–5; socioeconomic status 180–8
Crandall, Prudence 7
Cuba 13, 58–9
Cultural Revolution 10
culture: culture of reading 124, 129–30; definition 21; destroying cultures 9–13; factors influencing literate activity 18, 20–1; measured reading ability 41, 58; skill versus will 151; socioeconomic status 41
cunieform tablet 155
Curley, N. 129, 132
Cyprus 29
Czech Republic 41, 45, 115

Daily Sun 121
Dalai Lama 10
Daley, William 203
Dalton, Bridget 159
D'Angiulli, A. 177
Darling-Hammond, L. 30, 82, 188
databases 107, 110
Davies, Reverend Samuel 5
Deadspin 113

deep spelling systems 82
Delft 107
Denmark 31, 45, 70, 72, 130, 202
Deutsche Telecome 206
developing nations 19, 29, 58, 145, 198, 199, 200
Dewey, John 81, 150
The Diamond Age 154
Diary of a Pakistani School Girl 174
Dick and Jane 74
digital prosthesis 159
digital scaffolds 159, 161
digital texts: access to texts 19–20; bookstores 123, 124, 129, 134; digital divide 19–20; digital literacy in schools 165–6; economics of digitization 161; is digital reading hazardous to your health? 162–3; key firsts in digital reading 156; libraries 104–6, 110, 111; literacy definition 43; message of the standards 163–6; newspapers 117, 119–20; policy recommendations 166–7; secondary schooling 93; supporting literate cultures 135, 136; from tablet to tablet 153–8; trends in media use 153–68; unique affordances of digital texts 158–61; what is literacy? 17, 19
digital text supports 160, 166
distribution 118–9, 126
document literacy 43, 44, 45
Donga ILBO 115
Douglass, Frederick 2, 5–6, 7
Douglass, Margaret 6–7
Dugger, C.W. 179
The Dumbest Generation 80
Dweck, C.S. 189
Dyson, Freeman 61

"The Eagle" (Tennyson) 160, 161
early intervention 91, 92, 98
East Asia 42, 58, 193
Eastern Europe 42, 116, 197, 198
East Germany 80
ebooks 79, 125, 133–5, 154, 156, 157, 159, 161
The Economist 55, 115
Economist Intelligence Unit (EIU) 186
Eder, H. 133
education: comparing countries 81, 82–3; cost of literacy 6, 7, 8; crisis of elementary schooling 65–85; crisis of secondary and post-secondary schooling

86–99; how reading is taught 67–72; knowledge-based economy 196–8, 199, 202–6; libraries 103; long struggle for literacy 8, 14; measured reading ability 24, 50, 52, 53–6, 58, 59–60; message of the standards 163–6; peer influence 21; socioeconomic 170, 171, 176–80, 185–8; trends in media use 163–6, 167
Education Fever 56
Egypt 12, 102
elementary schooling 65–85; between country differences 72; crisis of secondary schooling 88, 92, 95; how reading develops 66–7; how reading is taught 67–72; lessons for policy 83; overview 65–6; "reading wars" 72–80; what can comparing countries teach us? 80–3
Elley, Warwick 19, 81
emigration 52, 60
The End of Ideology 193
Engelhardt, Tom 121–2
England 33, 36, 82, 149
Enjoyment of Reading Index 148–9
Equality of Educational Opportunity 171
Erasmus Project 186
Escalante, Jaime 21, 189
Esdaile, A.J.K. 102
Eslite Bookstore 125, 126
Estonia 197
Europe 59, 115, 116, 198, 202
European Union 186, 197, 204
Evans, Frederick 127
evening papers 114, 115
Ewing, J. 116
Exeter School Library 109
extrinsic motivation 145
ExxonMobil 206

Facebook 156, 166
Fahrenheit 451 9
Fakt Gazeta 115
family cultural capital 181
Festival of the Book 132
Filippetti, Aurélie 131
financial literacy 44
Finland: bookstores 130, 133; elementary schooling 81, 82–3; IALS 45; IEA Study 28, 29, 30; Knowledge Economy Index 202; libraries 110; measured reading ability 52–4, 55, 58, 59; PIAAC 50; PIRLS 36; PISA 38, 42; socioeconomic status 184, 187, 188

First Look Media 119
fixed mindset 189
fixed pricing 126, 130
Flesch, Rudolph 73, 74
Florida Center for Reading Research 77–8
fluency 66–7, 88
Forbes 206
Foyles 128, 134
France 29, 50, 57, 126, 129–31
Frankfurt Book Fair 131
Franklin, B. 121
Freud, Sigmund 11

Galbi, D.A. 105
Gardner, David 161
Gardner, Tom 161
Garfield High School 189
Gazeta Wyborcza 115
gender gap 30–1, 36, 41, 46, 50, 54, 58–60, 103, 130, 203
Gengras, Richard 113
Georgia 7
Germany: bookstores 131, 132; cost of literacy 10–2; elementary schooling 80, 82; IALS 43; knowledge-based economy 196, 204; newspapers 113, 115, 116; PISA 41; secondary schooling 95–6; socioeconomic status 41, 185, 187
Gerson, Michael 172
Ghent 107
Global Post 119
Goebbels, Joseph 12
Google 117, 125, 156, 206
government intervention 129, 130, 132, 136
government libraries 101, 110
Gray, William S. 24–5
Great Library of Alexandria 12, 102
Greece 38
growth mindset 189
Grundschule 95, 96
The Guardian 120
Guiding Curriculum 70
Gutenberg, Johannes 102, 113
Gymnasium 95, 96

Hammad, S. 131
Hangul (Korean alphabet) 69, 83
Hargrove, T. 114
Harian Metro 115
Harris, Christopher 154

Harris, Michael 100, 104
Harry Potter 13
Hartford Courant 137
Hart, Michael 156
Hay, John 192
Hebrew 82
Heine, Henirich 9, 11
Hertzman, C. 177
Herzog August Library 109
higher education 94, 186, 198
high schools 90, 109, 171
Hirsch, Samuel 10–1
Hispanics 121, 179
Holocaust 9, 11
Home Depot 134
Hong Kong 29, 33, 36, 38, 52, 126, 193, 202
Hopper, L. 108, 109
Host 156
Hp Keluskar Marg Municipal School No. 2 177–8
Huffington Post 113, 119
Hughes, E. 133
human voice narration 159
Hungary 29, 33, 115, 197
hyperdifferentiation 122, 123
hypermedia 159

IALS (International Adult Literacy Survey): history and purpose 42–3; measured reading ability 25, 42–6, 58–60; measurement 43–4; PIAAC 47, 50, 51; results 44–5; results in context 45–6
I am Malala 174
iBooks 161
Iceland 29, 110, 120, 132
Idriss, R. 124
IEA Study of Reading Literacy (International Association for the Evaluation of Educational Achievement) 26–31; elementary schooling 81; history and purpose 26; IEA results for 9-year-olds 28–9; IEA results for 14-year-olds 29–30; IEA results in context 30–1; literacy definition 26–7; measured reading ability 25, 52, 58; measurement 27; PIRLS 31, 32
illiteracy 2, 19
immigration 46, 50, 184
income 41–2, 58–9, 181
independent bookstores 128, 130, 131, 135

India: bookstores 126; knowledge-based economy 193, 198, 200, 204, 205; libraries 110; newspapers 112, 115–9
individualized education program (IEP) 68
Indonesia 29, 36, 38, 181
industrial economies 29, 103, 193–4, 204
informational reading 32, 33
initial teaching alphabet (i/t/a) 82
Instagram 166
instruction 88, 95, 96, 97–8
Intel 206
Intermediate International Benchmark 53
International Adult Literacy Survey *see* IALS
International Association for the Evaluation of Educational Achievement *see* IEA Study of Reading Literacy
International Federation of Audit Bureaux of Circulation (IFABC) 115
International Literacy Association 78, 97
International Monetary Fund 59
International Student Center (ISC) 31
Internet: bookstores 130, 135; elementary schooling 79; knowledge-based economy 204; libraries 106, 107, 108; literacy definitions 43, 47; measured reading ability 53, 55; newspapers 114, 116–7, 118, 119; secondary schooling 98; supporting literate cultures 137; trends in media use 154, 158, 159, 163–4, 166
intervention strategies 78, 92, 98
intrinsic motivation 145
iPads 135, 155, 156, 166
Iran 33, 36, 199–200
Iraq 8
Ireland 4, 30, 43, 51–2, 60
Italy 31, 33, 50, 57, 108

Jackson, J. 115
Jamalon 132
James, Peter 156
Japan: elementary schooling 81; knowledge-based economy 193, 202, 204; libraries 103; measured reading ability 52, 53, 59; newspapers 112, 117–20; PIAAC 50; PISA 38, 41
Jefferson, Thomas 103, 150
Jewish culture 10–11, 12
job-related reading 150
Johnson, K. 132
Johnson, Samuel 2

Joongang ILBO 115
journalism 112, 113, 121–2
junior high schools 86–7

Kahlenberg, R.D. 171, 172
KBE *see* knowledge-based economy
Kemeny, John G. 110
Kilroy, Matthew 3–4
kindergarten 67–71, 163, 177, 186
Kindle 156
Klein, Karen 166
Knezevic, M. 125
knowledge-based economy (KBE) 192–206; all countries see themselves as "in" 198–200; knowledge is product 195–6; multi-national agreements 203–5; new workforce, new education 196–8; overview 192–3, 205–6; power of literacy 14; pre-industrial, industrial, and post-industrial economies 193–4; technology is the driver 194–5; who's really in? 200–3
Knowledge Economy Index (KEI) 200, 201–2
Knuth, R. 10, 12
Kobo 125
Koran 12
Korea: bookstores 126, 130, 132; elementary schooling 69, 72, 82, 83; measured reading ability 52, 55–6, 59; newspapers 115; PISA 38, 41; secondary schooling 93–4; socioeconomic status 184, 187, 188
Kuwait 33, 59
Kyrgyzstan 38

Lane Technical High School 178–9, 180
Lang Law 131
language 20, 32, 50, 53, 124, 160
Latin 102
Latin America 116, 120
Latvia 33, 57
Leap schools 179–80
Learning to Read Home Survey 33
Learning to Read: The Great Debate 73, 75
LeGuin, Ursula K. 142
leisure time 20, 147, 150
Lerner, F. 101, 102, 103
Leu, Donald 164
Lewis, D.L. 105
Liberia 60

libraries: access to texts 19; bookstores 124, 133, 134; cost of literacy 10, 11, 12, 13; current libraries 104–10; IEA results 31; libraries of the future 110–11; libraries of the past 101–4; overview 100–1; supporting literate cultures 100–11, 135, 136, 137; unique affordances of digital texts 158
Library of Congress 101, 103, 104, 110
Library of Leningrad 103
Library of the Abbe of St. Gall 109
libricide 2, 12
Lifschutz, Alex 134
literacy: cost of literacy 4–13; definitions 16, 26–7, 32, 37, 43, 47; destroying cultures 9–13; factors influencing literate activity 18–21; keys to the literate kingdom 3–4; knowledge-based economy 194–5, 202, 205, 206; long struggle for literacy 1–15; measured reading ability 57, 59; overview vii–viii, 1–3, 13–14; power of literacy 1–3; what is literacy? 16–22
Literacy Instruction in the Content Areas 98
literary reading 32, 33
Lithuania 33, 36, 196
Locke, John 73
Lockheed, M. 58
Logar Province 8
Los Angeles 166
Loveless, Tom 77, 149
Luque, Javier 185
Luxembourg 38, 120

Macedonia 38
Malaysia 115
Malcolm X 2
Manley, W. 9
Mann, Horace 73
Mao Zedong 10, 13
Martial 153
Mashable 113
Master of the Revels 124
mathematical literacy 37, 38, 41, 42, 177, 185
Matsa, Katerina 121
Matthew Effect 202
McCarthy, Joe 13
McGuffee, Michael 19
McGuffey, William Holmes 73
McKenna, M.C. 151
McKinsey & Company 178

McLuhan, Marshall 135
measured reading ability 23–64; Finland 52–4; general insights 56–61; IALS 42–6; IEA Study of Reading Literacy 26–31; long view 24–6; Korea 55–6; Morocco 54–5; OECD and country profiling 52–6; overview 23–4; PIAAC 47–52; PIRLS 31–7; PISA 37–42
media 135, 136
media literacy 93
The Medium is the Message 135
megatrends 192, 193
Meiji Restoration 103
The Memory of Mankind 101
metacognition aids 160
Metro 115, 120
Metro Ahad 115
Mexico 38
Meyer, H.-D. 53, 58
Microsoft 206
Middle Ages 102
Middle East 198, 202, 203
middle schools 87, 90, 92, 94–6
Miller, J. 114
Miller, J.W. 110, 120
mindset 188–9
Mintz, S.L. 87
Missouri Botanical Garden Library 101
Mndini, Gcobani 179–80
Mohammed VI, King 55
Monastery Library, Ulm 109
Mongols 13
Montgomery, Hugh 3–4
Morgan Library and Museum 109
Morocco 33, 36
Morris, B. 131
motivation to read 60, 94, 144–8, 149–51, 159
Motley Fool 161
Mott, F.L. 113–4
Mourshed, M. 186–7, 188
Mudawana 54
Mueller, M.U. 116
Mujahedeen 12
multi-national agreements 203–5
Mumbai 118–9, 177–8, 180
Mumby, F.A. 127
Municipal Corporation of Greater Mumbai 178
Murphy, P.C. 123
Murray, J. 164
Murrow, Edward R. 113

museums 109
music industry 128–9, 154, 157
Muslim countries 4, 12

NAANDI Foundation 178
NAEP (National Assessment of Educational Progress): elementary schooling 73, 75, 76, 77, 83; secondary schooling 86, 87, 88; skill versus will 143, 151; socioeconomic status 177
NAFTA (North American Free Trade Agreement) 203
Naisbitt, John 192, 193
National Case Study Questionnaires 27
National Commission on Excellence in Education 73, 75, 87
National Defense Education Act (NDEA) 74
National Foundation for Educational Research in England and Wales 31
National Governors Association 69
national income 41, 55
National Library of Vienna 103
National Reading Panel 73, 76
A Nation at Risk 73, 75, 87
Nazism 9–12
NCLB (No Child Left Behind) 72, 77, 84
Ness, Molly 97
Netherlands: bookstores 127; elementary schooling 81, 82; IALS 43; IEA Study 29, 30, 31; Knowledge Economy Index 202; libraries 106, 107, 108; PIAAC 50; PIRLS 33, 36; socioeconomic status 181
Neues Deutschland 115
newspapers: bookstores 123–4; current newspapers 114–20; libraries 105; newspapers of the future 120–3; newspapers of the past 113–4; skill versus will 143; supporting literate cultures 100, 111, 113–23, 135–7
New York 112, 121, 177
New York Public Library 105, 109
New Zealand 29, 30, 38, 116
Nigeria 29
91–9 problem 79–80
Nineveh 101
No Child Left Behind (NCLB) 72, 77, 84
Noland, Marcus 55–6
Norman, M. 104
Norris, S.P. 97
North Africa 116
North America 116

North American Free Trade Agreement (NAFTA) 203
Northern Ireland 149
Norway: bookstores 130, 133; elementary schooling 82; IALS 45, 46; IEA Study 29, 31; Knowledge Economy Index 202; libraries 110; newspapers 120; socioeconomic status 184
NuroMedia 156
Nyheter 115

OECD (Organization for Economic Cooperation and Development): elementary schooling 72; Finland 52–4; IALS 43–6; Korea 55–6, 93; measured reading ability 52–6, 58, 60; Morocco 54–5; PIAAC 47, 48, 51–2; PISA 37, 38, 41, 42; skill versus will 150; socioeconomic status 185; trends in media use 165
Olmos, Edward James 21, 189
Oman 36
Omidyar, Peter 119
The Onion 121
Online Computer Library Center (OCLC) 110
online news 114, 116, 122, 158
online reading comprehension 61, 164
open libraries 102
"The Open Window" (Saki) 160
oral language development 66, 67, 124
ORCA Project (Online Reading Comprehension Assessment) 164
Organization for Economic Cooperation and Development *see* OECD
orthography 53, 66, 71, 82, 83
Ostend 108
Overman, L.T. 177

Pacific Rim 192–3, 203
Pakistan 174
Panama 38
Pandora 129
parental influence 41, 72, 92, 151, 169, 178
Parrett, W.H. 176
Partnership for Assessment of Readiness for College and Careers (PARCC) 61
Patrick, Deval 175–6
Pearson Publishing 186
peer influence 21, 147, 162, 171
penny papers 112, 113
People's Press 94

Peru 38
PetroChina 206
Pew Research Center 119, 121, 142, 157
Pfefferkorn, Josef (Johannes) 10–11
Philippines 29, 31
Phillips, L.M. 97
phonemes 66, 82
phonics 73, 74, 75
PIAAC (Program for the International Assessment of Adult Competencies): history and purpose 47; IALS 46; knowledge-based economy 200; literacy definition 47; measured reading ability 25, 47–52, 58–60; measurement 48; reading outside work 149; results 48–50; results in context 50–2; trends in media use 164, 166
Pierre-Louis, Millicent 172
pinyin 71, 83
Piper, P.S. 105
piracy 124
PIRLS (Progress in International Reading Literacy Study): elementary schooling 65, 67, 70, 81–3; history and purpose 31–2; knowledge-based economy 200, 202; literacy definition 32; measured reading ability 25, 31–7, 52–5, 57–60; measurement 32–3; OECD and country profiling 52–5; PIRLS 2001 results 33; PIRLS 2006 results 33–5; PIRLS 2011 results 36, 180, 182–3; results in context 36–7; secondary schooling 92, 93; skill versus will 143, 144, 151; socioeconomic status 58, 59, 180–4, 186
PISA (Program for International Student Assessment of 15-year-olds): elementary schooling 75, 83; history and purpose 37; IALS 44; knowledge-based economy 200, 202; measured reading ability 24–5, 37–42, 52, 53, 57–60; measurement 37–8; PIAAC 51–2; PISA 2000 results 38, 39–40; PISA 2012 results 39–40, 42, 180, 182–3, 185; results in context 41–2; secondary schooling 93; skill versus will 143, 147, 148, 151; socioeconomic status 180–6; trends in media use 165
Pittman, Sir James 82
Plato 145
Poland 43, 45, 115, 184–7, 196
policy change: elementary schooling 83; measured reading ability 23, 24, 60–1;

secondary schooling 96–8; skill versus will 150–1; trends in media use 166–7
Portugal 29, 30, 38, 45
post-industrial economies 193–4, 195, 198, 200, 204, 205
Postman, Neil 2
poverty: libraries 103; measured reading ability 24, 55, 58; secondary schooling 92; socioeconomic status 169, 170, 173–5, 177, 178
power of literacy 1–3, 13
pre-industrial economies 193–4
Preston, P. 114, 120
Preventing Reading Difficulties in Young Children 73
price controls 126, 130
print books: alternatives 20; bookstores 129, 133, 134; libraries 106, 107; literacy definition 47; readership 111; supporting literate cultures 135, 136, 137; trends in media use 153–7, 161, 166, 167
printing press 102, 104, 113, 153
print journalism 112, 113, 118
proficiency: elementary schooling 65; factors influencing literate activity 18, 19; long struggle for literacy 2; measured reading ability 50, 60; secondary schooling 88; skill versus will 143–7, 149–51; socioeconomic status 170; supporting literate cultures 136
Program for International Student Assessment of 15-year-olds *see* PISA
Program for the International Assessment of Adult Competencies *see* PIAAC
Progress in International Reading Literacy Study *see* PIRLS
Progressive movement 86
Project Gutenberg 156
prose literacy 43, 44–5
Prosser, Gabriel 5
prosthestic supports 159
public libraries 101, 103–8, 110, 158
publishers 12, 124, 126, 127, 133, 135, 166
publishing on demand 135

Qatar 33, 36, 38, 59, 184
quantitative literacy 43, 44, 45
Queensland 69–70

Race to the Top 74, 77
radio 113, 119
Rainie, L. 106, 107, 142, 157

Ramesh, S. 198
rankings 24–6, 57
Ray, R.K. 205
readership 111–2, 114, 120, 142
reading: attitude to reading 143, 146–7; comprehension 61, 66–8, 75, 143, 164; culture of reading 129–30; definition 16; elementary schooling 66–72, 81–3; factors influencing literate activity 18–20; how reading develops 66–7; how reading is taught 67–72; reading literacy definitions 26–7, 37, 41, 47; "reading wars" 65, 72–80; secondary schooling 95, 97–8; skill versus will 142, 143, 144–8; *see also* measured reading ability
Reading Excellence Act 73, 76, 77, 78
Reading First 74, 76, 77, 78
"Reading Journey" program 95
Reading Next 86, 98
reading outside work 149–50
reading proficiency *see* proficiency
reading rooms 103, 109
"reading wars" 65, 72–80
Ready to Learn report 185
Realschule 96
A Reason to Believe 175
record shops 128–9
recreational reading 94, 95, 96
Red Guard 10
reforms 72–80
Reich Chamber of Literature 12
religious libraries 101, 109
remedial services 86, 90, 92
Renaissance 102
research 77–8, 107, 198, 200
resilience 171–2, 177, 187
Response to Intervention (RTI) 70, 74, 78, 79
Reuchlin, Johann 11
Rijksmuseum Library 109
Rivkin, Jan 23
Robert Taylor Homes 175
Roeselare library 108
Romania 36, 115, 120
Roosendaal library 108
Rosenwald, M.S. 154, 156, 161
Rouet, Jean-François 164
Rousseau, Jean-Jacques 73, 81
Rowling, J.K. 13
RTI (Response to Intervention) 70, 74, 78, 79
Rushdie, Salman 13, 125

Russia/Russian Federation: elementary schooling 74, 75, 83; knowledge-based economy 204, 205; measured reading ability 33, 36, 52, 59; socioeconomic status 185–7
Rwanda 199

Sahlberg, P. 54
Sala Borsa 108
Salman, J. 127
sample stock system 133–4
Samuel, Herbert 101
Samuelson, R.J. 204, 206
Saraiva 135
Satanic Verses 13, 125
Sattari, Sorena 199–200
The Saturday Evening Post 75
Saudi Arabia 129
scaffolded supports 159, 161
Scandinavia 44–5
Schiller, K. 58
Schleicher, Andreas 197
Schnibben, C. 116, 117
School Excellence Programme 178
schooling *see* education
Schwartz, Alexandra 131
scientific literacy 37, 38, 41, 97, 205
Scribner's magazine 123
Seattle 132
secondary schooling 86–99; addressing the right achievement gap 88–9; China 94–5; Germany 95–6; history of secondary schooling 86–7; Korea 93–4; lessons for policy 96–8; what can we learn from other countries? 92–3; what has been done to address the problem? 91–2; why does the problem persist? 90–1; why do so many students experience difficulty? 88–9
Sejong 83
Seth, Michael 56
The Shallows 80
shallow spelling systems 82
Shanghai 38, 41, 52, 125
Shannon, Claude 154
Shaw, George Bernard 127
Shin Huang Ti 9–10
Shosun ILBO 115
Sibelius, Jean 187
Siegel, L.S. 177
Silander, T. 54
Simon & Schuster 156

Singapore: elementary schooling 83; knowledge-based economy 193, 196, 202; measured reading ability 29, 31, 33, 36, 38, 52, 59; socioeconomic status 181, 187
skill versus will 142–52; deconstructing motivation 144–8; lessons from other countries 148–50; overview 142–4; recommendations for policy 150–1
SKY universities (Seoul National, Korea, and Yonsei) 94
slavery 5–7
Slavin, Robert 91–2
Slovenia 36
Smarter Balanced 61
smart manufacturing 195
social media 20, 79, 80, 157, 162
socioeconomic status and literacy 169–91; countries 180–8; definition 181; individuals 172–6; measured reading ability 41, 58–9; overview 188–9; schools 176–80
Solidarity 185
South Africa 4, 32, 120, 121, 179–80
South Carolina 7
South Korea: elementary schooling 69, 81; knowledge-based economy 193, 202; measured reading ability 55–6; secondary schooling 93–4; socioeconomic status 184, 187
Soviet Union 12, 75, 185, 186
Spain 32, 50, 82, 116
spelling 82–3
Der Spiegel 117
Spotify 129
Sri Lanka 199
Stahl, N.A. 25
Stand and Deliver 189
standards 68–9, 77, 87–8, 163–6, 167
Starbucks 134
state censorship 124–5
State of Victoria Library 109
Statistics Canada 31
Stempel, G., III 114
Stephenson, Neal 154
Stockholm 120
storytelling 20
strategic aids 160
Striving Readers 74
struggling readers 88–9, 90–1
Sub-Saharan Africa 203
subsidization 126, 130, 131, 132

supported text 159, 160, 166
supporting literate cultures 100–41; bookstores 123–35; libraries 100–11; newspapers 111–23; overview 100, 135–7
Survey of Adult Skills 47
Svenska Bagbladet 115
Swat Region 174
Sweden: bookstores 133; elementary schooling 82; IALS 43, 44, 45, 46; IEA Study 29; Knowledge Economy Index 202; measured reading ability 59; newspapers 115, 120; PIRLS 33, 36; PISA 42; socioeconomic status 184, 187
Switzerland 43

tablets 101, 153–8
Tagholm, R. 126
Taiwan 125, 126, 193, 202
Taliban 8, 12, 174
Tan, T. 124
teacher education 24, 31, 54, 188
Teaching and Learning: Achieving Quality for All 202
technical schools 178–9
technology: bookstores 123, 135; elementary schooling 79, 80; knowledge-based economy 194–8, 204–6; libraries 104, 105, 106, 107, 111; newspapers 118; supporting literate cultures 136, 137; trends in media use 157, 159, 162–6
Ten Best Libraries in the World 101, 109
textbooks 154, 159, 161, 167
texting 18, 20
text supports 159, 160, 166, 167
Text to Speech (TTS) 159, 160
Thailand 29, 30, 31
Tibet 10
Tigris River 13
The Times (India) 115
Title I 73, 75, 91
Tolzmann, D.H. 101, 102
Trace, A.S., Jr. 75
Trelease, Jim 53
Trinidad and Tobago 29, 30, 57
Trinity College Library 109
Tröhler, D. 75
Tseng, Chun-Yao 197
Turbill, J. 164
Turkey 115
Turkle, Sherry 162

Turner, Nate 5
Turning High-Poverty Schools into High-Performance Schools 176
Twain, Mark 2, 154
Twitter 20

Ukraine 196
Understanding Media: the Extensions of Man 135
UNESCO (United Nations Educational, Scientific and Cultural Organization) 25, 26, 30, 54, 202
UNICEF (United Nations Children's Fund) 55, 178
United Arab Emirates 36, 59, 184
United Kingdom 114, 131, 134
United States: bookstores 128, 131, 132, 134; elementary schooling 68–9, 72–5, 81, 82, 83; IALS 43, 45, 46; IEA Study 28, 29, 31; knowledge-based economy 198, 202–6; libraries 103, 106, 109; long struggle for literacy 4–7, 12; newspapers 113, 115, 121; PIAAC 50; PIRLS 33, 36; PISA 38, 42; rankings and literacy growth 57; secondary schooling 86–7, 88, 92, 96; skill versus will 149; trends in media use 164
Unite for Literacy 19, 22
universal design 159–60
university libraries 101, 109
University of Illinois Library 101
urban revitalization 107, 108, 111
U.S. Department of Education 74, 83
Utrecht 127
Uzanne, Octave 123

Välijärvi, J. 54
Vallet, N. 107
Van Der Werf, H.H. 106
Vatican Library 101, 109
Venezuela 29, 30, 31
Venice 113
Verizon 206
Verschaffel, B. 111
Vesey, Denmark 5
Viadero, Debra 171–2
videos 17, 47, 158
Vietnam 181, 184, 185, 187, 202
Vinnychuk, O. 196
vinyl records 128–9, 154, 157
Virginia 5, 6, 7
Vision 2020 199

visual impairment 159
vocabulary 67, 68, 88, 90, 91
vocational education 94, 96, 186
Voltaire 192
von Neumann, John 60, 61

Walesa, Lech 185
Walker, J. 101
Walpole, Sharon 160
Warsh, D. 119
Washington Post 119
Waterstones 135
wealth 58, 59, 181, 184
Western Europe 116, 198, 202
West Germany 31, 80
Wharton School 122
What Works Clearinghouse 78
whole language movement 73, 75, 76
whole-word instruction 74
Why Johnny Can't Read 73, 74
Will, George 76
William Penn High School 97
Williams, Khadijah 172–3, 176
Willingham, Dan 145, 163
Wilson, Edmund 158

Winfrey, Oprah 173–4, 175, 176
women's rights 8, 46, 54, 103
word recognition 27, 66, 68, 82
workforce 196–8, 205
World Association of Newspapers and News Publishing 120
World Bank 30, 53, 200
World Digital Library 111
World Press Trends 115
World Public Library 111
World's Most Literate Countries (WMLC) study vii, 58
Writing Next 98
Writing to Read 98
written language 47, 71, 124, 137, 160

Yalta Conference 185
Yarden, A. 97
young adults 51, 162
Yousafzai, Malala 8–9, 174–5, 176

Zaman 115
Zickuhr, K. 106, 107, 142, 157
Zimbabwe 29, 31
Zuse, Konrad 156